CELEBRATE

CELEBRATE

A year of British festivities for families and friends

PIPPA MIDDLETON

With photography by David Loftus
and illustrations by Gill Heeley

MICHAEL JOSEPH
an imprint of
Penguin Books

MICHAEL JOSEPH

Published by the Penguin Group

Penguin Books Ltd, 80 Strand, London WC2R 0RL, England

Penguin Group (USA) Inc., 375 Hudson Street, New York,
New York 10014, USA

Penguin Group (Canada), 90 Eglinton Avenue East, Suite 700,
Toronto, Ontario, Canada M4P 2Y3 (a division of Pearson Penguin Canada Inc.)

Penguin Ireland, 25 St Stephen's Green, Dublin 2, Ireland
(a division of Penguin Books Ltd)

Penguin Books Australia Ltd, 707 Collins Street, Melbourne, Victoria 3008, Australia
(a division of Pearson Australia Group Pty Ltd)

Penguin Books India Pvt Ltd, 11 Community Centre, Panchsheel Park, New Delhi – 110 017, India

Penguin Group (NZ), 67 Apollo Drive, Rosedale, Auckland 0632, New Zealand
(a division of Pearson New Zealand Ltd)

Penguin Books (South Africa) (Pty) Ltd, Block D, Rosebank Office Park, 181 Jan Smuts Avenue,
Parktown North, Gauteng 2193, South Africa

Penguin Books Ltd, Registered Offices: 80 Strand, London WC2R 0RL, England

www.penguin.com

First published 2012
001

Text copyright © Pippa Middleton, 2012

Photography copyright © David Loftus, 2012

Illustrations copyright © Gill Heeley, 2012

The extract on page 218 is taken from *Winnie-the-Pooh* by A. A. Milne. Text copyright © The Trustees of
the Pooh Properties 1926. Published by Egmont UK Ltd and used with permission.

'Spring', 'Summer', 'Autumn' and 'Winter' © Victoria and Albert Museum, London.

Celebration /ribbon wallpaper © The Metropolitan Museum of Art/Art Resource/Scala, Florence.

Set in Gill and Mrs Eaves

Colour reproduction by Altaimage Ltd
Printed and bound in Italy by Graphicom srl

A CIP catalogue record for this book is available from the British Library

ISBN: 978-0-718-17678-5

To my family, for all their love
and support over the years.

CONTENTS

INTRODUCTION

It's a bit startling to achieve global recognition (if that's the right word) before the age of thirty, on account of your sister, your brother-in-law and your bottom.

One day, I might be able to make sense of this. In the meantime, I think it's fair to say that it has its upside and its downside. I certainly have opportunities many can only dream of, but in most ways I'm a typical girl in her twenties trying to forge a career and represent herself in what can sometimes seem rather strange circumstances.

I am by nature an optimist, so I tend to concentrate on the advantages. One of the most attractive has been the chance to publish *Celebrate*.

I've always loved to write, so it seemed natural to try to combine this passion along with my enjoyment for entertaining, an enthusiasm I hope to share with others.

I don't think there's a right way or a wrong way to celebrate. But I do strongly believe in the importance of bringing friends and family together. I have been lucky enough to grow up in a very close-knit family and this has played a central role in my life. The nurturing of friendship, family and home feels more important than ever to me in a world that sometimes appears to be moving so fast that we forget what really matters.

This book is designed to be a comprehensive guide to home entertaining, based on my experience in my family's party business, Party Pieces, and work for London-based events company, Table Talk. It is a useful and practical journey into British-themed occasions and I hope it offers welcome inspiration and ideas, most of which needn't leave you alarmingly out of pocket. Entertaining on any scale can be stressful and daunting so this is all about finding ways to manage and enjoy the process.

I hope you will see this as a feel-good book with ideas to look forward to each month, providing threads of lasting, happy memories, be it around a table lit with candles in winter, outside on a rug in summer or in the autumn, perched on a leaf-covered bench, hot drink in hand.

I have very fond memories of many of the events celebrated in this book and each seasonal introduction seeks to give you an insight into why I feel it should be there. I hope there's something here for everyone, whatever their age. In some cases I've harvested fascinating tidbits of history, which shed a little light on why we celebrate certain occasions in the first place.

The book is structured around the seasonal cycle and focuses on tradition, ritual and rhythm, providing a glimmer of anticipation and hope – like that warm feeling on your back on the first sunny day of the year or spotting the first signs of spring.

I know many of you will have picked up this book out of nothing more than curiosity. I can assure you that it feels even stranger to me than it probably does to you to have seen so much written about me when I have done so little to paint a picture of myself. This is my first chance to do that, and I've enjoyed every minute of it.

I hope you find *Celebrate* fun to read, practical to use and inspiring to look at. I've tried to make it as all-embracing as possible – but I'm having new ideas all the time, which I look forward to sharing with you in the future.

Thank you very much for your support.

Pippa Middleton, 2012

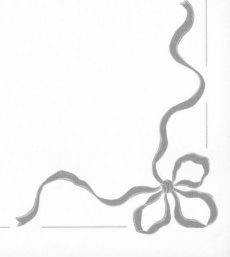

AUTUMN

HALLOWE'EN
SUNDAY LUNCHES
COSY SUPPER PARTIES
BONFIRE NIGHT

Autumn is a celebration of gathering and of golden light. Leaves turn to all shades of bronze, conkers carpet the dewy ground. The weather brings cooler days and fresh misty mornings. It marks the end of summer and a new start. Hedgerows boast ruby fruits among spindles and spikes, root vegetables swell and flavoursome game appears in butchers' windows, wholesome and plump. Stews, roasts and pies fill our plates.

Light as feathers the witches fly,
The horn of the moon is plain to see;
By a firefly under a jonquil flower
A goblin toasts a bumble-bee.

'Camomile Tea',
Katherine Mansfield

HALLOWE'EN

Hallowe'en is a chance to celebrate the macabre and brings out the impish spirit in us all. Ghost stories and fairy tales depict creatures howling at the full moon, bats flitting across troubled skies and pumpkin lanterns glowing on windowsills to ward off bad spirits – scenes that evoke fright and mystery. On this night, trick-or-treaters take to the streets: ghosts rub shoulders with trolls and hobgoblins, witches ride their broomsticks and Frankenstein's monsters seem to emerge out of nowhere.

Many of the elements of today's celebration have their origins in Celtic Ireland and the festival of *Samhain*, and are heralded by the falling leaves of autumn, which signify death. Spirits of those who had died in the previous year were thought to return to Earth in search of living bodies to inhabit. The Celts would disguise themselves in ghoulish costumes, hoping that the spirits would mistake them for one of their own kind and pass them by.

Hallowe'en lends itself to a family celebration: adults get involved with the preparations, helping children carve pumpkins, create costumes and have fun with face painting and traditional games. As a child, I felt that Hallowe'en was a time when creatures of the night suddenly came to life – we would turn off all the lights in the house and let flickering candlelight conjure up scary shadows and create the effect of imaginary figures lurking in dark corners. It was also a time for sugary treats – we feasted on creepy edible morsels, Hallowe'en-themed chocolates and spookily named concoctions, which often looked better than they tasted.

Nowadays, I frequently celebrate Hallowe'en over a supper with friends. It's a wonderful excuse to let your imagination run riot with gory-looking food and special effects: stir witchy cauldrons of pumpkin soup, hang homemade spiders inside window nooks, string cobwebs on tables and haunt gardens, attics and stairways with ghosts made from sheets.

Shops are well stocked with fancy dress and decorations in a palette of garish colours – pumpkin orange, bat black and the sinister purple of unspeakable potions. Mix and match shop-bought items with things you have at home and make your celebration as elaborate or as low-key as you like, depending on how much time you have, the size of your venue and its location. It needn't cost a fortune, just a simply carved pumpkin lit up among glimmering candles will go a long way to producing the right atmosphere.

EXTEND A SPOOKY WELCOME

At Hallowe'en your home should look the part on the outside to greet your guests and any passing spooks and spirits. Decorate your windows with stained-glass bats (page 17). String outdoor fairy lights around trees and shrubs, and light the pathway with a few paper lanterns. A scarecrow made like a Bonfire Night Guy (page 77) sat under a tree and lit with a torch will set the scene from a distance. A few mournful ghosts floating around will add to the effect: simply blow up white balloons, tie each one to a bamboo cane and drape a white sheet over it. Tie around the 'neck' with string and use a black marker to draw the face. Stick the canes in the ground where you want each ghost to stand.

You can buy cobweb-effect decorations, but they are easy enough to make yourself using cotton wool or ripped muslin (which you can buy from department stores). Swathe liberally over tree branches, doorknobs, in doorways and on light fixtures, and hang pompom spiders from them. These are made using black pompoms (page 178) for the spiders' bodies and pipe cleaners for legs. You can add some googly eyes for extra scare tactics. Scrawl a menacing message on a sign for the front door to prepare the unwary for what lies within. You might like to welcome guests into a pitch-black hallway or garage, devoid of electric lighting, with only candles and torches available to help them find their way inside. It's amazing how creepy even the most familiar places can seem when plunged into darkness.

Arrange glowing pumpkins in a prominent position where they will light up windows and the front door, welcoming wandering souls and frightening off supernatural beings. As well as the classic scary face, you can also carve out stars, names, numbers and other Hallowe'en motifs (use a stencil for these).

HALLOWE'EN CRAFTS

The jack-o'-lantern (or pumpkin) is now the most recognisable symbol of Hallowe'en, but it's not the only fun craft to do in the run-up to the event. For a gothic touch, cover a cauldron or saucepan with aluminium foil and fill with popcorn balls (page 93) to hand out to visitors at your front door.

SWEETIE WREATH

A twist on the classic door wreath, you can make this trick-or-treat version with wrapped sweets, such as toffees, or any other kind of treat that comes in shiny paper.

I: Curve a 1m length of gardening wire into a circle, weaving the two ends together to fasten. 2: Using 1m of fishing thread, knot together 3 wrapped sweets and tie the thread tightly around the circled wire. 3: Repeat with 3 sweets at a time. 4: Each time you knot the sweets on, bunch them up to create a full-looking wreath.

SPOOKY BOTTLES

Stack some aged 'spell books' beside these candlesticks dripping with blood for maximum eerie effect.

I: Prepare a label for your bottle by printing or writing with a marker pen on plain paper an evocative description of the contents (i.e. 'Witches' Wine', 'Bats' Blood', 'Spooky Syrup'). 2: Cut into a label shape, burn the edges, dab with a wet teabag and sprinkle with coffee granules. Leave to dry and then stick to your bottle with PVA glue. 3: Place a white candle into the neck of the bottle, then light a red candle and allow it to drip over the white candle and the bottle. The messier it gets, the better! Experiment with other coloured candles, such as slime-green or purple, if you prefer.

STAINED-GLASS BATS

Add the finishing touches to your room with these Hallowe'en bat window decorations, or vary the template and cut out star, moon or pumpkin shapes.

I: Draw around a plate on black card. In the centre of your circle, position a bat template and draw around the outlines of the bat. 2: Cut around the bat and the circle. 3: Stick tissue paper to the back of the silhouette with PVA glue, or use colourful sweet wrappers instead (in which case use a glue stick).

Transform your dining table into a Hallowe'en focal point. If the weather is good enough you can place your table outside for an autumn tea. Spread a multi-coloured knitted blanket over it as a tablecloth or overlap scarves in brilliant oranges, yellows and reds to add warmth and texture. Long-necked butternut squash and plump root vegetables (carved or covered with glitter using PVA glue) fit the autumnal theme and add variety to the table.

LOLLIPOP-STUDDED PUMPKIN

A great table centrepiece, the lollipops can be handed out as going-home treats. You can also skewer pumpkins with other nibbles, such as cocktail sausages, tomatoes and mini mozzarella balls or chunks of fresh fruit.

1: Cut a white paper napkin or a piece of kitchen roll into quarters. 2: Place one piece of napkin over the head of the lollipop and tie tightly at the neck with a piece of white cotton thread. Draw on eyes with a black marker pen. 3: Repeat until you have enough lollipop 'ghosts' to cover your pumpkin.

A HARVEST HALLOWE'EN TABLE

If you want your table to have a grown-up, pagan feel to it, go for a Hallowe'en harvest look using the colours of the season. Scatter your table with leaves, clusters of conkers and sweet-chestnut husks, acorns and other seedpods – go on a nature walk to collect various bits and pieces in advance. This style of decoration is perfect for a bare wooden table. Alternatively, cover your table with a dark-coloured cloth or hessian (which you can buy in department stores and haberdashery shops).

Pewter, stone and slate offer a stark contrast to rich autumn shades so, where possible, use these natural materials – slate looks particularly good as placemats or dinner plates. Inject an element of magic and mayhem with a scattering of edible (or plastic) creepy crawlies and make silhouetted place cards, handwritten in silver pen, or cut out a colony of bat silhouettes using black card and fix them to the wall. Light lots of candles, dripping with red blood (page 17), stack up old 'spell' books and close curtains, blinds or shutters to conjure up a moody atmosphere. Autumn branches and ferns in tall vases with hanging spiders make simple, structural centrepieces. Intersperse with branches of physalis with their papery orange lanterns, or use other orange-hued flowers, such as mango calla lilies, burgundy sunflowers, russet hydrangeas or gerbera daisies and dahlias.

There is no such thing as overdoing it when it comes to Hallowe'en, but there's no need to buy lots of expensive decorations: make simple crafts or be inventive and adapt household items to transform the party room into a cavern of ghoulish wonders.

ALL HALLOWS' FEAST

Whatever you choose to eat on Hallowe'en, dress your food for the occasion and add some hair-raising dishes to your table. Children will love to get involved, so help them to make delicious cookies or a jelly bowl crawling with worms. You could also let them mash up blackberries for a flavoured butter with the gory appearance of entrails to seep into crumpets or spread liberally on toast.

Dishes with spooky names will both feed the imagination and satisfy the stomach, so prepare your guests to eat toad-in-the-hole, witches' fingers and devil's food cake. You can accessorise dishes with a trickle of tomato ketchup 'blood' and black plastic spiders perched on serving trays or in drinks.

WORM-RIDDEN JELLY BOWL

Have some jelly worms 'escaping' to make everyone's toes curl. Add in any other spooky gummy sweets you can find.

The night before you want to serve this, make a layer of lime jelly according to the packet instructions in a clear glass bowl. Add a few jelly sweet 'worms' before putting into the fridge overnight to set. The next morning, make up some blackcurrant jelly and pour over the first set layer, adding more worms. Put back into the fridge to set. The steps can be repeated again with different coloured jellies to create an impressive layer effect.

 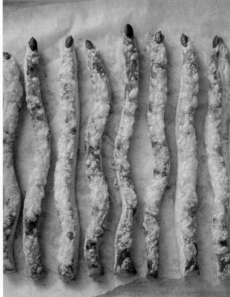 

HALLOWE'EN COOKIES Makes 16

These cookies use white chocolate and cranberries to represent ghosts and blood, dark chocolate and raisins for bats and witches. Shape them using Hallowe'en-themed cookie cutters if you like. The raw dough mixture can be frozen once wrapped in clingfilm. Simply defrost thoroughly before rolling out.

Preheat the oven to 180°C/gas 4 and line a baking tray with greaseproof paper. In a large bowl, beat 250g softened unsalted butter and 150g caster sugar together until creamy. Stir in 1 teaspoon baking powder, 2½ tablespoons golden syrup and 3 egg yolks. Gently mix in 500g plain flour to form a dough.

Split the dough in two and put half into a second bowl. Add 100g white-chocolate chips and 50g dried cranberries to one half, and 100g dark-chocolate chips and 50g raisins to the other half. Mix each batch. Place one dough on the work surface and shape into a sausage. It may seem a little crumbly, but keep working with your fingertips to bring it together. Repeat for the second dough. Wrap each dough in clingfilm and place in the fridge to rest for 30 minutes. Once chilled, cut each sausage in half, for ease of handling. Roll out each half to about 1.5cm thickness, then cut out your cookies using a cutter. Place the cookies on to your baking tray and cook in the preheated oven for 10–12 minutes, until golden brown.

BLACKBERRY BUTTER Makes 2 jam jars

Gently heat 300g blackberries, 2 tablespoons lemon juice and 4 tablespoons icing sugar in a small pan for 5–6 minutes, until the berries look soft and syrupy. Allow to cool completely. Soften 300g unsalted butter and, using an electric whisk or food processor, beat the blackberries into the butter to create a lovely ripple effect. Spoon into jam jars and use on crumpets. This can be stored in the fridge for up to 4 days, or frozen for 1 month.

TIPS: *The soup can be frozen for up to 3 months in a sealed container. • Fry sage leaves in a little oil to create sage crisps for a soup garnish, or try adding drops of pumpkin-seed oil to the finished dish. • If you don't have enough pumpkin flesh, bulk it out with chunks of butternut squash. Alternatively, you can always cheat by adding shop-bought cartons of butternut squash or carrot and coriander soup.*

PUMPKIN SOUP

Served in its own raw or baked 'carcass', this soup is one of my favourites for this time of year. Hollowing out the pumpkins always proves a challenge — many an evening has been spent carving them in front of the TV — but the final result is well worth the effort. Witches' fingers cheese straws are great to dip into the soup, or as a pre-dinner nibble with drinks, served in tankards.

SERVES 8

For the soup

2.5kg pumpkin flesh (using 8–10 small or one large)

100g unsalted butter

3 medium onions, peeled and finely chopped

4 garlic cloves, peeled and crushed or finely chopped

a large pinch of dried chilli flakes

¾ teaspoon freshly grated nutmeg

sea salt and freshly ground black pepper

1.7 litres chicken or vegetable stock

To serve

double cream

toasted pumpkin seeds

Cut the tops off the pumpkins and set aside. Remove the seeds and fibres from the middle of each and discard. Using a sharp knife and a spoon, carefully hollow out the pumpkins. Scoop out the flesh and roughly chop.

In a large pan with a lid, melt the butter over a low heat then add the onion and garlic. Cook gently for 10–15 minutes, until softened and golden brown. Add the chopped pumpkin, the chilli flakes and the nutmeg, then season with salt and pepper. Increase the heat to medium and cover with the lid. Sauté for 6–8 minutes.

Pour in the stock, bring to the boil, then simmer for 40–45 minutes, stirring occasionally. Remove the pan from the heat and allow the soup to cool slightly. Hand-blend until smooth. When ready to serve, fill the hollowed-out pumpkins with soup (these can be used raw or baked with their lids on at 170°C/gas 3 for 20–25 minutes, drizzled with a little olive oil). Swirl with a little cream and scatter with toasted pumpkin seeds. Hand around cheese straws for dipping.

WITCHES' FINGERS CHEESE STRAWS Makes 24

Cut 375g ready-rolled puff pastry in half, and roll each half out on a lightly floured surface into a strip about 24cm long. Brush them with 2 beaten egg yolks mixed with a little water, sprinkle with 1 teaspoon paprika and 75g grated Cheddar cheese. Cut the pastry into 2cm-wide strips with a sharp knife — uneven strips make the knobbliest fingers. Press a pumpkin seed on to the tip of each to make a 'fingernail'. Bake on a lined baking sheet for 10–15 minutes at 200°C/gas 6 or until lightly browned. Remove to racks to cool. These can be frozen for up to 3 months in a sealed container. If cooking from frozen, add 3–5 minutes to the cooking time.

MUSHROOM CAPPUCCINO

After a damp afternoon spent kicking up the autumn leaves, this velvety, earthy soup will warm you up. Transform it into a magic potion with a cloud of foam and serve in little china cups. A drizzle of truffle oil will really lift the flavour. Serve with garlic croutons or garlic bread to keep evil spirits at bay.

SERVES 8

700g mixed mushrooms (chestnut and Portobello), wiped clean and chopped

12 spring onions, trimmed and chopped

4 garlic cloves, peeled and chopped

2 tablespoons olive oil

25g butter

1 litre chicken or vegetable stock

250ml skimmed milk

¼ teaspoon ground white pepper

To serve

15g dried porcini or chanterelle mushrooms, finely chopped

sea salt and black peppercorns

200ml skimmed milk

In a large pan, sauté the mushrooms, spring onions and garlic in the olive oil and butter over a high heat for 3–4 minutes. Pour in the stock, cover the pan and continue to cook for another 3–4 minutes. Add the milk and white pepper, then blitz the soup with a stick blender until very smooth. Keep hot. (At this stage the soup can be frozen for up to 3 months.)

To serve, grind the dried mushrooms, sea salt and peppercorns into a fine powder using a pestle and mortar and set this aside. Heat the milk until very hot, then use a milk frother or electric beater to create billows of light foam. Fill two-thirds of each serving cup with hot soup, spoon a little of the froth on top and sprinkle with the ground mushroom powder.

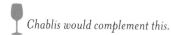 *Chablis would complement this.*

TIPS: *This makes a lovely starter, but double the quantities if you're serving it in soup bowls. • To make garlic croutons, cut 2 slices of crusty bread into small cubes, toss them in 2 tablespoons olive oil with 1 crushed garlic clove and season with salt and freshly ground black pepper. Fry over a medium heat until golden brown all over.*

TOAD-IN-THE-HOLE
WITH ONION GRAVY

Although it's a supper staple throughout the year, this is perfect for Hallowe'en — when better to put a toad on somebody's plate? Buy the sausages from a local butcher and choose interesting flavours for variety. The batter is flavoured with rosemary, but you could also try a few pinches of paprika or replace the mustard powder with a tablespoon of wholegrain mustard. Dish up with a rich onion gravy.

SERVES 8

16 pork sausages

16 slices Parma ham

2 tablespoons olive oil

450g plain flour

8 eggs

500ml milk

1 teaspoon mustard powder, or to taste

2 tablespoons chopped fresh rosemary

salt and freshly ground black pepper, to taste

For the onion gravy

2 tablespoons olive oil

2 large onions, peeled and finely sliced

4 teaspoons Dijon mustard

2 pints dark beef stock

Preheat the oven to 200°C/gas 6. Wrap the sausages in Parma ham. Pour the oil into the bottom of two 33cm x 24cm x 4cm-deep baking trays and arrange the sausages in a single layer in each tin. Place in the preheated oven and bake for 10 minutes.

In a bowl, mix together the flour, eggs and half the milk. Gradually mix in the rest of the milk until smooth. Add the mustard powder and rosemary, and season with salt and pepper.

Remove the pan from the oven. Ladle the batter over the sausages until they are three-quarters covered. Return to the oven and bake for 20–25 minutes, until risen and golden brown.

To make the onion gravy, heat the olive oil in a heavy-based saucepan. Add the sliced onion and cook over a gentle heat until soft, golden and caramelised. Stir in the mustard and pour in the stock. Bring the mixture to the boil, then reduce for 10 minutes, or until the liquid has thickened and reduced by half.

 *Rich and savoury red wine like Rioja works well with this dish.*

TIPS: *Try serving this with mashed potato. Colcannon is traditional at Hallowe'en and is a useful way of introducing greens to the table by adding chopped kale or green cabbage to the mashed potato. A healthy variation could be a colourful sweet potato mash, or for crunchy cheesy mash, add handfuls of grated Cheddar and a sprinkling of Parmesan on top before baking in the oven. For an extra kick, add a small amount of grated fresh horseradish.*

BUTTERNUT SQUASH LASAGNE

A large dish of this lasagne will bring the season to the table. This recipe may be vegetarian but it's so delicious that many a carnivore will consider converting. Serve with a mixed green salad.

SERVES 8

olive oil

1½ large onions, peeled and thinly sliced

1.2kg butternut squash, peeled, deseeded and sliced into 0.5cm thick crescents

1 large bunch of sage leaves, half left whole, half chopped

4 large garlic cloves, peeled and sliced

450g fresh spinach

a generous grating of nutmeg

sea salt and freshly ground black pepper

12–15 fresh or dried lasagne sheets

2 x 125g balls of mozzarella

For the béchamel sauce

125g butter

125g flour

800–850ml milk

75g grated Parmesan, plus 50g extra for sprinkling between layers

Preheat the oven to 200°C/gas 6. Drizzle a little oil on to a large baking tray, add the onion, butternut squash, chopped sage and garlic, then roast in the oven for 15-20 minutes until soft.

To make the béchamel sauce, melt the butter in a medium saucepan, then add the flour. Stir together until you have a paste and cook for 1–2 minutes. Slowly add the milk, constantly stirring until the sauce thickens, and add 75g Parmesan.

In a separate pan heat a little oil, add the spinach and nutmeg and season. Cook for a couple of minutes until the spinach has wilted, squeezing out any excess water.

If using dried lasagne sheets, blanch them in a pan of salted boiling water for 2 minutes until soft. Put a layer of pasta into a large earthenware baking dish, top with a layer of the butternut-squash mixture, a layer of béchamel sauce, some spinach and a sprinkling of Parmesan. Repeat the layers, ending with a final layer of pasta. Smooth over the remaining béchamel sauce. Rip the mozzarella into pieces and scatter these over the top with any remaining grated Parmesan. Place in the preheated oven for 25–30 minutes until the mozzarella bubbles and browns. Garnish with the whole sage leaves, flash-fried in a little hot butter.

*Aromatic and fullish whites like Chenin Blanc or a white Rhône.*

TIP: *This can be kept in the fridge for two days if covered in clingfilm or frozen for up to 3 months. Defrost fully before cooking.*

DEVIL'S FOOD CAKE

This chocolate cake reminds me of holidays in the Lake District when I was a child. A friend who lived there would make this cake and leave it in an old Roses tin for us to enjoy during our stay. It's comforting, not too rich and stays moist for ages (a treat for the rest of the week). Serve big wedges with a thick blood-red raspberry coulis to complete it as a pudding.

SERVES 8–10

85g margarine

285g caster sugar

2 medium eggs, lightly beaten

55g cocoa powder

220ml water

170g self-raising flour

For the icing

125g margarine

250g icing sugar

2 tablespoons cocoa powder, plus extra for dusting

2 tablespoons milk

For the raspberry coulis

300g raspberries

lemon juice, to taste

3 tablespoons icing sugar

Preheat the oven to 150°C/gas 2. Grease and line 2 x 20cm sandwich tins. Cream the margarine and caster sugar together until soft and fluffy. Then gradually add the beaten eggs, mixing well after each addition. Blend the cocoa powder with the water. Add alternately with the flour into the margarine mixture, until all is blended smoothly. Divide the cake mixture between the two tins and bake in the centre of the oven for 25 minutes until firm and just coming away from the side of the tins. Turn out and leave to cool on a rack. (At this stage the sponges can be frozen for up to a month.)

To make the icing, beat the margarine and icing sugar together until light and fluffy. Add the cocoa powder and milk and beat until combined. Sandwich the cakes together using half the icing, then use the remainder to top the cake. Decorate with a simple dusting of cocoa powder.

For the coulis, blend the raspberries, lemon juice and icing sugar until smooth, then sieve to remove any seeds.

TIP: *To make chocolate curls to decorate the cake, melt 100g dark chocolate (70% cocoa solids) then pour on to a flat surface (such as a baking sheet) and spread it out thinly. Allow to cool until set, then carefully drag a sharp knife from one end of the chocolate to the other to form curls.*

SOUL CAKES *In the Middle Ages, 'soul cakes' made of bread, currants and spices were laid out, along with glasses of wine, as an offering to the souls in Purgatory. On All Hallows' Eve and All Souls' Day, families sent their children out 'souling': walking from house to house begging for these cakes. For each cake received, they would say a prayer for the souls of the donor's dead relatives.*

CREEPY COCKTAILS

BLACKBERRY COLLINS Serves 4

Blend 100g blackberries with 1 tablespoon icing sugar to make a blackberry purée. Strain this through a sieve into a wide shallow bowl. Pour a little caster sugar into another bowl, then dip the rims of 4 tall glasses into the purée and then into the sugar. Fill the glasses with crushed or cubed ice. Add the blackberry purée to a cocktail shaker, with 100ml blackberry liqueur or cassis and 200ml gin. Shake well over cubed ice before carefully pouring into your sugar-rimmed glasses. Stir in a little soda water and finish with a couple of blackberries.

SHIRLEY TEMPLE Serves 1 (make to order)

For this alcohol-free option, adding grenadine syrup at the end gives the effect of blood trickling down the edges of the glass. Make these up individually to achieve the best layering effect. Fill a tall glass with ice and pour over old-fashioned lemonade (or use the juice of 1 large lemon and 120ml soda water) until it is three-quarters full. Top up the glass with orange juice and add a few teaspoons grenadine syrup. Garnish with a slice of orange and a maraschino cherry on a cocktail stick.

ESPRESSO MARTINI Serves 1 (make to order)

This cocktail can be served after dinner in lieu of pudding. Make each to order to get the best flavour and froth. Put just a few cubes of ice in a cocktail shaker and pour over 50ml vodka, 25ml good-quality coffee liqueur (such as Illyquore or Kahlua), 25ml espresso and a dash of sugar syrup (page 104). Shake well and strain into a chilled martini glass. Garnish with coffee beans and dust with cinnamon.

BLOOD AND SAND Serves 1 (make to order)

It's all in the name. Fill a cocktail shaker with ice cubes and pour in 30ml Scotch whisky, 30ml blood orange juice, 20ml Italian sweet vermouth and 20ml cherry liqueur. Shake and pour into a chilled martini glass or Champagne coupe. Garnish with an orange twist.

> RAISING A TOAST *Lambswool, a cocktail of mulled ale with sugar, spices and the pulp of roasted apples, served with spiced pieces of brown toast floating on the surface, was historically drunk at Hallowe'en. (The custom of floating toast on drinks is said to be the origin of people raising a toast.)*

FUN AND GAMES

For parties, make sure all your guests are in character. Provide a dressing-up box and face paints, then organise a variety of activities and games. Stage rounds of bobbing for apples and eating doughnuts dangling from a tree, or for a quieter activity set up a leaf-rubbing table. And don't forget to spook the children by telling them ghost stories to heighten the atmosphere.

DRESSING UP AND FACE PAINTING

Generations of adults and children have devised increasingly imaginative ways of dressing up as scary and supernatural creatures. My Hallowe'en costumes as a child were usually homemade mismatches from the dressing-up box. Traditional characters include witches, ghosts, skeletons, vampires and cats. In more recent years, these Hallowe'en regulars have been joined by zombies, aliens and superheroes from popular sci-fi and horror films.

A black jumper and leggings or trousers can be embellished to create a whole host of different characters. Try adding:

- *A cape and an arrowhead tail for a devil costume.*
- *Ears and a tail for a black cat.*
- *A pointy hat, fake hair and a broom for a witch's outfit.*
- *A pair of white gloves and a ghoulish mask for a skeleton look.*
- *A hairband with corks stuck to it and sprayed silver (as bolts) for Frankenstein's monster.*

Another easy idea is to use old white torn-up sheets to create a ghost or a mummy (add an extra wrapping of loo roll for the full effect). A flour bag or calico bag with slits for eyes, nose and mouth can also be the basis for a dressing-up costume – think scary escaped convict . . .

Face paint, make-up and grisly accessories are vital for a convincing costume. Have plenty of white and red face paint for zombies, some horns for your little devils and orange face paints and stripy scarves for pumpkins. Beards and brows can be applied using soot from a cork burnt in a candle flame. Make sure you have some false teeth for vampires, black eye-pencil for scars and cat features, and red lipstick for blood. You can buy fake body tattoos for a bit of fun, and face-paint stencils if you'd like a professional finish.

PUMPKIN BOWLING

This is a seasonal take on ten-pin bowling. In the run-up to Hallowe'en, save ten small drink bottles for pins. You can give them the appearance of ghosts by pouring in 5cm white gloss paint and a drop of paint thinner and shaking. Add faces to the outsides with black marker pen. You'll also need small pumpkins with short stems for bowling balls. If you can't find any, oranges work just as well.

Add some gravel or water to each bottle so they don't topple over too easily. Arrange them in a triangle and mark out the boundaries of your 'alley' with twigs and branches or string if you are indoors, plus a starting line. Then, following the rules of ten-pin bowling, each player gets two goes at bowling to try to knock down as many ghost 'pins' as possible.

THE MUMMY CHASE

You'll need a garden to play this game (or a quiet street and understanding neighbours), plus a stockpile of loo roll.

Divide the players into teams. Each team nominates a mummy. Give each team a couple of loo rolls and put on some Hallowe'en-themed music. As the music plays, team members must wrap their mummy from head to toe, leaving just a small gap for the eyes and nose. Teams must use up all their loo rolls.

Once the mummification is complete, everyone goes outside. Set up a starting and finishing line for a race between the mummies, who must complete it without their wrappings coming off. If the paper starts to unravel mid-race, the mummies must return to the starting line where their team-mates can perform emergency repairs. The first mummy to cross the finishing line with bandages intact is declared the winner.

APPLE BOBBING

This has many variations, but here I've turned apple bobbing into a team relay for enhanced exhilaration. Play outside, or have lots of towels on hand to mop up! Blindfolding the players can be hilarious, and remember, the deeper the container, the harder it is to bite the apple. Fill two large bowls with water, fill them with enough apples for each team member and place each bowl on a chair about 30cm apart. Divide the players into two teams and stand behind the starting line several metres away from the bowls. On the command 'Go!', the first players on each team run up to the bowls and try to get an apple out of the water by kneeling or standing in front of the bowl and using their teeth. No hands allowed! As soon as an apple is out of the water and dropped on the floor, the successful player races back and tags the next player. The winning team is the first to empty their bowl. To keep things moving and ensure that everyone gets a go, set a limit of a minute per person.

LEAF RUBBING

This is a lovely activity to make the most of the splendours of the season. Set up a table with coloured wax crayons and paper, and send the children on a hunt to find autumnal leaves in interesting shapes and textures. Lay the paper over the foliage and rub using the sides of the crayons to create skeletal pictures of nature.

THE WITCH'S LAIR

Sometimes you want a game that's more of an experience than a contest. One Hallowe'en game I particularly remember playing with friends involved taking turns to delve into bowls of unusual objects and 'guess the body part'. In advance of your party, gather a selection of 'body parts'. Here are some suggestions, but let your imagination run riot:

- *Eyeballs: peeled or oil-covered grapes, olives, lychees.*
- *Guts: cooked spaghetti, sausages with most of the sausagemeat removed from the casings or marshmallows soaked in water, strung together and coated with oil.*
- *Brain: overcooked cauliflower.*
- *Heart: a skinned beef tomato.*
- *Toenails: shells from pistachio nuts or walnuts.*
- *Veins: cooked vermicelli or egg noodles.*

Put your body parts into separate bowls and hide them out of sight of your guests or cover the bowls with tea towels. When it's time to play, gather your guests and blindfold them. Tell them a Hallowe'en story about a local witch who has been collecting body parts to use in her potions. Lead your blindfolded victims to the 'body parts' and share with them the grisly items the witch has left behind, guiding hands into the bowls and asking your victims to identify what they're touching. Invariably, the game ends in howls of horror and disgust.

GHOULISH GAMES AND GHOST STORIES

THE DOUGHNUT TREE

This is best played outside, before it gets too dark and cold, but if you play indoors, line the floor with plenty of newspapers. If you have time to prepare the tree in advance, hang other spooky decorations from it to conjure up a witchy atmosphere.

You'll need a tree with accessible branches. Hang up a ring doughnut for each player, spacing them out and dangling them from various heights to accommodate both the short and the tall. (If you're playing indoors hang them from a length of string across the room.) Players stand by the doughnuts and when the umpire shouts 'Eat!' everyone must devour their doughnut as quickly as possible without using their hands. The first player to finish wins. Umpires must demand to see an empty mouth as proof of victory.

GHOST STORIES

Share stories as the light begins to fade, with just a torch for illumination. Get an enthusiastic storyteller to read from a classic children's book: some brilliant reads include the Dr Seuss books, the Meg and Mog series, Grimm's fairy tales, *Frankenstein*, *Dracula*, *The Worst Witch* and Roald Dahl's ghost stories. Or you could let everyone take turns adding a few sentences to a story and see where it leads. Serve hot blackcurrant squash (vampire's blood) and Hallowe'en cookies (page 23) and tell your younger guests that they've been made using a secret 'spell' to rachet up the tension and multiply the chills running down their spines.

When mighty Roast Beef was the Englishman's food,
It ennobled our brains and enriched our blood.
Our soldiers were brave and our courtiers were good
Oh! the Roast Beef of old England,
And old English Roast Beef!

'The Roast Beef of Old England'
Henry Fielding

SUNDAY LUNCHES

A Sunday roast with all the trimmings is something to look forward to when the summer months are coming to an end and we move from refreshing salads and sizzling barbecues in the fresh air to indoor feasts. As the nights draw in, the kitchen once again becomes the nucleus of the household, wafting tantalising aromas of roasting meat and baking, attracting everyone in the house and echoing the natural instinct in us all to batten down the hatches and prepare for the cold months ahead.

The Sunday roast has a long and distinguished history in Britain; traditionally a piece of meat was rotated before an open fire or else dropped off at the baker's on the way to the church to cook slowly in the cooling bread ovens (bread wasn't baked on Sundays). It was seen as a weekly treat; Sunday was the only rest day after a six-day working week, and this meal gave families the opportunity to sit down together. Modern life has reinvented the nature of Sundays, however – many shops are open, and some people now work, while others choose to go out for the day, leaving little time to dedicate to cooking and being homely.

Cooking a roast is a traditional domestic ritual that does require some time, but it can be a great focus for a casual celebration, perhaps centred around a family get-together, birthday or other special event. It's worth putting in the effort to make an occasion of it and having a sit-down lunch as a regular feature of your home life. Sunday lunch offers the perfect slot in the weekend to rejoice in the company of those close to you, to push the pause button and to take stock before the madness begins again the following week. In my boarding-school days, a family Sunday lunch gave us a good reason to come back from school, even just for the day – we would be fed the full works, pudding and all, to prepare us for the school week ahead (a great way to fend off the dreaded Sunday-night blues).

What I like about this ritual is the fact that it's essentially unfussy – there's nothing to dress up, not even the food. It should be an occasion, like the Christmas meal, where everyone pitches in to help – laying the table, carving, clearing up and chatting together, so you'll need to pay less attention to the finer details. It's also a great way to feed many people with relatively little effort. With a clever choice of cut, and various preparation shortcuts, the perfect roast can be something you can almost forget about in the oven. You can even cheat with a few of the ingredients if you simply haven't got time to prepare things yourself – remember, it's all about being gathered round the table, talking and enjoying the meal together.

RELAXED SUNDAYS

What you choose to cook for your Sunday lunch all depends on what plans you have over the weekend. Visit your local butcher's and experiment with different cuts of meat and seasonal game – don't worry about getting a piece a little bigger than you need, as roasts make for delicious leftovers for the rest of the week. The traditional choice is a classic roast but it can be quite a feat bringing all the components to the table at the same time (particularly the gravy). If you're planning a walk before lunch, consider slow cooking or pot roasting. You might want to encourage your children to get involved and help plan the menu; this way they can feel part of the occasion and will – hopefully – inherit a love for this time-honoured ritual.

Starters are rarely necessary, as this meal is often substantial enough to keep everyone full throughout the afternoon, but some spiced nuts (page 62) and vegetable crisps are great to pick at between bouts of table-laying and vegetable prepping. Serve a few jugs of Bloody or Virgin Mary alongside. Use colourful autumn leaves as place names for the table. Stick on a pretty feather with PVA glue and staple to a piece of card or hessian. Write the name with a gold pen.

HOW TO CARVE A ROAST

Carving a roast at the table makes a real ceremony of the meal. Always let the meat stand for 10–20 minutes after you take it out of the oven, depending on how large the joint is, to keep in the juices and make carving easier. This also gives you time to get the trimmings ready and make the gravy. When it comes to carving, make sure you have a very sharp, long-handled knife and a pronged fork (with a guard) to hold the meat. Use a carving board with a lip or well around the edges to catch the tasty juices – you can add these to the gravy. Carve the meat using long, sweeping motions and firm pressure – avoid sawing or pressing down too hard, as this will create distorted or ragged-edged slices. Have a warmed platter ready for the carved slices and cover them with foil until you need them. Don't forget to serve some of the crispy ends, skin and brown meat, as these are often the tastiest morsels.

LEG OF LAMB

Cut a few slices in the same direction as the bone to create a flat base. Holding the protruding bone end of the lamb steady with your fork, start at the shank end and slice down towards the bone at a slight angle (across the grain). Turn the knife slightly to free each slice from the bone as you go, or do it at the end by turning the knife parallel to the bone and freeing all the slices at once. Turn the leg over and do the same on the other side.

RIB OF BEEF

Steady the joint with the fork and carve downwards with the chine (thick end) parallel to the rib bones, starting on the right side if you are right-handed and on the left if left-handed. Cut vertically along the bone. I like thicker slices for beef, but carve to your preference.

CHICKEN

You can cut up your chicken into portions consisting of the drumstick, thigh, breast and wing. With the legs pointing away from you, lever the whole leg away from the body and cut through the skin and joint. Then separate the drumstick from the thigh by cutting down through the joint (if it's turkey, you can carve slices off the drumstick first, slicing at an angle). Remove the wing by cutting it at the joint with the body. Turn the chicken so the neck is facing you and cut each breast away from the breastbone either in slices or as a whole slab, – you can then carve the whole breast on the diagonal. Don't forget to remove the 'oysters' under the carcass – these tasty little nuggets are the 'carver's reward'.

POT ROAST
TARRAGON CHICKEN

This is a great way to cook a whole chicken while keeping the meat juicy. This recipe serves four people, but is easily doubled if you have room in the oven. The chicken can be shredded in its sauce (reduce it if it's too runny) and will make a great pie filling.

SERVES 4

1.6kg free-range
whole chicken

salt and freshly ground
black pepper

I lemon, halved

2 tablespoons olive oil

2 medium onions, peeled and
cut into wedges

2 celery sticks, roughly
chopped

2 garlic cloves, kept whole,
but squashed

125ml white wine

250ml chicken stock

½ bunch of fresh tarragon

For the sauce

300g button mushrooms,
brushed clean and halved

20g butter

200g crème fraîche

I–2 tablespoons wholegrain
mustard (optional)

2 tablespoons chopped fresh
tarragon leaves

Preheat the oven to 180°C/gas 4. Season the chicken with salt and pepper and stuff the lemon halves into the cavity. Heat the oil in a large pan (which has a lid) over a medium to high heat. Add the seasoned chicken and brown on all sides. Remove to a plate. Into the same pan, toss the onion, celery and garlic. Sauté for 2–3 minutes. Sit the chicken back in the pan on top of the vegetables. Pour in the wine and chicken stock before adding the tarragon. Bring the liquid to the boil, put the lid on and then cook in the oven for I hour IO minutes. To check it's cooked, insert a skewer into the thigh and the juices will run clear.

Remove the chicken from the pan and transfer to a plate. Strain the onions, tarragon and celery through a sieve. Let the remaining liquid sit for a few minutes before skimming any fat from the surface. In another pan, brown the mushrooms in the butter, remove from the pan and set aside. Pour in the reserved liquid gradually, then whisk in the crème fraîche, mustard (if using) and tarragon. Stir well until combined and cook until starting to thicken, before finally adding the mushrooms. Serve the chicken whole to the table in the pot and carve, or joint the rested chicken and serve in a dish with the sauce poured over. This is lovely with the roast potatoes on page 54.

 *Hunter Valley Semillon Sauvignon Blanc or a Pinot Noir.*

ROASTING TIMES FOR CHICKEN

For a traditional, oven-roast chicken, allow 20 minutes per 450g at 190°C/gas 5, plus 10—20 minutes at 220°C/gas 7 at the end to crisp the skin. Check and baste the meat frequently and adjust the timings for your particular oven.

TRADITIONAL ROAST RIB OF BEEF

The ultimate Sunday lunch dish, roast beef and Yorkshire pudding is a quintessential British combination, well known from the middle of the eighteenth century when the French started referring to the English as 'les rosbifs'. Rib of beef is one of the tastiest cuts as it's cooked on the bone, which also makes for a flavoursome gravy. Ask the butcher to trim the bones for a neat finish. I like to cheat a little and use shop-bought fresh or frozen Yorkshire puddings. Remember to remove the meat from the fridge half an hour before cooking to allow it to come to room temperature.

....

SERVES 8

....

3- to 4-bone trimmed rib of beef, approximately 3kg

4–6 tablespoons Dijon mustard

salt and freshly ground black pepper

For the horseradish sauce

100g hot horseradish sauce

4 tablespoons crème fraîche

a squeeze of lemon juice

For the gravy

4 tablespoons plain flour

800ml good-quality beef stock

200ml red wine

Preheat the oven to 220°C/gas 7. Place the rib of beef in a large roasting tray and spread the mustard all over the meat. Season well with salt and pepper. Roast in the preheated oven for 20 minutes then reduce the heat to 170°C/gas 3 and roast for the remaining calculated cooking time (see box below). Baste occasionally with the roasting juices. Once the meat is cooked to your preference, remove it from the oven, transfer to a board and cover with foil. Reserve the roasting juices. Allow the meat to rest for at least 25–30 minutes. Combine the horseradish sauce, crème fraîche and lemon juice in a bowl. Season to taste.

To make the gravy, drain all but 3–4 tablespoons of fat from the roasting tray. Place the tray on the hob over a medium heat and stir in the flour. Once combined, gradually whisk in the stock and red wine. Continue to whisk until smooth and allow to reduce until thickened. Season with salt and pepper to taste, add the roasting juices and strain before serving.

 A red Claret.

> ### ROASTING TIMES FOR BEEF ON THE BONE
> *For rare: allow 12 minutes per 450g, plus 15 minutes. For medium, allow 16 minutes per 450g, plus 20 minutes. For well done, allow 20 minutes per 450g, plus 25 minutes. Check and baste the meat frequently and adjust the timings for your particular oven.*

SLOW ROAST LEG OF LAMB

The ultimate lazy roast, and delicious served with whole roasted bulbs of garlic (page 62). To add extra flavour and tenderise the meat, marinate it in the red wine, herbs and garlic overnight before cooking as instructed. You can also use lamb shanks in this recipe, if you prefer (see tip below).

SERVES 8

2.2–2.5kg bone-in leg of lamb

salt and freshly ground black pepper

2 tablespoons olive oil

4 red onions, peeled and cut into wedges

4 carrots, peeled and cut into chunks

4 garlic cloves, peeled and crushed

3 bay leaves

3 sprigs of rosemary

1 x 750ml bottle red wine

400ml lamb or beef stock

8 plums, cut in half and stoned

15g butter, softened

15g plain flour

1–2 tablespoons redcurrant jelly

Preheat the oven to 160°C/gas 3. Season the lamb with salt and pepper. Heat the oil in a pan and cook the onion and carrot for a few minutes until softened. Place the lamb in a very large, thick-bottomed, lightly oiled roasting tin. Add the softened vegetables, garlic, bay leaves and rosemary. Pour in the wine and stock, cover tightly with foil and cook in the preheated oven for 3 hours, basting occasionally with the cooking juices. Remove the foil and cook, uncovered, for another 30 minutes, then add the plum halves and cook for a further 20–25 minutes until the lamb is tender, almost falling off the bone, and the liquid has reduced slightly.

Remove the lamb, vegetables and plums from the tin, set aside and keep warm. Remove the bay leaves and discard. Place the roasting tin on the hob over a high heat. Mix together the softened butter and flour in a small bowl until it forms a smooth paste, then whisk into the sauce. Simmer for 10 minutes or until the sauce has thickened and reduced. Stir in the redcurrant jelly and season to taste. Return the lamb and accompaniments to the sauce and warm through.

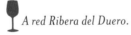 *A red Ribera del Duero.*

TIP: *Substitute the leg of lamb with 8 seasoned lamb shanks. Brown them in a little olive oil in a large casserole pot. Remove from the pot, add the onion and carrot and cook for a few minutes until soft. Stir in the garlic, bay leaves and rosemary and return the shanks to the pan. Pour in the wine and stock, bring to the boil then reduce to a simmer for 8–10 minutes. Cover with a lid, transfer to the preheated oven and cook for 2 hours. Add the plum halves and cook, uncovered, for a further 20–25 minutes. To finish the recipe, continue as per the leg of lamb recipe above.*

...AND TWO VEG (OR MORE)

Depending on what vegetables are in season, serve them freshly boiled or steamed on the side. They can be cooked at the last minute and neatly arranged on a platter. Alternatively, parboil them ahead of time, chill in ice-cold water and reheat in butter or oil and herbs when needed. Look out for mini versions of vegetables when in season, such as carrots, leeks, courgettes and asparagus, which look tidy and don't require peeling or chopping. Aside from the classic sides here, you could serve roast parsnips and carrots (page 147), or a potato dauphinoise (page 257), which can be made ahead of time.

GARLIC AND ROSEMARY ROAST POTATOES Serves 8

Preheat the oven to 225°C/gas 7. Peel 1.8kg Maris Piper, King Edward or other floury potatoes, and cut any large potatoes in half so that they are all a uniform size. Put them into cold salted water, bring to the boil and cook for 6 minutes. Drain, return the potatoes to the pan and shake them with the lid on to 'fluff' the edges up, then allow to cool.

Place 3 tablespoons each of goose fat and vegetable oil into a heavy-based roasting tin and heat in the oven for 5–10 minutes, until the oil is smoking. Add the potatoes with 4 roughly chopped sprigs of rosemary and 12 fat garlic cloves with their skins on, and season well. Make sure everything is well coated in the oil and not too crowded in the tin. Cook for 40–45 minutes until golden and crispy, turning the potatoes every 10 minutes.

HASSELBACK POTATOES Serves 8

Preheat the oven to 200°C/gas 6. Parboil 8 unpeeled medium baking potatoes for 10 minutes, then drain. Using a sharp knife, make slices widthways across each potato about 3–5mm apart, but don't cut all the way through the potato (see the photograph on page 71). When all the potatoes have been sliced, place them cut side up in a shallow baking dish or small roasting tin. Drizzle with 2 tablespoons melted butter, then season with salt and pepper.

Bake for 15–20 minutes. Remove the potatoes from the oven and drizzle with another 2 tablespoons melted butter. Sprinkle 4 tablespoons finely grated Pecorino cheese and 2 tablespoons breadcrumbs on top of the potatoes and season with a little more salt and pepper. Return to the oven and bake for another 20 minutes, or until nicely browned.

CAULIFLOWER AND BROCCOLI CHEESE Serves 8

Preheat the oven to 180°C/gas 4. Cut a large cauliflower into florets and boil in salted water for 4–5 minutes, until just tender. Cut a large head of broccoli into florets and add midway through the cooking, as it takes less time to cook.

For the cheese sauce, melt 50g butter in a medium saucepan. Add 50g plain flour and 1 teaspoon mustard powder, stir well and cook for 1–2 minutes. Gradually whisk in 650ml milk and cook over a low heat for 6–8 minutes, stirring frequently, until the sauce begins to thicken. Stir in a generous pinch of freshly grated nutmeg. Remove from the heat and mix in 200g mature Cheddar and 50g Parmesan (both finely grated), until the cheese has melted and the sauce is smooth. Arrange the cauliflower and broccoli in a 30cm x 22cm ovenproof dish. Pour over the sauce, making sure everything is evenly coated. Sprinkle with more Parmesan and some grated nutmeg, then bake in the oven for 30–35 minutes, until golden brown and bubbling.

RED CABBAGE Serves 8

In a large pan, melt 30g butter and sauté 1 red onion, peeled and thinly sliced, for a few minutes to soften. Remove and discard the core from a red cabbage and shred the rest finely, then add to the pan along with 4 tablespoons red wine vinegar, 5 tablespoons dark brown sugar and a cinnamon stick. Stir together for a few minutes before adding the juice and zest of 1 orange and 75ml water and seasoning with salt and freshly ground black pepper. Bring to the boil then reduce the heat, cover with a lid and simmer for 35–40 minutes until the cabbage is tender and the liquid has evaporated. Garnish with orange zest to serve.

FAVOURITE BRITISH PUDDINGS

Traditional puddings are a key element of a Sunday lunch. I've included a few of my favourites, but if time is short, the supermarkets are well stocked with steamed puddings, tarts and fresh custard, all of which are quick to heat through. For a more continental option, drown vanilla ice cream in a shot of espresso to make an 'affogato', an instant dessert that's a quick and light end to a meal.

STICKY TOFFEE PUDDING Serves 8

The sponge can be frozen for up to a month, tightly wrapped in clingfilm. Reheat with toffee sauce drizzled over.

Preheat the oven to 180°C/gas 4. Lightly grease a large (26cm x 24cm) rectangular baking tin. Mix 100g chopped dates and 1 teaspoon each of vanilla essence and bicarbonate of soda with 450ml water. In a separate bowl, cream 60g softened unsalted butter and 170g soft light brown sugar together until pale and fluffy, then gradually beat in 1 egg. Sift 225g self-raising flour and gradually add this to the creamed mixture with 1 teaspoon mixed spice and ½ teaspoon ground cinnamon, then add the date mixture, stirring to combine. Pour into the baking tin, and bake for 40 minutes until it's spongy to the touch. To make the sauce, put 100ml double cream in a pan with 30g unsalted butter and 60g dark brown sugar. For extra spice, you can also add 3 balls of chopped stem ginger to the sauce. Stir over a low heat until the sugar is dissolved. Serve over the sticky toffee pudding and drizzle with cream.

APPLE AND BLACKBERRY CRUMBLE Serves 8

Fruit crumble always goes down well. Apple and blackberry wins the filling contest for me, but peach and banana, gooseberry or rhubarb are all delicious. Make up a batch of crumble and freeze in an airtight container.

Preheat the oven to 180°C/gas 4. Lightly grease a 2 litre/25cm ovenproof dish or 8 individual ramekins. Melt 100g unsalted butter in a large non-stick pan. Add 800g peeled, cored and roughly chopped Bramley apples with 100g caster sugar, 100ml apple juice and the zest of 1 lemon and cook for 6–8 minutes, stirring frequently until the apples are softened. Add 250g blackberries and toss together, adding more sugar if necessary, then transfer the mixture to the prepared dish. Sift 150g plain flour into a large bowl and add 75g cold unsalted butter cut into cubes. Rub the butter into the flour until the mixture resembles fine breadcrumbs. Stir in 150g golden caster sugar, 75g porridge oats or muesli, 50g roughly chopped almonds and 2 teaspoons ground cinnamon. Spoon the topping over the filling, sprinkle with light brown sugar and bake for 30 minutes or until the top is golden brown. Serve with custard.

FUN AND GAMES

Games are not only fun but are also useful for keeping children at the table. A Sunday lunch merits a good walk afterwards to at least attempt to burn off some of the excess calories. Give each child an egg box, or even a matchbox, in which to collect nature's treasures and tell them to find as many objects as they can to fit into it.

FICTIONARY DICTIONARY

Scan the dictionary for a suitably obscure word and read it out. Everybody invents a definition and writes it down on a piece of paper. Write down the real definition, collect the papers from the group and read them all out. Everyone votes for the definition they think is true and the person who fools the most people is the winner.

COIN RUGBY

This is a game for two players sitting opposite each other. To start, someone balances their two-pence piece on their edge of the table so that half is resting on the table, while the other half is hanging off the edge. From this position, the player has three moves to slide the coin further across to the other side of the table, where it should end up hanging half over the edge again. The first move should be with a flattened palm – the player simply hits the overhanging coin further on to the table. The second and third moves can be flicks or nudges but sustained contact with the coin in the form of a push or a drag is forbidden. If the player doesn't manage to achieve overhang at the other side of the table in his three goes, then it is the other player's turn to play. If, however, he does succeed, then he can attempt to score a 'try'. To do this, he must flick the overhanging coin into the air with one of his fingers and then catch it with the same hand. A point is awarded for a successful 'try'.

BOUCHON

For this family favourite, players sit round a table with a number of corks in the centre, one fewer cork than there are players. Appoint a game 'leader' and decide how many 'lives' players will have before they are eliminated. From a full pack of cards select four cards of the same number or rank for each player, ie for four players select all the fours, aces, eights and jacks. Shuffle this selection and deal each player four cards. To start a round, each player places one of their cards face down on the table. When the leader says 'pass', cards are passed one at a time to the left while they are received from the right. The aim is to collect four cards of the same kind. Once someone has achieved this, he takes a cork and calls out 'Bouchon' ('cork' in French). The other players must snatch a cork as quickly as possible. The one who fails to do so loses a 'life'. When a player is eliminated remove one set of four-of-a-kind cards from the pack and one cork from the pile and carry on with the game with one less player, and so on ...

STOP THE BUS

Ask everyone to draw a simple grid on a piece of paper with columns for categories such as colours, parts of the body, breeds of dog, etc. The first column must be blank and labelled 'Bus Route'. Randomly select a letter of the alphabet – this becomes the Bus Route and should be entered on the first line of each player's grid in the Bus Route column. One of the players 'Starts the Bus' and the idea is to fill each column with an entry that begins with this chosen letter. The first player to complete every column shouts 'Stop the Bus'. Everyone stops writing and reads out their answers. Players are awarded 2 points for a unique entry, 1 point for a non-unique entry and no points for a blank entry. Select another random letter for the next round. After a set number of rounds, add up the final scores to determine the winner.

That the speed of eating should be
moderate, dinner being the last affair of the
day, and that the guests behave like travellers
who aim to arrive at the same destination.

La Physiologie du Goût,
Jean Anthelme Brillat-Savarin

COSY SUPPER PARTIES

Not tied to a specific calendar event, informal suppers span the seasons and cover a multitude of occasions, from a low-key birthday to a house-warming event or simply because it's a Friday evening and you can enjoy some respite at the end of a busy week. See this chapter as a celebration of the everyday and the chance to reconnect with important friends, something that seems increasingly difficult with the pressures of work and family life.

Historically, the dinner party was a largely nineteenth-century creation, which reflected broader changes in society. But this sort of evening isn't about the 'pomp' and pretentiousness often associated with a dinner party, nor is it about fancy decorations and presenting a procession of expensive gourmet delights. It's about creating a welcoming and private space for people to unwind after a day's work. You could be sitting at a dining table, a kitchen counter, perched on a stool or relaxed on the sofa for a TV supper in front of a big sporting game. As with traditional Sunday lunch, the focus here is on breaking bread, sharing good food and wine in an intimate and more personal way, not about slaving over a hot stove for hours on end. Good friends shouldn't and won't expect this – the company and atmosphere should reign above all else.

For these sorts of low-key occasions, often the foods that everyone enjoys the most are old friends themselves, familiar and reliable. Nothing could be more welcoming than walking into a home that smells of glorious comfort food (by this I'm talking about pies and stews bubbling in the oven). Lots of friends I know serve the same 'signature' dishes when they have people for supper, often because they don't have lots of time and their recipes are guaranteed to work. Similarly, these fail-safe dishes often mean you can prepare them on autopilot and ideally freeze them ahead of time, so when guests are over you're not fussing about the food in the kitchen and being kept from the company for too long. A personal touch, such as a thoughtful place setting, an unusual dessert from the supermarket if you've run out of time or a fun after-dinner game, is a quick and inexpensive way to make the evening your own. But these are added extras, if the occasion calls for it.

SET THE SCENE

A relaxed supper with friends needn't be a tablecloth occasion. Keep everything low-key: a bare wooden table with a simple table runner, bistro-type glasses and plenty of candlelight. If anything, be creative with place names; quick ideas include Scrabble letters or used corks (cut a groove into one edge and slot in a place card). Buy a bunch of fresh flowers for a side table and scented candles for the bathroom.

GREET YOUR GUESTS

Offering something other than wine as an aperitif when your guests arrive will help everyone relax and unwind. Set up a help-yourself gin and tonic or martini bar (page 65), with an ice bucket, knife and small board for slicing lemons and limes, or perhaps a dry sherry and spiced nuts. Have jugs of water infused with ribbons of cucumber and mint.

NIBBLES AND STARTERS TO SHARE

Your friends will need something to graze on to keep hunger pangs at bay, especially if they've arrived straight from work. Drizzle some whole heads of garlic with olive oil and sea salt, then roast at 190°C/gas 5 for 30–40 minutes until soft. Serve halved with French baguettes. Vegetable crisps and spiced nuts (see below) or good-quality salted potato crisps with dips are always extremely popular, however unoriginal! Starters should be quick and easy: a Camembert baked in a hot oven for 10–15 minutes (page 333) or a board of charcuterie and antipasti can be put together in minutes and shared at the table with warm ciabatta bread and small bowls of olive oil and balsamic vinegar for dipping. Lovely antipasti ingredients include meats such as Parma ham, chorizo, Iberico ham and salami, as well as olives, artichoke hearts, mixed roasted peppers, sun-blush tomatoes and caperberries.

SPICED NUTS Serves 8

Heat a large, non-stick frying pan over a medium heat and dry roast 400g mixed plain nuts (hazelnuts, pecans, whole almonds, cashews and walnuts) for 5–6 minutes, until golden. Transfer to a large bowl. Melt 50g butter in the hot pan and add 50g dark brown sugar, stirring gently until the sugar dissolves. Mix ¼ teaspoon each of ground cumin, cayenne pepper and mixed spice with a pinch of chilli flakes and ¼ teaspoon sea salt. Return the nuts to the pan, add the spices and stir to coat evenly with the sticky mixture. Tip on to a tray lined with baking parchment, and leave to cool and harden before serving.

Manzanilla or Fino Sherry, a red Chilean Merlot or Rioja, or a white Chenin Blanc.

MADE-TO-MEASURE MARTINIS

It can be fun to set up a bar dedicated to martinis where guests can mix their own concoctions. On a small side table set out the basic ingredients: bottles of vodka, gin and dry vermouth that have been chilled in the freezer; a small jug of chilled 'dirty' water (the olive brine); dishes of cucumber, olives and citrus fruit for garnishes – lemons, oranges and limes are classics, or try grapefruit rind (for garnish ideas see page 104). Make sure you have a cocktail shaker, strainer and stirrer, as well as plenty of ice. Your guests can opt for shaken, stirred, poured, clean or 'dirty'. Typically, a martini should be stirred, not shaken, as the gin can 'bruise' and become bitter, but of course James Bond has popularised what was traditionally known as a 'Bradford' martini. Chill martini glasses to give them a lovely opaque look by putting them in the freezer along with your gin and vodka. To keep the glasses cool on the bar, fill them with iced water until you need them. It's likely that one friend might like to take charge if they know what they're doing and make them for everyone. Have a menu card handy with notes on how to mix a dry or wet martini or some other variations so guests can experiment.

THE BEST VODKA MARTINI Serves 1 (make to order)

There has been so much written about this legendary cocktail in a seemingly endless quest for the perfect mix. For gin-based versions, the classic garnish is an olive or three, or a cocktail onion (this is called a Gibson). I prefer a vodka martini, simply garnished with lemon. For refreshing alternatives, try a passion-fruit martini (page 161), a pear martini (page 133) or a White Lady (page 250).

Slice pieces of rind from a lemon of around 2.5cm in length and 1cm wide (one per drink). Fold the rind in half lengthways over a frozen martini glass to catch any escaping zest and rub the folded edge around the rim of the glass before placing it inside.

Fill a cocktail shaker with ice. Pour a capful (10–15ml) of vermouth into the shaker and put the lid on. Shake gently and strain away any excess vermouth so that the ice is only covered in it (there should be no liquid left in the shaker). Pour 90ml frozen vodka into the shaker with the ice. Shake vigorously for 10–20 seconds. Strain into the glass and serve immediately. Garnish with a lemon twist.

TIP: *The lick of vermouth will take the edge off the vodka so you don't get that horrible shudder when you sip it, but too much makes the martini sickly. Try varying the amounts of the ingredients and you'll see what I mean. It is a glass of vodka after all, and there's a fine line between sublime and undrinkable.*

STEAK, GUINNESS AND KIDNEY PIE

This pie evokes the rustic charm of traditional village pubs. An essential comfort food, it's ideal for feeding friends over to watch a football or rugby match. If you don't like kidneys, just add more steak or mushrooms.

SERVES 8

For the filling

1.5kg braising steak, trimmed of fat and cut into cubes

450g ox or lamb kidneys, cleaned and cubed

salt and freshly ground black pepper

6 tablespoons plain flour

6 tablespoons sunflower oil

30g butter

300g small button mushrooms

2 onions, halved and thinly sliced

2 cloves of garlic, peeled and crushed

2 celery sticks, chopped

2 carrots, peeled and chopped

4 large sprigs of thyme

1 tablespoon caster sugar

400ml Guinness

400ml beef stock

2 tablespoons Worcestershire sauce

3 bay leaves

For the pastry

4 beaten egg yolks mixed with water, for glazing

flour, for dusting

500g pack of puff pastry, chilled

Season the steak and kidneys well, then coat in the flour. Heat 4 tablespoons sunflower oil in a large casserole dish or saucepan and brown the meat in batches. Remove and set aside. Add another tablespoon of oil and half the butter into the pan and brown the mushrooms, scraping off all the residue from the meat, then remove and set aside with the beef. Add the last of the oil and butter to the pan and cook the onions over a medium heat until soft, then add the garlic, celery, carrots, thyme and sugar and sweat for a further 5 minutes.

Return the meat and mushrooms to the pan, pour in the Guinness, stock and Worcestershire sauce and add the bay leaves. Partially cover with a lid and simmer for 1½ hours, stirring occasionally to ensure nothing sticks to the bottom. Remove the lid and continue to simmer, uncovered, for a further 30 minutes, until the meat is tender and the sauce has thickened. Season well.

Preheat the oven to 200°C/gas 6. Spoon the beef mixture into a 4-litre pie dish (or into 8 individual pie dishes). Brush the edges of the pie dish with a little of the beaten egg and roll out the pastry on a lightly floured surface until it is just larger than the dish. Arrange over the dish and trim off any excess so it fits the dish nicely, pressing the edges down to secure. Use any trimmings to decorate the pie as you wish, and secure them to the pastry with a little of the egg-yolk mixture.

Brush the top of the pastry with the remaining egg wash and make a cross in the middle to allow the steam to escape and keep the pastry crispy. (You can use a pie funnel in the centre if you have one.) Put the dish in the middle of the preheated oven for 25–30 minutes, until the pastry is golden. Allow to stand for a few minutes before serving.

A French regional red, or real ale.

TIPS : *Other fillings, such as game, are also very popular, or for a chicken pie filling, see page 48. • You can freeze the finished uncooked pie for up to 3 months. It is best cooked straight from frozen, but you need to add 15 minutes to the cooking time.*

FISH PIE

Mash is a classic topping for this pie, but for something lighter use a mix of breadcrumbs and Parmesan or simply a scattering of good-quality crisps for a crunchier texture. Try adding a couple of handfuls of washed spinach to your filling just before topping with the mashed potato. You could substitute coley for the cod — a more sustainable fish with similar white flesh — or use scallops instead of prawns, and serve with garden peas. You can make this the night before.

SERVES 8

8 eggs

800g cod loins, skinned and bones removed

800g undyed smoked haddock fillets, skinned and bones removed

1.4 litres milk, plus extra for the mash

4 bay leaves

2 lemons, cut into slices

16 black peppercorns

2.5kg Maris Piper potatoes, peeled and halved

salt and freshly ground black pepper

130g butter, plus extra for the mash

130g plain flour

a large pinch of freshly grated nutmeg

a large handful of chopped flat-leaf parsley

400g raw tiger prawns, peeled and deveined

Preheat the oven to 180°C/gas 4. Bring a pan of water to the boil and cook the eggs for 8 minutes. Run under cold water, peel and cut into quarters. Set aside.

Place the cod and smoked haddock in a saucepan, cover with the milk and add the bay leaves, lemon slices and peppercorns. Bring to a slow simmer for 4–5 minutes. Remove the fish with a slotted spoon and set aside. Strain the milk into a large jug and reserve. Cook the potatoes for 12–15 minutes until tender. Drain in a colander, return to the pan and mash. Season well, add a knob of butter, a splash of milk and beat until smooth.

To make the white sauce, melt the butter in a medium saucepan. Add the flour, stir well and cook for 2–4 minutes. Gradually whisk in approximately 1.2 litres of the reserved milk from poaching the fish and cook over a low heat for 6–8 minutes, stirring frequently, until the sauce begins to thicken. Stir in the nutmeg and the parsley and season to taste.

Pour the sauce into a large ovenproof dish. Scatter the prawns and flake the fish evenly over the sauce. Divide the eggs over the fish, followed by the rest of the sauce and top with mash, fluffing it up with a fork. Dot the pie with butter, and bake in the oven for 30 minutes until the top is golden brown and the sauce is bubbling.

 *A crisp Chablis suits this creamy dish.*

VENISON AND BEETROOT STEW

This is a lovely, dramatic deep burgundy colour. I always enjoy cooking stews, particularly with venison in early autumn. This recipe will freeze for 3 months in a sealed container.

SERVES 8

8 tablespoons plain flour

salt and freshly ground black pepper

1.3kg stewing venison, trimmed and cut into 4cm pieces

16 tablespoons olive oil, plus a little extra

350g smoked streaky bacon, cut into pieces

16 juniper berries, crushed

4 teaspoons thyme leaves

2 bay leaves

2 teaspoons pink peppercorns

4 garlic cloves, peeled and crushed

8 medium raw beetroot, peeled and cut into wedges

zest and juice of 2 oranges

300ml red wine

300ml port

400ml beef stock

4 red onions, peeled and cut into wedges

300g whole shallots

75g butter

1½ tablespoons sugar

Preheat the oven to 160°C/gas 3. Place the flour in a large bowl and season well with salt and pepper. Add the venison pieces and toss to coat evenly. Heat the olive oil in a large pan and brown the venison pieces, in batches if necessary, until evenly coloured. Remove from the pan and set aside. Add the bacon and cook for a few minutes until golden. Stir in the juniper berries, thyme leaves, bay leaves, peppercorns, garlic, beetroot wedges and orange zest and juice. Cook for several minutes, stirring frequently. Return the venison to the pan.

Add the red wine, port and beef stock. Bring to the boil, then reduce the heat and cover with a lid. Transfer to the oven and cook for 1½ hours, until the sauce has thickened and the venison is tender. (If you are making the stew in advance, reduce the cooking time by 30 minutes so that the meat doesn't overcook when you reheat it.) While the meat is cooking, caramelise the onions and shallots in the butter with the sugar, stirring until soft and golden, then add to the stew for the last 30 minutes of cooking. Season to taste. Serve with baked or hasselback potatoes (page 54) topped with sour cream and chopped chives.

 A Tuscan red wine.

SEALING THE MEAT *The word 'stew' is said to have come from the old French word 'estruier', meaning to enclose, suggesting the importance of sealing the juices in the meat before stewing it and adding flavour.*

PUDDINGS

BROWN BREAD ICE CREAM Serves 8

This is best eaten as soon as it comes out of the freezer when the caramelised breadcrumbs are at their crunchiest. You can make this up to a month in advance.

Preheat the oven to 200°C/gas 6. Mix 100g brown or wholemeal breadcrumbs with 100g soft brown sugar in a baking tray and place in the oven. Cook for 12–15 minutes until the sugar has caramelised and the crumbs are golden and crisp, keeping an eye on them and turning them once or twice. In a saucepan, heat 600ml double cream to just below boiling point. Meanwhile, separate 2 eggs. Beat the yolks and 100g caster sugar together and, beating continuously, pour in the cream to make a custard. Heat gently, stirring constantly, until the mixture thickens enough to coat the back of a spoon. Leave to cool. Whisk the egg whites until stiff. When the custard is cold, fold in 1 teaspoon vanilla essence, most of the cooled breadcrumbs (reserving some for serving) and the egg whites. Freeze the ice cream for 5–6 hours, stirring once after 30 minutes, and again 30 minutes later. Serve sprinkled with the reserved breadcrumbs.

POACHED PEARS IN RED WINE Serves 8

A lovely, light and elegant pudding. It looks great too. You can make these 1–2 days ahead.

Place 75cl (1 bottle) red wine, 300ml port, 2 split vanilla pods, 4 star anise, 2 cinnamon sticks, 250g caster sugar, 4 tablespoons honey and the peel and juice of 2 oranges into a wide saucepan and heat gently until the sugar has dissolved. Peel 8 firm pears carefully so they remain neat and with stalks intact. Sit them upright in the saucepan (slice off the bottoms if necessary) and submerge them in the wine. Cover with a lid and simmer very gently for 25–30 minutes, until they are a deep red colour and tender. Allow the pears to sit in the liquor for 1 hour to let the colour develop, then transfer the fruit to 8 serving bowls. Bring the poaching liquor to the boil and allow to reduce for 15–20 minutes until syrupy, then strain it and pour over the pears. Serve with vanilla ice cream.

BLOOD ORANGE POSSETS Serves 8

These are delicious, but if blood oranges aren't in season, use the juice and zest of 5 large oranges and 2 lemons.

Gently heat 900ml double cream and 250g sugar in a large pan, stirring to dissolve the sugar. Simmer for 3–4 minutes, being careful not to let it boil. Remove from the heat and whisk in the juice and zest of 7 blood oranges, retaining a little zest to garnish, and the juice and zest of 2 lemons. Pour into 8 small glasses or ramekins. Allow to cool, then transfer to the fridge for 1–2 hours or until set. You can chill these overnight. To serve, garnish with ribbons of orange rind.

Remember, remember the fifth of November,
Gunpowder, treason and plot.
I see no reason why gunpowder, treason
Should ever be forgot.

BONFIRE NIGHT

At the beginning of November the skies are alive with kaleidoscopic streams of colour and the air is filled with the crack and fizz of fireworks. It's Bonfire Night, and amber-outlined crowds silhouetted against the light of towering bonfires gather together to stop the cold and darkness from stealing in. Everyone is wrapped up, their faces glowing from the heat of the fire, their breath freezing in clouds in the night air. Sharing warming drinks and simple, hearty food enhances the sense of camaraderie among the revellers.

The unique sights, sounds, smells and tastes of this festival make it a particularly evocative one. I remember the noise of the bells ringing at school as the effigy of Guy Fawkes we'd prepared earlier was carried out on a canvas stretcher, hoisted on to the huge bonfire and set alight. Then the revelry would begin. My school friends and I would all have sparklers that we passed around, lighting one from another, the lingering gunpowdery scent of them so distinct. We devoured hot tomato soup, garnished with melting chunks of Cheddar cheese, as we stood in the dark so we wouldn't miss a minute of the night's many thrills.

The celebrations of 5 November commemorate the failed attempt by a group of Catholic conspirators in 1605 to blow up the Houses of Parliament and assassinate the Protestant King James I. One of the conspirators, Guy Fawkes, was found with forty barrels of gunpowder in the cellars beneath Parliament. To celebrate the fact that the Gunpowder Plot had failed and that King James I had survived, people lit bonfires around London. Months later, the introduction of the Observance of 5th November Act enforced an annual public day of thanksgiving. Within twenty years, bonfires and tar barrels were being lit annually across the country and the occasion had become known as Bonfire Night.

Bonfire Night is a wonderful way to celebrate the beginning of winter and perhaps the last chance to make the most of the great outdoors before the freezing weather sets in. There are few other dates in the calendar that give us such an enjoyable excuse to celebrate part of British history.

THE ORIGINS OF 'BONFIRE' *A bonfire was originally a 'bone-fire' — the first syllable of the word may have derived from the French word 'bon' ('good'), suggesting the idea of fire cleansing and doing good. Smoke was thought to have medicinal qualities, and the smell of burning bones was believed to drive away dragons.*

HOW TO MAKE...

BRILLIANT BONFIRES

My father and brother have built some amazing flaming structures and have spent hours explaining to me how to get it right. If you don't have space in your garden for a bonfire, there are some cheap and easy alternatives. Braziers and firepits work almost anywhere and are very easy to use. The key to the best fires is a good 'heart'.

I : Clear the area where you want to have your fire of anything flammable, and check it is away from trees (find out what direction the wind is coming from and make sure there isn't anything downwind that sparks could ignite). 2 : Map out the parameter of your fire with a circle of logs. Build the heart in the centre with firelighters first, then use kindling and small dry twigs to build up vertically. 3 : Using the heart as a base, construct around it in layers to form a wigwam, starting with small sticks and branches, and building up with loose layers of longer sticks leaning inwards. Try to leave a small gap in the construction so that when it's time you can reach the firelighters. 4 : Cover the bonfire with a tarpaulin or plastic sheeting to keep it dry until you are ready to light it. If you want to burn your Guy on the fire, make sure there is a stake to sit him on running through the centre of the bonfire tower.

A GUY TO BURN

To complete your bonfire you'll need a Guy. Hold a competition for the best brown-paper mask creation.

I : Collect some old clothes – men's trousers, a shirt or jersey and a pair of old boots. Leaving a gap for inserting stuffing, fasten up all openings in the clothes using string and pack them tightly with straw, hay or scrunched-up newspaper. Once the legs and torso of the Guy are well stuffed, staple them together. 2 : The head can be formed from old tights or fabric, the hands from gloves, and padded out like the body and legs. Cover the head with a paper bag, on which you can draw the Guy's face or use a balloon for the head and draw on the features with a black marker pen. 3 : Finish your Guy off with a tatty old jacket and a hat with a peak or a brim if you can find one.

'PENNY FOR THE GUY' *Traditionally, children wheel a stuffed effigy of Guy Fawkes on the streets, calling 'Penny for the Guy!' in the run-up to Bonfire Night.*

OUTDOOR ORGANISATION

Now that you've built your bonfire, it's time to get everything ready for the outdoor celebrations. The fireside is where everyone will gather, sitting, standing or simply staring, hypnotised, into the flickering flames. A well-tended bonfire can keep you company into the small hours and is a focal point for fellowship and warmth.

SEATING AND LIGHTING

Seat as many guests as possible by the fire. Hay bales and tree stumps to perch on are practical ways to seat many; benches and folding canvas chairs provide more comfort. Keep the bales a safe distance from the flames and the seating area on the upwind side of the fire. To lock in the warmth, fill baskets with blankets, hand-warmers and mini hot water bottles for added luxury.

For extra lighting use paper lanterns with battery-operated tea lights on flat surfaces, and carefully positioned garden torches to circle the camp. If you use an outdoor extension cable you can also bring over a standard lamp for a retro but effective touch. Torches and head torches are useful for finding lost objects, picking up rubbish and lighting fireworks.

FIRESIDE TABLE

Set up a table where you can lay out food, drinks and utensils — use tinfoil as a reflective tablecloth. You can store boxes of sparklers and empty trays, for clearing away, underneath the table. This is also a useful place to keep packets of marshmallows for roasting later on in the evening, as well as bottles of warming liqueurs. Have a few bin-liners for rubbish.

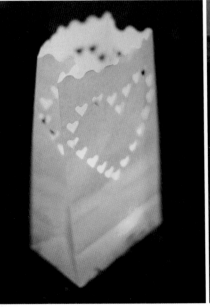

FILLING FOOD FOR A COLD NOVEMBER NIGHT

Bonfire Night provides the perfect occasion for serving autumnal favourites. Choose foods that are robust and comforting, which can be balanced on your lap or held in one hand, leaving the other free for a drink or sparkler. The likelihood is that you will be perched on a bench, hay bale or log, so it's important they are not too fiddly to eat. For other outdoor food see Barbecues, Picnics and Camping.

Individual portable portions in cups, bowls and on sticks are easy to negotiate in the dark and cold. Baked potatoes and stuffed peppers are ideal because the foil acts as a bowl and the skins, soaked in flavour, can be devoured with your fingers once you've eaten the filling. Simple flasks of soup, a bowl of chilli con carne (page 391), sausages, and spicy dips served with tortilla chips will also take the chill out of the night. Hot drinks will warm freezing hands, and boozy ones the insides.

EATING OUT

Disposable paraphernalia makes eating and clearing away easy, and your tableware should mirror the simplicity of the food. When it comes to arranging the food so that it is ready to serve, do so in your kitchen beforehand. Try the following ideas:

- *Transport your food outdoors using baking trays and baskets lined with tea towels and foil for insulation.*

- *Wrap cutlery in napkins and assemble in baskets or upright in tankards or small sturdy jugs. Bamboo cutlery, plates and cups are eco-friendly, and can be disposed of in the bonfire after use.*

- *Use sticks and skewers for finger food; they are more practical for those with gloves on.*

- *Enamel and melamine cups and plates are durable and perfect for the outdoors. Thermos flasks keep drinks and soups warm.*

- *Terracotta and earthenware serving dishes are sturdy and practical — line them with torn sheets of baking parchment for rustic food presentation.*

- *Use stemless glassware, such as tumblers, for cold drinks and wine, or provide paper cups that can be burnt on the bonfire after use (serve soup in these).*

- *Fill wheelbarrows and buckets with ice to cool drinks, and attach a bottle-opener on a string so that it's always to hand. Wheelbarrows are also great for collecting empties at the end of the night.*

HONEY AND MUSTARD SAUSAGES Serves 8 (makes 24)

Roast 24 cocktail sausages (allow 3 per person) lightly coated in oil in a preheated oven at 200°C/gas 6 for 15–20 minutes, or until browned and cooked through. Mix 1½ tablespoons good-quality clear honey with 2 tablespoons wholegrain or Dijon mustard. Drizzle this over the sausages, stirring and shaking until well coated, then return them to the oven for 5 minutes, turning them halfway. Serve sprinkled with toasted sesame seeds.

TIPS : *Serve these in a hollowed-out loaf of bread.* • *For a fruitier version, replace the honey with marmalade.*

TOMATO SOUP Serves 8

Chop 8 rashers of bacon into chunks and place in a hot pan with 2 peeled and finely chopped large onions. Cook for 4–5 minutes, until the onions have softened. Add 800g tinned chopped tomatoes, 500g passata, a pinch of smoked paprika (optional), 800ml beef stock, a good pinch each of sugar, sea salt and freshly ground black pepper and a splash of sherry, then simmer on a gentle heat for 15–20 minutes. Using a hand-held blender, purée the soup until smooth. Serve in cups with chunks of Cheddar cheese on top.

SALSA Serves 8

Finely chop 800g tomatoes, 1 peeled shallot, a small bunch of fresh coriander and 2–3 mild red or green chillies. Combine with a pinch of caster sugar, the juice of 2 limes and 6 tablespoons extra virgin olive oil. Garnish with chopped fresh coriander.

BABA GHANOUSH Serves 8

Preheat the oven to 225°C/gas 7. Heat 5–6 tablespoons olive oil in a large non-stick ovenproof frying pan over a medium heat. Add 5 large peeled and chopped aubergines, 5 peeled and crushed garlic cloves and 2 teaspoons ground cumin and cook until golden. Transfer to the oven and cook for 8–10 minutes. Place the aubergine into a food processor with a large bunch of fresh mint, 4 tablespoons tahini paste and 2 tablespoons extra virgin olive oil. Blend to a rough paste, stir in 2 tablespoons thick yogurt, season and serve.

GUACAMOLE Serves 8

Mash the flesh of 4 avocados until smooth. Add the juice of 1–1½ limes, 2 peeled and finely chopped garlic cloves and a small handful of chopped fresh coriander. Add Tabasco sauce to taste and leave to one side for 20 minutes to allow the flavours to develop. Dust with a little paprika before serving. To add some freshness, mix in a couple of spoonfuls of salsa.

SHEPHERD'S PIE
BAKED POTATOES

Hand these out with just a fork and an optional squirt of ketchup or Worcestershire sauce. Each singed crust, where the topping has caught the heat, makes the potato look as if it's been touched with gunpowder. For variation, mix the cooked potato flesh with a Welsh rarebit mixture (page 130).

SERVES 8

8 large baking potatoes

I tablespoon olive oil

2 large onions, peeled and finely chopped

3 large carrots, peeled and finely diced

Ikg minced lean lamb

3 heaped tablespoons tomato purée

I x 400g tin chopped tomatoes

a generous grating of nutmeg

I teaspoon picked fresh or dried thyme leaves

2–3 tablespoons Worcestershire sauce

400ml lamb stock

100ml milk

50g butter, plus a little extra

I egg yolk

sea salt and freshly ground black pepper

Preheat the oven to 180°C/gas 4. Put the potatoes on a baking sheet and place in the preheated oven for I hour until the skins are crisp and the potatoes are cooked.

Heat the oil in a medium-sized saucepan. Add the onion and carrot and cook on a gentle heat for 10 minutes until soft. Add the lamb mince, turn up the heat and cook until it turns brown. Spoon away any excess fat. Add the tomato purée and fry for a minute, then add the chopped tomatoes, nutmeg, thyme leaves and Worcestershire sauce and fry for a few more minutes. Pour in the stock, bring to the boil then simmer on a low heat, covered, for I hour.

Remove the potatoes from the oven and carefully slice a 'lid' off the top of each one. Spoon the centre out from each one into a bowl, leaving a sturdy outer 'shell'. Add the milk, 50g butter and egg yolk to the potato in the bowl, then season with salt and pepper and mash together.

Divide the mince between the hollowed-out potato skins, top with the mash and little knobs of butter and ruffle with a fork. Place the potatoes back into the preheated oven for a further 15 minutes until golden. To serve, fold foil around each potato and scrunch it into a bowl shape.

 *Warming reds such as Argentinian Malbec or Chilean Cabernet Sauvignon.*

TIP: *Traditionally, potatoes were baked in the embers of the fire. Cover in oil and salt, prick them and wrap in foil, placing in the hot embers for 1–2 hours.*

SPICY BEAN-STUFFED PEPPERS

Different coloured peppers have varying flavours — I've used yellow and red for their Bonfire Night colours. You can also use pimento peppers with this recipe. For a side dish, allow half a pepper per person and for vegetarians serve two halves as a main course. Add a generous scattering of fresh coriander or, for an extra kick, a sprinkling of chopped chilli and Tabasco sauce.

SERVES 4 (OR 8 AS A SIDE DISH)

2 large red peppers

2 large yellow peppers

1 tablespoon olive oil

1 small onion, peeled and finely chopped

2 garlic cloves, peeled and finely chopped

2 teaspoons ground cumin

1 teaspoon tomato purée

2 carrots, peeled and finely chopped

1 celery stick, finely chopped

1 x 410g tin red kidney beans in chilli sauce

1 x 400g tin chopped tomatoes

a small handful of fresh coriander, chopped

1 fresh red chilli, halved, deseeded and chopped

sea salt and freshly ground black pepper, to taste

50g grated Parmesan cheese

Preheat the oven to 200°C/gas 6. Cut the peppers in half lengthways and scoop out the seeds and membrane. Place the peppers on a baking tray, drizzle with oil and roast for 10–15 minutes.

Meanwhile, heat the oil in a large non-stick frying pan. Add the onion, garlic and cumin and cook for 5 minutes, until soft. Add the tomato purée, carrots and celery and fry for 2 minutes, then add the remaining ingredients, except the cheese, and simmer for 15–20 minutes until the vegetables are soft and the juice has reduced.

Remove the pepper halves from the oven and divide the filling between them, making sure each one is filled right to the corners. Wrap them in foil and continue to cook in the oven for a further 10–15 minutes. Remove from the oven, open the foil and drain the juices.

Sprinkle a generous handful of Parmesan over each pepper and return to the oven for 10–12 minutes, until the cheese melts. Serve with forks, letting the foil act as a bowl. These are really good with the guacamole from page 82 and a little sour cream or crème fraîche.

An Italian red such as Sangiovese matches the spicy flavours in this dish.

TIP: *Try filling the peppers with a spicy chilli con carne (page 391).*

APPLE PIES IN POTS

This is a classic autumnal staple, a pudding that everyone loves and which can be served in 8 small individual ramekins, cups or bowls, or as 12 mini apple pies. You can also make these with a lattice topping — just cut the rolled-out pastry into strips and lay it over the pie filling in a criss-cross pattern, then trim to size. Make the filling ahead and freeze for up to a month.

MAKES 8 POTS

For the filling
100g butter
100g soft light brown sugar
5 Cox apples, peeled, cored and chopped
7 Bramley apples, peeled, cored and chopped
1 teaspoon ground cinnamon
zest and juice of ½ a lemon

For the pastry
flour, for dusting
800g ready-made sweet shortcrust pastry

For the glaze
2 egg yolks, beaten
a splash of milk
caster sugar, to sprinkle

Preheat the oven to 180°C/gas 4. Melt the butter in a large pan on a medium heat. Add the sugar and mix until slightly golden. Add the apples, cinnamon and lemon zest and juice. Cook the apples on a low–medium heat for 10–15 minutes until soft but with a little bite. Add a splash of water and allow to cool.

Dust a little flour on your work surface and rolling pin. Flatten the pastry out on the surface, then, working from the centre outwards, roll the pastry out into a large circle until it is as thick as a pound coin. Cut out 8 circles of pastry for pie lids, cutting each one larger than your chosen ramekins or bowls. (To make mini pies, see below.)

Fill 8 ramekins, cups or bowls with the cooled pie filling, and then top with the pastry lids. Use your fingers to crimp and pinch the pastry to seal the pies. Mix the beaten egg with the milk and brush this glaze over the top of each pie, followed by a sprinkling of sugar. Bake for 20–25 minutes, until the pastry is golden brown.

TIPS: *To make one large pie, follow the recipe above but divide the pastry into two when rolling out. Line a 20cm pie dish with half the pastry, add baking beans and bake blind for 8 minutes at 190°C/gas 5. Remove the beans and bake for a further 4 minutes to colour the pastry. Add the filling, then cover with the remaining pastry lid, glaze and bake for 20–25 minutes as above. • Squeeze the lemon juice over the apples after you've cored them if you have other preparation to do, as this will prevent them discolouring.*

MINI APPLE PIES
Grease a 12-hole shallow bun tin. Cut out 12 circles of pastry using a cutter and press into each hole. Divide the filling between them, cut lids or lattice strips from the pastry, place on top, then glaze and follow the baking instructions in the main recipe.

PARKIN

A hearty, comforting ginger cake made with oatmeal and black treacle, parkin originated in the north of England and is customarily eaten on Bonfire Night. It gets better and stickier with time so, once cool, store in an airtight tin for a minimum of three days before tucking in. It will keep for up to two weeks.

MAKES 16 SQUARES

200g softened, unsalted butter, plus extra for greasing

100g light brown sugar

75g black treacle

200g golden syrup

150g porridge oats (medium oatmeal)

175g self-raising flour

2 teaspoons baking powder

3 teaspoons ground ginger

2 teaspoons mixed spice

2 large eggs, beaten

2 tablespoons milk

Preheat the oven to 140°C/gas 1.

Lightly grease a 20cm square cake tin and line with baking parchment. In a large, heavy-based saucepan melt together the butter, sugar, treacle and golden syrup over a low heat. Do not allow the mixture to boil.

In a large bowl, stir together all the dry ingredients. Gradually add the melted butter mixture, and beat with a wooden spoon until it is well combined. Beat in the eggs one at a time, then stir in the milk. Pour the mixture into the prepared tin and cook for 1½ hours, or until firm to the touch and a dark, golden-brown colour on top.

Remove from the oven and leave to cool in the tin for 10 minutes. Remove from the tin and cut into 16 equal squares, then store in an airtight container.

TIP: *Parkin can be used as the base for an autumn-flavoured trifle or served with a fruit compote (page 222). It's delicious as a pudding with custard or just buttered with a cup of tea. Ginger is also a perfect partner to whisky — try serving this with one of the drinks on page 192, or with a Whisky Mac (page 194).*

TOFFEE APPLES Makes 8

Toffee made with treacle was a Bonfire Night tradition, known as bonfire toffee or plot toffee — it was set so hard it had to be broken into pieces using a hammer. These toffee apples are a lovely sticky treat, especially for children. They can be prepared up to two days in advance and stored in a dry place.

Place 8 tablespoons golden syrup, 450g light brown sugar and 50g butter in a saucepan and pour over 140ml water. Bring to the boil, stirring to dissolve the sugar and melt the butter. Reduce the heat and leave to simmer, without stirring or moving the pan, for 20–25 minutes, or until a sugar thermometer inserted into the mixture reads 138°C.

Meanwhile, prepare 8 medium Braeburn apples, or your favourite type of eating apple. Wash them well to remove any wax as this will help the toffee to stick. Push a cleaned twig from the garden about halfway into each apple. Line a baking sheet with baking parchment.

Once the toffee mixture has reached the correct temperature, remove the pan from the heat and place it in a shallow container of cold water. Leave the pan for a few minutes to cool and thicken the toffee, then tip it a little so the mixture pools at one side. Carefully, but working quickly before the toffee sets, dip each apple into the mixture, holding it by the stick and spinning it around to completely coat it. Stand the apple on the baking sheet, stick pointing up. Repeat for all 8 apples, then leave to cool and harden before serving.

TIP: *Making toffee can be dangerous, due to the high temperatures involved, so keep children well away until the apples are ready to be eaten.*

POPCORN BALLS Makes 24

Perfect to snack on by the bonfire, these are light, airy and deliciously childish. Pop your own kernels, but if you're short of time you can buy ready-popped plain popcorn. Serve in popcorn boxes.

In a saucepan over a medium heat, combine 110g golden syrup, 30g butter, 1 teaspoon cold water and 75g pink or white marshmallows. Heat and stir until the mixture comes to the boil. In a large bowl, carefully combine the hot mixture with 125g plain popped popcorn, stirring to coat it well. When the mixture has cooled and can be handled, grease your hands with a little sunflower oil and quickly shape it into 24 squash-ball-size portions before it cools completely. Lay the popcorn balls on a large tray lined with baking parchment and refrigerate to set until ready to serve. These will keep overnight if stored in an airtight container.

AUTUMNAL FLASK-FILLERS

A good blanket against the chill, these hot drinks can be poured from flasks into mugs or paper cups. For grown-ups, flavoured spirits and fruit liqueurs such as a home-brewed sloe gin or raspberry vodka (page 405) are ideal for hip flasks, and warm drinks such as a spiced apple warmer or hot toddy (page 194) will bring comfort to cold hands and bodies.

BULL SHOT Serves 8

This is a hot, spicy, savoury drink, good for the outdoors. Serve it for elevenses with sausage rolls (page 360). Place the following ingredients in a large saucepan and bring to the boil: 2 x 400g tins beef consommé, 50ml vodka or sherry, 1 teaspoon Tabasco, a pinch of freshly ground black pepper, 1 teaspoon Worcestershire sauce, a good squeeze of lemon juice and a pinch of salt. Turn the heat down and simmer to keep warm until ready to serve. (Add 500ml tomato juice for a richer, longer drink.)

WINTER PIMM'S Serves 8

This is less well-known than the summer variety, but easy to make in large quantities and equally as delicious. Mix 400ml brandy-based Pimm's Winter (No.3) with 1.2 litres of warmed cloudy apple juice. Serve in cups, garnished with slices of peeled fresh ginger or apple.

SPICED APPLE WARMER Serves 8

A child-friendly autumn drink. Add rum for the adults or replace the apple juice with cider for a 'mulled cider'. Gently simmer I litre cloudy apple juice and 500ml water with 4 cored and sliced apples, 4 cinnamon sticks and 6 star anise for 5–10 minutes. Stand off the heat until all the flavours have infused. When ready to serve, warm through, adding sugar or honey to taste.

TOFFEE VODKA Makes I x 35cl bottle

One shot of this really delicious (and strong) vodka will make you want another! Pour a little vodka out of a 35cl bottle and then add a 50g tube of smashed butter toffees. Leave the vodka overnight, or for at least 8 hours. Speed up the process by putting the sealed bottle in the dishwasher on a hot cycle. When done, the toffees will have dissolved. Keep in the fridge and shake before serving. Try using chocolate bars such as Mars or After Eights for different flavours.

SLOE GIN OR WHISKY Makes I x I litre bottle

Traditionally you should always pick sloes after the first frost. The liqueur takes at least 3 months to mature, but is even better after a year. Freeze 500g ripe sloe berries in a single layer to burst their skins, then defrost and place into a large sterilised kilner jar (page 402). Pour over 250g sugar and I litre gin or whisky, close the lid, shake well then store in a dark cupboard, shaking every day until the sugar has completely dissolved. After three months, bottle the gin by straining through a muslin and store in a dark place for another year (I can never wait that long).

OUTDOOR GAMES AND ACTIVITIES

Have a couple of games up your sleeve in the build-up to the bonfire and firework display. Take the chance to have some fun with your Guy before you burn him. One good idea is to divide everyone into teams, provide a selection of old clothes and scrap materials and ask them to dress the Guy as a character from history. Once their time is up, the other team needs to guess who it is supposed to be. Make use of conkers for a classic contest, and marshmallows before you roast them by constructing marshmallow towers, and, of course, lay on plenty of sparklers when it's time to start the fireworks.

SARDINES

Sardines is best played at dusk when the light begins to go as it makes this game a bit harder and more fun to play. To start, one player runs off to hide. Everyone else counts together to a previously agreed number (up to 20 or 50). Once they have finished counting they go in search of the player who has hidden. When somebody finds this player, they join them in hiding. The group of hidden players grows larger and larger until there's one person left still searching. This person is the first to hide in the next round of the game.

CONKER FIGHTS

I remember playing these at school: we all used to get really competitive (the trick was to paint clear nail varnish on the conkers to make them very tough and less likely to break – outrageous cheating, of course!). Each player has a conker threaded on to a piece of knotted string (use a skewer to make the hole, and wear gardening gloves to protect your hands) and pairs of players take it in turns to hit each other's conker. The conker should hang perfectly still, ready for your adversary to strike. If you hit your opponent's conker, you have another go; if you miss, it's their turn. The game is won when one conker is destroyed or knocked off its string.

SKY LANTERNS AND GLOW-IN-THE-DARK GAMES

Sky lanterns add a wonderful dimension to outdoor parties after dark, and come in a huge range of shapes and sizes, as well as all the colours of the rainbow. Buy eco-friendly 100% biodegradable versions and get everyone to let one go and make a wish just before they float up into the sky. They only work well on a calm night, so don't release them if it's windy. Another way to light up the night is with glow-in-the-dark games. I've bought Frisbees, boules sets and even golf balls for previous Bonfire Night parties, which are fun to play later in the evening.

BONFIRE-ROASTED MARSHMALLOWS

Spear any leftover marshmallows on long-handled forks or sticks that have been soaked in water for a few hours, and then pile them up in baskets ready to roast over the flames. They are also delicious in a warming mug of hot chocolate. Use a good-quality chocolate powder or homemade hot chocolate spoons (page 395) mixed with hot milk, then add a squirt of cream. You can put mini marshmallows on top, or dip your toasted ones into the drink. Try sandwiching them between two biscuits to make s'mores (page 395).

MARSHMALLOW TOWERS

Split into two teams. Each team is given a bag of marshmallows and a packet of spaghetti. The aim is simple – to build the tallest tower possible from your marshmallows and spaghetti, using the sweets as the joints and the pasta as the framework. Set a time limit – this will vary according to architectural ambitions! First-timers might like to give themselves ten minutes, while more expert builders could take anything up to half an hour. Once the time is up, the team with the tallest tower wins. The best bit is that the winners get to gobble up their opponents' tower (without the uncooked spaghetti, of course).

SPARKLERS AND ...

Children and adults alike love sparklers. Have a bucket of sand or water at the ready for sticking spent stubs into. If children are too young to handle them safely, mini torches, glow sticks and bands will keep them occupied.

There's a great game called 'Just a Sparkler', a seasonal take on Radio 4's famous quiz show *Just a Minute*. Have a stash of sparklers at the ready, and choose a Bonfire Night topic such as 'Guy Fawkes', 'mittens' or 'matches'. A sparkler is lit. The first player must attempt to speak on the set topic without hesitation, repetition or deviation until the sparkler burns out. If they fail, the next player takes over. The person who is talking when the sparkler burns out is the winner. You can play around with who holds the sparkler – the person who's speaking might use it to gesticulate wildly and hammer home their points, passing it to the next player when they make an error. Or you could elect an umpire who holds the sparkler and uses it to adjudicate. Either way, sparks will fly!

...FIREWORKS: ENDING WITH A BANG!

Your guests have been fed, night has fallen and the bonfire is ablaze. If you're having fireworks, now is the time to light them. Public displays cannot be beaten for their sheer awe-inspiring spectacle, but it is hugely satisfying to put on a private show in your own garden just for you and your family and friends, even if it is short and sweet.

Think in advance about the effect you want to achieve, and how to get your audience to look at different levels of the sky. If you can, alternate lower fireworks with those that shoot high into the sky to explode. The easiest to work with are 'batteries' — these involve lighting one fuse that triggers several fireworks to go off in sequence; although they can be expensive they provide a spectacular display. Burning times are usually given, so do check these first. Individual rockets can also be effective — as long as you are prepared to do a lot of running around to set them off! There are dozens of online retailers offering a huge choice to suit all budgets.

FIREWORK SAFETY

Safety is paramount, so adhere to the firework safety code and handle with great care.

- *Read the instructions for each firework closely and follow them properly.*

- *Ensure you have a big enough space for the display you are planning, and warn your neighbours.*

- *Head torches are very useful for those responsible for setting off fireworks, as they allow both hands to be kept free.*

- *Keep pets safely indoors. Dogs may be more settled inside with the radio or television as background noise to distract from the loud bangs outside.*

EASY ENTERTAINING

Informal drinks parties are a great way to entertain a crowd for a short time in the early evening. They're always popular, and can be very useful if you want to thank people for invitations you've received throughout the year. Don't be intimidated by the logistics of catering for lots of guests; with some simple tips they can be enjoyable occasions to host as well as attend.

ESSENTIAL SUPPLIES

Keep these items in your kitchen and cupboards for parties and celebrations. Some you'll have already, but others are simple and affordable supplies that are useful to stock up on.

- **Cookie cutters and chef's rings:** *for shaping biscuits, canapé bases and sandwiches.*
- **Serving platters:** *see 'Canapé Presentation' (page 105).*
- **Large plastic buckets or bins:** *for chilling drinks when fridge space is limited and emptying dregs from used glasses.*
- **Vases in assorted shapes:** *for flower arrangements (page 282). Column vases can be filled with whole fruits and used as decoration on the bar.*
- **Candles and candle holders:** *scented candles, tapered candles and lots of tea lights to cluster in groups.*
- **Glassware:** *wine and highball glasses, as well as Champagne coupes or martini glasses, can be hired or bought very cheaply in bulk from supermarkets.*
- **Plastic wine glasses and Champagne flutes:** *emergency spares in case you run out of clean glassware.*
- **Cocktail napkins, skewers and cocktail sticks:** *keep a stock of these handy.*
- **Paper plates, bamboo and disposable cutlery:** *bamboo servingware, mini paper plates and party boxes are all great for 'mini meals' for children.*

CANAPÉ PLANNING

Allow 10–12 canapés per person for a two-hour drinks-only reception, 6–8 if you're serving dinner too. Bolster these with a few bowls of nuts and crisps on side tables for early guests. Aim to hand out your first canapés about 20 minutes after your first guests arrive, and have plenty of cocktail napkins to hand. Sweet canapés can be a subtle way to signal that the evening is drawing to a close (or just stop topping up glasses and your guests will soon start to disperse!). You can buy all sorts of ready-prepared items — see 'Time-saving Tricks' (page 105) — or there are recipes for homemade canapés throughout the book. Just remember to keep them bite-size.

DRINKS PARTY DOS AND DON'TS

• Do move any clutter from the space you're entertaining in and push large items of furniture back against the walls (but provide lots of side tables for nibbles and empty glasses).

• Do designate a space for guests' coats. Empty pegs or coat racks so guests can use them, leave a number of spare hangers on stair banisters or open a bedroom for the purpose.

• Do set up a bar area away from the entrance to your party to encourage guests to move into the space. Make sure the bar is well stocked with a little more than you think you'll need (many wine merchants will trade on a sale or return basis). Cover the table you're using with a large cloth to hide supplies underneath, provide a slosh bucket for dregs and a bin-liner taped to the side of the bar for rubbish.

• Do offer drinks on a tray as people arrive to cut wait times at the bar. Have a few soft drinks along with the alcoholic option, and use garnishes of different citrus fruits (page 104) to differentiate between drinks.

• Do mark glasses for your guests at smaller gatherings, so they don't lose track of their drink (easily done!). Buy glass tags online or make your own to fit the theme of the evening. Write guests' names with glass paint that comes off in the dishwasher, or use pretty twine or ribbons in a rainbow of colours (at Christmas my mum has a ribbon tied to hers because she's always losing her own glass and takes everyone else's!).

• Don't go it alone. Enlist help to make things run smoothly. Get a few friends or family members to help you greet guests and take their coats, top up and clear away glasses, hand round food, man the bar and keep the kitchen tidy.

• Don't offer too wide a selection of drinks that require different sorts of glasses. For example, if you're serving Champagne or sparkling wine in flutes, use only one other type of glass for soft drinks, wine and cocktails.

• Don't forget the ice. Properly chilled drinks make such a difference. Buy bags of ice cubes, or fill trays with water well before your party and make plenty in advance. Clear space in your fridge for wine the night before, and for large quantities of bottles use a sink filled with ice. Adding salt to ice and cold water will lower the temperature and chill bottles more quickly.

• Don't lose the corkscrew. Attach it to the bar on a string (have a few spares).

• Don't underestimate how much food you'll need. Plan quantities per person (see 'Canapé Planning', page 102) and stagger when and where you hand them out so you don't run out too early or end up with lots of leftovers.

• Don't worry about accidental spills. If you don't have red-wine stain remover, it's best to remove the stain when it's still wet. Blot with a clean cloth, pour a little white wine over it or soak up the stain with a pinch of salt or talcum powder.

DRINKS AND COCKTAIL KIT

- **Cocktail shaker set**: *with liquid measure, bar spoon for mixing and strainer.*

- **Bottle openers, corkscrews and foil-cutter.**

- **Muddler**: *for crushing sugar or bruising mint and fruits (or use the end of a rolling pin).*

- **Ice, wine buckets, jugs and tongs**: *plus a large bowl and a ladle for serving cocktails, punches and mulled wine.*

- **Straws, cocktail sticks and umbrellas**: *various thin, short and long straws.*

- **Small chopping board, knife and garnishes**: *citrus fruits, glacé or maraschino cherries and olives.*

- **Sugar syrup**: *shop-bought or homemade (see right).*

- **Flavoured cordials and fruit liqueurs**: *to spruce up soft drinks, wine and sparkling wine.*

- **Fruit juices and pureés.**

SUGAR SYRUP

This is useful in all sorts of cocktails, as well as for glazing fruits and edible flowers (page 285). Best of all, it doesn't even require a recipe — just boil together 2 parts of water to 1 part of sugar (e.g. 1 litre water with 500g sugar) until all the sugar is dissolved. Store it in a sterilised bottle in the fridge for up to three months, but it's best to make up a small batch as you need it.

CITRUS GARNISHES

These add visual effect to cocktails and the citrus peel releases the oils held in the rind, adding an extra zesty flavour. Avoid the pith as much as possible and use fresh fruits so that the skin is firm — it won't work with old, soft fruit.

- **Twists or Spirals**: carve round the diameter of the fruit using a deep-channelled zester, making sure you get a lovely length of peel. For a tight curl, wrap around a straw or chopstick. Drape off the rim of the glass.

- **Knots**: using a narrow zester, peel a medium length of rind and tie it into a knot.

- **Wheels**: use a narrow or deep-channeled zester to score the length of the fruits, leaving even spaces between each. Slice the fruit to create wheels.

- **Peels**: peel a wide unbroken strip of the rind with a potato peeler and gently squeeze to release the oils from the rind and then use as a garnish.

CANAPÉ PRESENTATION

Collect pretty bowls, patterned plates and other interesting serving dishes from markets and holidays. Decorate simple platters with natural items or use themed accessories. Assemble fiddly food on to mini forks, or thread on to cocktail sticks and skewer them into watermelons (page 304) or pumpkins (page 19). Scoop out the insides of a loaf of bread and fill with cocktail sausages, or serve seafood canapés in cleaned oyster and scallop shells.

- **Wooden and porcelain boards:** simple and practical, these are great for summer gatherings, charcuterie and antipasti. Small, handled boards are easier for passing around.

- **Silver trays, round or square table mirrors:** these add a shimmer to foods and are perfect for special occasions, particularly Christmas and New Year.

- **Natural slate:** dark tones set off delicate canapés; use chalk to label foods.

- **Baskets:** line with cellophane, baking parchment or straw for rustic entertaining.

- **Chinese-style spoons:** use to assemble individual portions on a tray. Particularly good for messier bites where guests can't use their fingers.

- **Paper cones:** buy or make your own. Use them to serve crudités, popcorn and fruits.

- **Mini galvanised buckets and tankards:** stand foods, such as cheese straws, upright in these.

TIME-SAVING TRICKS

These instant nibbles can take you from casual suppers with friends to more formal entertaining:

LARDER

- *Good-quality potato and vegetable crisps, cheese straws, mixed nuts and savoury popcorn.*

- *Stuffed olives and other jarred antipasti, such as roasted peppers and artichokes in oil.*

- *Instant canapé bases: croustades, crostinis, cheese thins, mini oat cakes, poppadoms, blinis and tart and vol-au-vent cases.*

- *Ready-made sauces, such as Hollandaise, sweet chilli dipping sauce, tartare sauce and mayonnaise.*

- *Quick garnishes, such as red-onion marmalade (page 404), fig jam and inexpensive caviar and truffles.*

- *Good-quality white, dark and milk chocolate: use melted for dipping fresh and dried fruit or breadsticks.*

- *Ready-made petits fours, biscotti, mint thins, amaretti biscuits and Turkish delight.*

FREEZER

- *Ice (crushed and cubed): buy in bulk for delivery from wine shops, or make batches of your own and store in freezer bags.*

- *Ready-rolled pastry (puff, shortcrust and filo) for canapés, tarts, samosas and spring rolls.*

- *Smoked salmon, uncooked cocktail sausages and mini Yorkshire puddings (always popular).*

- *Pre-cooked canapés: test out and stock up on ones you like, such as Indian or Oriental selections.*

- *Pizza bases, pitta, rye, thin ciabatta baguettes and other breads, to cut out and use for quick canapé bases.*

WINTER

CHRISTMAS
NEW YEAR'S EVE
BURNS NIGHT

Days grow short and icy winds blow; it's time to bundle up. Sharp frosts dust the roofs and bare trees stand dark against a metallic sky. Coldness bites on wintry walks, breath rises in clouds and grass crunches underfoot. The red-breasted robin perches on a branch: a quintessential Christmas card image. There's a chance of snowfall and we all hope it settles.

CHRISTMAS

*'Happy, happy Christmas, that can win us back to the delusions of
our childish days; that can recall to the old man the pleasures of his youth;
that can transport the sailor and the traveller, thousands of miles away,
back to his own fire-side and his quiet home!'*

The Pickwick Papers, Charles Dickens

One of the best things about Christmas is the anticipation. There's something in the air throughout December, and it's not just the cold weather. Window displays sparkle with gift ideas and stocking fillers, lights twinkle above streets, and markets spring up out of nowhere. When I was a child, my December weekends were spent making cards, decorating the tree, hanging the wreath and preparing brandy butter and peppermint creams. Bowls brimming with walnuts, shiny wrapped chocolates and piles of clementines would appear around the house. There was always a distinctive smell, too: pine and cinnamon and the heady scent of mulled wine and pomanders that merged into one festive bouquet.

No matter how much we may adapt other celebrations, come December we tend to repeat our own familiar customs year after year – and this is perhaps key to the magic of Christmas. Looking back, I don't remember the presents I received, nor whether the sprouts were overcooked or the turkey dry. But what I do remember are all the small rituals that we revelled in. It's inevitable that as we get older, Christmases become more complicated, and as one of the biggest events of the social calendar, raised expectations and high stress levels are unavoidable. Families grow, the dynamics change, and, as children become adults and parents themselves, the innocent thrill of opening a stocking is replaced by the responsibility of ensuring a memorable Christmas for their own children, relatives and friends.

HISTORY AND ORIGINS OF CHRISTMAS *Pagan midwinter festivities were recorded throughout Europe for hundreds of years (probably longer) before the birth of Christ, marking the onset of winter, a time of darkness. The Romans illuminated buildings with bright lights and decorated their houses with evergreens, exchanged presents, feasted, drank, danced and played games. The Germanic peoples of Northern Europe celebrated Yule on December 25, lighting fires to assist in the revival of the waning sun.*

It was against this background that the Christian Nativity feast developed. The early Christians, seeking to spread their faith throughout Europe, chose midwinter to mark the birth of Christ as it was a potent and symbolic time in the year. The result was a festival that combined both pagan and Christian elements. But it was the sentimental Victorians who provided most of the traditions — cards with elaborate snow scenes, crackers, an extravagantly decorated tree and the turkey feast — that we know and cherish today. They established Christmas as a celebration of the domestic arts, of hospitality and warmth and, above all, of reuniting with friends and family.

THE COUNTDOWN TO CHRISTMAS

You won't have time to do everything from scratch but pick and choose what you can manage making yourself. Have a kitchen clear-out before the festive period and make separate lists for different shops you might visit: the butcher's, wine store, greengrocer's, florist, supermarket and department store. Putting the lists on your fridge door will make them easily accessible. The priority is to get all the food planned and organised as far in advance as possible, freezing where you can. With lots of shops closed around this time it's harder to nip out and get last-minute goods so getting ahead will allow you to put your feet up after Christmas Day.

Christmas Planner

END OF NOVEMBER Advent calendar: buy or make (page 115). Cards: gather addresses, buy or make (page 115). Christmas pudding: buy ahead, or make on the last Sunday in November (page 112). Browse online for stocking fillers and present ideas.

4 WEEKS TO GO Crafts: buy or make wrapping paper and crackers (page 115), tree decorations (page 123) and wreath (page 119). Christmas tableware: use the 5 C's checklist (crockery, cutlery, candles, crackers, centrepiece); check linen and napkins, then buy any extra supplies you need.

3 WEEKS TO GO Write and send Christmas cards. Order turkey, meat and other food, such as cheeses, for collection the week before Christmas.

2 WEEKS TO GO Plan meals and order non-perishables and drinks for delivery. Christmas tree: buy on second weekend in December. Decorate the tree and house (page 120). Make berry ball (page 119), edible gifts (page 116) and mince pies (page 112).

1 WEEK BEFORE CHRISTMAS Collect turkey and buy food perishables, plants and flowers. Prepare ahead: freeze meals for the period between Christmas and New Year, and any food for New Year's Eve (page 162). Wrap presents and stocking fillers.

A FEW DAYS BEFORE CHRISTMAS Sort seating plans for Christmas meals. Set out a corner for a jigsaw puzzle and some other games. Make ahead any food for Christmas Day.

CHRISTMAS EVE Set out stockings, a mince pie for Father Christmas and reindeer food (page 134). Last-minute wrapping. Set the table (page 138) and chill relevant drinks. Pour yourself a large glass, and put on Christmas carols.

PREPARE-AHEAD FOOD

These recipes can be frozen or prepared ahead, so you won't feel quite as stressed when it comes to entertaining over the Christmas period.

STORE COOKED FOR UP TO 6 MONTHS

- **Christmas pudding** (*page 112*): *keep covered in a cool, dark place, and reheat before serving.*

FREEZE UNCOOKED FOR UP TO 3 MONTHS

- **Mince pies** (*page 112*): *bake from frozen, adding 5 minutes to the cooking time.*

- **Cheese biscuits dough** (*page 130*): *allow to stand for 10 minutes, slice into rounds and then bake, adding 5 minutes to the cooking time.*

- **Gingerbread dough** (*page 116*): *defrost thoroughly before rolling out.*

- **Pheasant goujons** (*page 130*) **and pigs in blankets** (*page 147*): *defrost thoroughly before cooking.*

- **Stuffing** (*page 147*): *freeze in balls and bake from frozen, adding 5 minutes to the cooking time.*

- **Brandy butter** (*page 150*) **and spiced Christmas butter** (*page 137*).

FREEZE COOKED FOR UP TO 1 MONTH

- **Twice-baked cheese soufflé** (*page 143*): *freeze this after first cooking. Bake from frozen to complete second cooking.*

- **Chocolate yule log** (*page 150*): *freeze the sponge only for up to a month. Defrost, unroll, fill and decorate with chocolate ganache.*

- **Giblet gravy** (*page 146*): *defrost, reheat until piping hot and add the roasting juices from the turkey on the day.*

- **Bread sauce and cranberry sauce** (*page 146*): *Defrost thoroughly before heating through.*

- **Parsnip soup espresso** (*page 130*): *cook and freeze before adding the milk and cream.*

UP TO 3 DAYS IN ADVANCE

- **Peppermint creams** (*page 116*): *store in an airtight container.*

- **Crostini and toasted bases for Christmas canapés** (*pages 129–30*): *store in an airtight container, then assemble the toppings on the day of serving.*

- **Boxing Day ham** (*page 154*): *store cooked but unglazed in the fridge before roasting.*

- **Stilton** (*page 154*).

24 HOURS BEFORE SERVING

- **Celeriac remoulade** (*page 129*).

- **Smoked trout paté** (*page 143*).

- **Shellfish tian** (*page 143*): *prepare the base mixture ahead, but finish on the day.*

- **Brussels sprouts** (*page 147*): *blanch and refresh in iced water, store in the fridge and finish cooking on the day.*

ON THE DAY

- **Canapés** (*pages 129–30*): *prepare toppings and assemble.*

- **Drinks and cocktails** (*page 133*).

- **Pear, walnut and Roquefort salad** (*page 143*).

- **Roast turkey** (*page 144*), **roast potatoes** (*page 54*), **honeyed carrots and parsnips** (*page 147*).

STIR-UP SUNDAY

Stir-up Sunday (the last Sunday before Advent) is the traditional day to make Christmas pudding, giving the flavours plenty of time to mature. Ask everyone to take a turn stirring the mixture (from east to west to echo the journey of the Three Wise Men) while making a wish. It's also the perfect time to bake the first batch of mince pies.

CHRISTMAS PUDDING Serves 8-10

The ritual and tradition of Stir-up Sunday might spur you on to make a pudding yourself rather than buy one.

In a large bowl, mix together 600g mixed dried fruit, 125g candied peel, 1 large peeled and grated cooking apple, 1 teaspoon each of mixed spice and ground cinnamon, the finely grated zest and juice of 1 lemon, 150g soft brown sugar, 75g halved glacé cherries, 1 large peeled and grated carrot, 150g ground almonds, 2 tablespoons black treacle, 50g plain flour, 125g vegetable suet, ½ teaspoon salt, 100ml brandy or Calvados, 25ml stout or dark ale and 2 beaten eggs. Give them a good stir and leave them for 2 hours or preferably overnight. Pour the mixture into a 1.2 litre pudding basin. Cover securely with a lid or foil, stand the basin on a metal trivet to stop it touching the bottom and steam the pudding in a large pan half-full of boiling water for 7 hours. Keep the water topped up. To reheat, steam for 1–2 hours until warmed through, or wrap in clingfilm, pierce holes to allow steam to escape and microwave for 5 minutes. Allow to stand for 3 minutes before serving.

MINCE PIES Makes 12-18

For really delicate mince pies, roll the pastry out very thinly. Make a variety of sizes — mini ones are great for drinks parties and normal-sized ones are perfect for tea or pudding (warm them in the oven before serving). For a pretty alternative to traditional mince-pie tops, use Christmassy cutters like stars or snowflakes.

Roll out 500g of ready-made shortcrust pastry very thinly and cut circles with a 6cm plain or crimped cutter. Press these into the greased holes of a bun tin. Spoon 400g of ready-made mincemeat between them. Roll out the remaining pastry and cut tops from it. Seal the pies, brush with beaten egg and sprinkle with a little caster sugar. Bake for 10–15 minutes at 180°C/gas 4, until golden. Cool in the tin for 5 minutes and then remove to a wire rack. These will keep for 3–4 days in an airtight container.

HOW THE TRADITIONS BEGAN... *Christmas pudding was traditionally made with thirteen ingredients to represent Christ and the twelve disciples. A coin was often added to the ingredients and cooked in the pudding (supposedly bringing wealth to whoever found it on Christmas Day). Family recipes are often handed down the generations and it remains a symbol of Christmas.*

The earliest type of mince pie was a medieval baked or fried pastry containing chopped meat or fish along with hard-boiled egg, dried fruit and other sweet ingredients. By the sixteenth century 'minced' or 'shred' pies had become a Christmas speciality and later the meat filling had disappeared from 'mincemeat', leaving us with the fruit version we know today.

CHRISTMAS CRAFTS

In the build-up to Christmas it can be fun to make a few things: Christmas is, after all, about the exciting sense of anticipation. Buying cards sold in aid of charity is a good way of supporting worthy causes but children might enjoy making them. Similarly, it's nice to add a personal touch to Christmas wrapping using various ribbons, accessories and even potato printing on to plain paper.

RED ROBIN CHRISTMAS CARDS AND GLITTER PEGS

Red robins are symbols of Christmas, but you can experiment with other seasonal motifs and designs. Use images from old cards as well as lace, buttons, felt, cotton wool for snow — the possibilities are endless. Glitter pegs add a little sparkle to cards pinned on to ribbon. Hang the ribbons on either side of doorways.

I: Cut a bird shape from some pretty paper and glue it to folded card using a glue stick. 2: Glue a button for the eye and coloured card for the red chest and draw feet. 3: To make glitter pegs use a brush and coat one side of a wooden clothes peg with PVA glue. Dip it into a shallow plate filled with glitter and shake off the excess, leaving to dry on a sheet of newspaper.

CHRISTMAS CRACKERS

It's lovely to make your own Christmas crackers and for the recipient to find personalised gifts inside.

I: For each cracker, cut two 30cm x 35cm sheets of crêpe paper and roll around 3 loo-roll tubes (lined up end to end), gluing down the seam to prevent unravelling. 2: Place a gift, joke and a snap into the middle roll and tie a ribbon at either end. 3: Remove the 2 outer rolls and fluff up the end of the crêpe. Decorate the top of the cracker with a dried leaf stuck on with a glue stick and write your guest's name on it.

A MATCHBOX ADVENT CALENDAR

I first came across this idea when a schoolfriend's mum made her a matchbox advent calendar. It's amazing what you can fit into a matchbox — this is all part of the challenge!

I: Number 25 matchboxes. Add a button or a short split pin to each drawer as a handle. 2: Fix the matchboxes together, drawer-side out, using double-sided tape. Stack the boxes in 5 tiers, with number 25 at the top. 3: Glue a strip of wrapping paper round the edges.

EDIBLE GIFTS

Homemade treats can be served as dessert canapés or handed out as gifts. Buy a few to save time – things like florentines, chocolate-covered orange peel and candy canes – then put the effort into wrapping them in pretty cellophane, boxes and festive tins lined with Christmas tissue paper. Gingerbread-house kits are fun to make and can sit on windowsills or as a centrepiece for a small table; gingerbread stars look lovely hanging from the Christmas tree.

CHRISTMAS TRUFFLES Makes 12–15

Make the truffles using the recipe on page 216 and turn them into mini Christmas puddings. Dust them with cocoa powder and decorate them using white fondant icing shaped to look like snow. Use an icing pen to stick the fondant to the truffle. Finish with mini red Smarties for the berries and use green icing pens to draw on holly.

GINGERBREAD STARS Makes 15–20

Preheat the oven to 170°C/gas 3 and line 2 baking trays with parchment. Melt 130g butter, 100g dark muscovado sugar and 6 tablespoons golden syrup in a medium saucepan, stirring occasionally. Once the sugar is dissolved, remove from the heat. Sift 350g plain flour into a bowl with 1 teaspoon bicarbonate of soda, 2 heaped teaspoons ground ginger and a good pinch of mixed spice. Pour the melted ingredients over the dry ingredients, stirring together to make a dough. Cover in clingfilm and place in the fridge to cool for 20–30 minutes.

Turn out the dough on to a lightly floured surface and roll to a thickness of about 0.5cm. Dip star-shaped biscuit cutters into flour before cutting the dough. Place the shapes on the baking sheets and bake for 12–14 minutes until light golden brown, then remove from the oven. (If hanging them from your tree, use a skewer or cocktail stick to make holes in the warm biscuits to thread ribbon through.) When completely cool and hardened, finish with glacé icing and decorate. Store in an airtight container for up to a week.

PEPPERMINT CREAMS Makes 40

Whisk 1 large egg white in a clean bowl until it forms stiff peaks. Add a few drops of peppermint essence and 400g icing sugar (and a few drops of green food colouring if you like), and mix well until it combines to form a stiff paste. Dust your work surface, your hands and a rolling pin with icing sugar and roll out the paste to 0.5cm thick. Use small cutters to cut out shapes, place them on a tray or plate and refrigerate for 3-4 hours until set.

EVERGREEN DECORATIONS

A CHRISTMAS WREATH

A wreath can make a welcoming first impression when hung on a front door. Regularly mist with a water sprayer every few days and the wreath will last you well into the New Year. Laid flat, it also makes a good tablecentre.

1: Soak a ring of florist's foam in water and attach a loop of ribbon for hanging. Gather together your foliage – rosemary, bay and sage, along with eucalyptus, spruce or ruscus, work well. Create the shape of your wreath by pushing similar lengths of foliage, as well as some thistles, into the ring until it is evenly covered. 2: Add groups of roses around the wreath, making sure they are spaced evenly so it looks balanced. 3: Finish the wreath by adding wired bundles of cinnamon sticks and dried fruit, such as apple or orange slices, then hang on the door with a wide bow.

A FESTIVE BERRY BALL

Hang your berry ball above a door or suspend it from a light fitting. You can replace the berries with mistletoe for a romantic twist. To ensure maximum freshness, water the centre of the ball every few days over a sink or outside, keeping it damp. Allow to drip before hanging inside again. It should last a couple of weeks.

1: Wrap a ball of florist's foam with chicken wire and secure the seams with cable ties or wire. Soak the ball in water. 2: Using a loop of ribbon, hang the ball up to decorate. Using foliage, such as mistletoe, eucalyptus or olive, mark out the top, bottom and sides to create the shape and size of your ball. 3: Fill in the rest of the shape with foliage of similar lengths until the ball is covered. Add clusters of seasonal berries to inject a bit of colour.

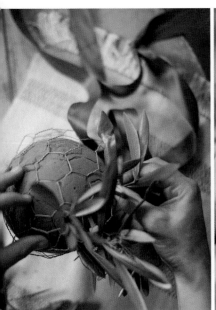

THE CHRISTMAS TREE

The Christmas tree has its origins in Germany, and first became popular among Europe's nobility in the early nineteenth century, adorned with nuts, dates, apples and sweets and lit by candles. We have Prince Albert to thank for bringing the custom to Britain, where it has evolved into a symbol of the happy family gathering. Even today, the tree remains the main visual attraction in homes during the festive period, so before you buy one, decide in advance where it will look best. Roughly calculate the height of the tree you want, allowing enough space for the tree-topper, and for the tree base or pot. Avoid positioning your tree beside a radiator or fireplace, and make sure there are power sockets nearby (or use an extension cable) for the fairy lights.

CHOOSING THE RIGHT TREE

Whether you choose your tree from a nursery or a stall on a street corner, try to source a local grower to guarantee freshness. Consider which variety will best suit your domestic set-up. Families with small children or pets might prefer an evergreen fir as these don't drop their needles; for those who want a traditional-looking tree the Norwegian Spruce is ideal, their fuller branches give you plenty of scope for an abundance of decorations.

- **Norwegian Spruce:** the classic British Christmas tree. As it tends to drop its needles, it is also the cheapest variety and shouldn't be bought too far in advance.
- **Nordmann Fir:** more expensive than the spruce, but less likely to lose its needles (which are short and soft). It has more space between its branches, giving it a graceful shape rather like a tiered cake stand. Another variety that retains its needles is the Noble Fir, used for almost all wreaths and other decorative foliage.
- **Blue Spruce:** the most expensive type of Christmas tree. It is a wonderful pale, silvery blue with short, stiff, pointed needles and a strong, fragrant smell.

DECORATING THE TREE

Decorating the Christmas tree is a ceremony for the whole family. Make a weekend of it and get into the Christmas spirit with mince-pie baking (page 112) and mulled-wine making (page 133) with carols in the background. When it comes to decorations, individual style is everything. I prefer trees decorated with lots of plain white fairy lights (no tinsel) and a variety of baubles (wooden, glass or felt) with a few edible gingerbread stars (page 116) or foil-wrapped chocolates. The ceremonial finale to the decorating is placing the tree-topper: a fairy, angel or star. Inevitably all the children will want to do it so, to save arguments, let them all have a go.

TREE DECORATIONS

CRANBERRY AND POPCORN GARLAND

Drape these around tree branches (as you would tinsel) or hang above the mantelpiece. Use stale popcorn if possible, as it is easier to thread. Once Christmas is over, leave them outside for the birds to nibble at.

Thread fresh cranberries and popcorn in sequence on to strong embroidery thread, using a needle if required. When it reaches the desired length, tie a knot to secure.

PAPER BIRDS

Paper birds are easy to make and add a homemade personal touch to your tree (see the picture on page 121).

I: Cut round a bird template on both card and patterned paper and glue them together using a glue stick. 2: Stick on buttons for the eyes. 3: Cut a slit in the card where the wings should go. Cut a sheet of coloured tissue paper to size, accordion-fold it and insert it through the slit, fanning out the paper and gluing in place if necessary. 4: Make a hole with a hole punch in the centre of the bird and thread wool through, fastening with a knot.

PEG ANGELS OR FAIRIES

Girls will particularly love to make these; they look so pretty hanging from branches or as a tree-topper.

I: Draw a face on the rounded top of an old-fashioned wooden peg and wind wool coated with a little PVA glue around the head to make hair. 2: Cut 8cm of pipe cleaner to create arms and glue to the back of the doll. 3: Cut a 12cm circle out of a doily, crêpe paper and netting, with a hole in the centre of each to put the doll through, and secure to the peg with masking tape. 4: Glue a loop of ribbon around the bodice with PVA and use the remainder of the ribbon to hang the doll. 5: Glue feathers to the back and paint shoes with glitter glue. (See the picture on page 121 for the finished doll.)

FABRIC-COVERED BAUBLES

A practical way to revive older, tired-looking baubles, and to make the most of fabric scraps.

I: Cut a circle of fabric big enough to cover the bauble and mould it around, sticking it down with PVA glue. 2: Tie a festive ribbon around the top and add a loop to hang.

GLITTER PINE CONES

You can hang these on the tree or use them as part of a table display in bowls mixed with baubles.

I: Using a paintbrush, cover the edges of a pine cone with PVA glue. 2: Sprinkle with glitter and shake off the excess. 3: Glue a small loop of ribbon to the base of the cone.

DECK THE HALLS

GREENERY, FRUITS AND FLOWERS

Get creative and bring your house to life from the outside in. Greenery and fruits can instantly transform a home – sprigs of pine, ivy, soft ruscus and berries are beautifully effective when they form the base of the decorations for the mantelpiece and banisters. Lift the dark green foliage with clusters of battery-operated fairy lights. Sprigs of holly look neat above picture frames and mirrors.

Assemble everyday containers that work with your decorations and fill them with long-lasting seasonal flowers and branches, such as ilex berries and pussy willow. These should last well into the new year. Flowers can be expensive and are often out of season around this time of year, so potted bulbs and houseplants are best. Cyclamen, jasmine, narcissi and amaryllis are fresh alternatives to the ubiquitous poinsettia. As with the Christmas tree, position them away from radiators and in cooler parts of the house, keeping them well watered.

Stud oranges with cloves to make scented pomanders to sit in bowls. Choose clementines with their leaves still on and clusters of whole nuts (with nut crackers) on side tables for casual grazing. Dried orange slices hanging from ribbons make lovely decorations. Cut some oranges into 0.5cm slices, lay them on a rack over a baking sheet and dry them out in the oven on its lowest setting for about 4 hours. You can also use just the dried peel as firelighters because of their natural oils. When they burn, the scent is wonderful.

ADDING A TWINKLE ...

DECORATIVE AND SCENTED CANDLES

Candles are perfect for Christmas, traditional and welcoming whether they are on a table, reflected in shiny glassware or twinkling on a mantelpiece or windowsill. Scented candles in accents of orange, clove, cinnamon or sandalwood will add an evocative, spicy fragrance to rooms – a large round one with three wicks will give hours of burning time and last for several months. Wrap the bases of plain white pillar candles with cinnamon sticks: put a rubber band around a white pillar candle and insert cinnamon sticks underneath it, side by side. When the candle is surrounded by the sticks, tie a ribbon around it to hide the rubber band. Or decorate pillar candles with sprigs of pine, rosemary, eucalyptus and dried apple slices and place in storm lanterns (these also look lovely filled with faux snow and decorated with red Christmas ribbon). To decorate tea lights, wrap ivy or other wintry leaves around inexpensive tea-light holders. To do this, arrange the leaves upside down on newspaper and lightly mist with adhesive spray. Wait for a few seconds and then place on the holder, overlapping the leaves slightly. Tie hessian string around the leaves and the holder to keep them in place.

FLICKERING FIRELIGHT

The fireplace is the natural focus of the room. It is, after all, where Father Christmas enters the house, so it's worth dressing up. Hang your stockings or suspend long socks, the toes stuffed with tissue paper, on either side of the mantelpiece to set a traditional scene. Stand a rattan reindeer (some come with decorative fairy lights) to guard the fire. If you have a fireplace that's unusable, fill the hearth with an assortment of candles and storm lanterns.

PAPERCHAINS AND BAUBLES

Children will enjoy helping to decorate rooms with colourful paperchains. I used to love making these at Christmas and hanging them in my bedroom at home. Assembling them from shop-bought packets is easier and less fiddly than creating your own. Christmas tree baubles need not be confined to the tree – dot them around on tables and in bowls, hang from twigs sprayed white or silver (a great alternative to a full Christmas tree) or tie ribbon to baubles and hang them at staggered heights from light fixtures.

A SPRINKLING OF GLITTER AND SNOW

A dusting of glitter on pine cones, acorns and seasonal fruits, such as pomegranates, will add a festive twinkle (just use PVA glue and glitter). Fake snow can be sprayed from cans on to windows to welcome guests, or the loose powder (which can be bought online) can be scattered around fireplaces – great for Christmas morning to delight expectant children.

FESTIVE CANAPÉS

If you throw only one drinks party a year, it's likely to be in the run-up to Christmas. Whether it's an informal gathering or a more organised affair, it's an occasion you'll need to plan. Stock your freezer in the weeks before Christmas (page 112). Accessorise serving trays with evergreen sprigs, bundles of cinnamon sticks, pine cones or tree decorations. For more ideas on hosting drinks parties, see page 102.

DEVILS ON HORSEBACK Makes 24

Allow 3 per person. Preheat the oven to 200°C/gas 6. Remove the stones from 24 prunes or use pitted ones. Wrap half a slice of streaky bacon around each. Place on a baking sheet and drizzle over 2 tablespoons olive oil and the juice of 1 small orange. Cook for 8–10 minutes, or until the bacon is crisp.

SMOKED SALMON AND BEETROOT CROSTINIS Makes 24

Allow 3 per person. Preheat the oven to 180°C/gas 4. Cut 24 rounds of 3–4cm from thin slices of walnut bread and place on to a non-stick baking sheet. Brush with 2 tablespoons olive oil and bake in the oven for 3–4 minutes, or until golden brown. Remove and leave to cool. Mix together 2 cooked grated beetroot, 2 teaspoons horseradish and 1 tablespoon crème fraîche and season well. Cut 120g smoked salmon into thin strips. Place a teaspoon of the beetroot mixture on to each toasted round and top with a small twist of smoked salmon and a dollop of crème fraîche. Sprinkle with ground black pepper and decorate with a few snipped chives.

BRESAOLA WITH CELERIAC REMOULADE Makes 24

Allow 3 per person. Peel and coarsely grate a small celeriac and mix with 5 tablespoons mayonnaise, 1 tablespoon grainy mustard, 3–4 teaspoons lemon juice and season well. Fold 24 slices of bresaola in half (or leave whole if smaller slices), place 2 teaspoons of the remoulade on top and roll up into a parcel. Tie each with a chive to serve.

QUAIL'S EGG CROUSTADES Makes 16

To keep expense down, allow 2 per person. Preheat the oven to 180°C/gas 4. Put 16 croustade cases on a baking tray. Crack a quail's egg into each and cook for 4 minutes until the whites have set. Spoon over ½ a teaspoon of warmed ready-made Hollandaise sauce and garnish with a shard of pan-fried crispy pancetta. To save time, buy pre-cooked pancetta or bacon and just warm through.

PARSNIP SOUP ESPRESSO Makes 24

Allow 1–2 per person (and freeze the excess for up to a month). Melt 30g butter in a large saucepan over a medium heat. Add 1 peeled and chopped onion and cook for about 5 minutes until soft but not coloured. Peel 3 parsnips and 1 medium pear, and chop into 1cm cubes. Peel and finely chop 2 cloves of garlic, then add the parsnips, pear and garlic to the pan and continue to cook for another 2 minutes. Pour in 600ml chicken stock and 350ml whole milk. Simmer for about 20 minutes, until the parsnip is soft. Remove the pan from the heat and purée the soup with a stick blender. Garnish with truffle shavings and a few drops of truffle oil.

PHEASANT GOUJONS Makes 24

Allow 3 per person. Beat 1 egg in a bowl with a splash of milk, and season. Cut 300g pheasant breast fillets lengthways into thin strips, add to the beaten egg and mix well. Mix the zest of ½ a lemon and a small handful of chopped fresh parsley with 80g white breadcrumbs, then spread on a large plate. Coat the pheasant strips evenly in the crumbs. Heat a little sunflower oil in a frying pan and, in batches, shallow-fry the goujons for 2–3 minutes until crisp and golden. Drain on kitchen paper and serve with tartare sauce.

WELSH RAREBIT AND CRANBERRY TOASTS Makes 24

Allow 3 per person. Preheat the grill to high. Cook 25g butter and 1 tablespoon plain flour together in a saucepan for a minute or two until it makes a smooth paste. Add 200g grated mature Cheddar cheese, 1 teaspoon each of English mustard and Worcestershire sauce, 3–4 tablespoons dark ale and a dash of Tabasco. Season well and stir constantly over a gentle heat until smooth. Toast 12 thin slices of ciabatta under the grill until both sides are golden, then cut in half. Spread the mixture on each piece. Return to the grill for 2 minutes or until golden brown. Garnish with cranberry sauce and parsley sprigs.

CHEESE BISCUITS Makes 24

This is a great recipe I learned at the Grange Cookery School. Allow 3 per person. Preheat the oven to 200°C/gas 6. Grate 55g strong cheese, such as mature Cheddar or other leftovers, and blend in a food processor with 55g softened butter, 75g plain flour and 1 teaspoon each of oregano and coriander seeds until it forms a ball. Using greaseproof paper, roll the dough into a sausage shape about 3cm in diameter. Roll the sausage in 1 tablespoon crushed peppercorns or 2 tablespoons sesame seeds. Slice into 0.5cm rounds and cook on a baking tray lined with baking parchment for 10 minutes, or until golden brown. Cool on a wire rack. Top with cream cheese, a few slivers of sun-dried tomato and a basil leaf.

CHRISTMAS DRINKS

A Christmas canapé party requires suitably festive drinks, mulled wine being a classic – or try a Horse's Neck, a Christmas variation on a Moscow Mule (page 161). Pomegranate ice cubes also add a touch of festive charm to any clear drink. Carefully pick out the seeds from a halved pomegranate. Drop a few in each compartment of an ice-cube tray, fill with water and freeze.

MULLED WINE Serves 8

Peel 4 oranges and set aside the peel. Juice the oranges into a bowl, then stud the orange peel with 20 cloves. Pour 2 bottles of fruity red wine, such as Merlot, into a saucepan with a pinch of ground ginger and 4 cinnamon sticks, then add the orange peel and orange juice. Measure out 140g soft brown sugar and add a little at a time – the amount of sugar you need depends on how sweet you like your mulled wine, so taste as you go. Simmer gently for 10 minutes until the sugar dissolves (do not allow to boil), and serve warm.

EGG NOG Serves 8

In a saucepan, warm 1 litre whole milk. Mix together in a jug 6 free-range egg yolks, 80g caster sugar and 1 teaspoon vanilla extract or 1 whole vanilla pod. Add this to the warmed milk along with 200ml brandy and heat through gently, without boiling, until the mixture thickens enough to coat the back of a spoon. Be very careful here – you don't want to scramble the eggs. The egg nog can be chilled at this stage for a few hours until needed, or served warm. Heat gently for 5–7 minutes and grate over nutmeg before serving in small cups.

CLASSIC CHAMPAGNE COCKTAIL Serves 1 (make to order)

Place one brown sugar cube into the bottom of a Champagne flute and soak it with two dashes Angostura Bitters. Add 15ml brandy, top with Champagne or sparkling wine and stir to dissolve the sugar. Garnish with a knot of orange rind. To make many of these in advance, add the sugar cubes, Angostura Bitters and brandy to each flute and wet with just a little Champagne. When you come to top up, this will prevent the Champagne fizzing over.

PEAR MARTINI Serves 1 (make to order)

Shake 40ml pear vodka, 60ml cloudy apple juice and 5ml sugar syrup (page 104) with ice cubes and serve in a martini glass with a squeeze of lime, garnished with a slice of pear or dried apple crisps. If you can't get hold of pear vodka, use plain vodka and the syrup from canned pears – use the fruit for garnish. Make in a jug for larger numbers.

CHRISTMAS SLOE GIN COCKTAILS

Gin and tonic: Add some festive colour and warmth to a classic. Replace regular gin with sloe gin (page 95), serve over ice, add tonic and garnish with a candied orange slice or sliver of peel.

Sloe gin fizz: A wintry English take on the classic French Kir Royale. Add sloe gin to the bottom of a Champagne flute and top with Champagne or another sparkling wine.

For colourful aperitifs, serve New World sparkling wines, Cava or Prosecco with fruit liqueurs.

CHRISTMAS EVE

Christmas Eve is the day to put all the finishing touches to your preparations. Wrap last-minute gifts first thing (try to keep this to a minimum) and, if you can, lay the table for Christmas lunch (page 138) to save time the following day. Come late afternoon, children's excitement will have reached fever pitch at the prospect of Father Christmas arriving, so keep them occupied with some simple activities. Hide a few foil-wrapped chocolate coins for a Christmas treasure hunt or encourage them to mix up oats and glitter to scatter outside the door or down the garden path to guide the reindeer. Later on, help them prepare the traditional offering of mince pies and a glass of sherry for Father Christmas to have when he comes down the chimney.

STOCKINGS

Each family has its own special place for hanging stockings, be it on either side of the fireplace or at the end of the bed. Wrapping stocking presents in tissue paper is not only cheaper and faster than using giftwrap, it makes opening them easier, too. Wrist Sellotape dispensers are essential when wrapping lots of stocking fillers. A great tip is to colour-coordinate presents for each stocking so they don't get mixed up. For more wrapping ideas, see page 197.

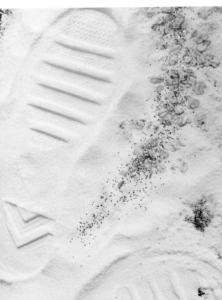

CHRISTMAS DAY

CHRISTMAS MORNING

Christmas morning is a magical time, with stockings first thing amid a flurry of excitement and strewn wrapping paper. Fillers can be the simplest of things; essentials for me are a tube of jelly beans poking out from the top of the stocking, a satsuma and a bag of chocolate coins. If Christmas lunch is planned for much later in the day, serve something satisfying and filling for breakfast, such as smoked salmon with scrambled eggs. For those with a sweeter tooth, raisin bread with spiced Christmas butter (see below) is delicious, and for kids make hot chocolate spoons (page 395).

CHRISTMAS MENU

Light starters
Twice-baked cheese soufflé *or*
Pear, walnut and Roquefort salad *or*
Shellfish tian *or*
Smoked-trout pâté quenelles

Main course
Traditional roast turkey
Gravy, bread sauce and cranberry sauce
Roast potatoes
Brussels sprouts, pancetta and chestnuts
Honeyed carrots and parsnips
Pigs in blankets and stuffing

Desserts
Christmas pudding and brandy butter
Chocolate yule log
Stilton

Loire Chenin blanc
A good-quality red or white Burgundy
Sauternes, Port or Piedro Ximénez

Christmas butter: add 75g diced cranberries, 40g soft brown sugar, a good pinch each of mixed spice and cinnamon, the zest of 2 clementines and 50g chopped mixed peel to a 250g pack of unsalted, softened butter. Mix to combine. Refrigerate in 2 sterile jam jars or wrapped in clingfilm and baking parchment.

CHRISTMAS LUNCH

This lunch only comes once a year so stick to a traditional menu. It's also a time to bring out special wines. The turkey with all the trimmings is the star attraction, so if you're serving a starter, keep it light or offer festive canapés (page 129) with drinks. Cooking the turkey might be a heroic solo effort but it's a meal everyone can muck in with: peeling vegetables, carving the meat, serving up and clearing away.

THE CHRISTMAS TABLE

White table linen is an effective backdrop to any Christmas colour scheme, but if you have a wooden tabletop in good condition consider leaving it bare, or just add a bit of softness to it with a Christmassy-coloured table runner.

TRADITIONAL

I prefer a traditional table with strong colours of rich reds and evergreens because it feels warm and nostalgic. Add touches of gold (or silver) to bring a special feel to the table on glassware, china or festive charger plates. Shiny pebbles and wrapped chocolates can be grouped in small bowls or scattered sparingly along the length of the table. If you are using natural foliage to decorate your table, you'll need plenty of light to keep it from looking heavy and gloomy (battery-operated fairy lights and tea lights are perfect for this). You could turn your door wreath (page 119) into a table centrepiece with the well in the middle filled with candles. Otherwise, stemmed cut-glass bowls filled with frosted fruits, berries and baubles, as well as decorative storm lanterns, can act as prominent features.

Pick out a particular colour or texture from your tablecentre and mirror this in smaller details, such as the napkins, place names and crackers. The beauty of homemade crackers (page 115) is that you can match your materials to the theme of your table. Napkins tied with tartan ribbon will complement holly and berries, or attach a bundle of cinnamon sticks and faux berries to each place setting. Name cards can be wedged into pine cones, along with colourful pompom balls, or tied with raffia string to the stalks of festive fruits, such as pears, clementines and figs.

CONTEMPORARY

For a more contemporary table, use crisp white linen and silvery-grey accessories as your base colour. For the tablecentre, a collection of elegant candlesticks at varying heights, interspersed with silver foliage, will create a twinkling, magical feel. Clusters of white, glass and silver tea lights or homemade lace-paper lantern jars (page 204) on table mirrors will catch the light, as will glass nuggets, acrylic gems and silver-foil chocolate coins scattered loosely on the table. A minimalist palette relies on texture and pattern, such as cut glassware and embroidered linen, but a splash of red will bring a Scandinavian feel.

Add personal touches, such as Christmassy decorations on place settings or on the backs of chairs. Attach name cards to mini bauble holders or to glass stems using glitter clothes pegs (page 115). Look out for pretty silvery napkin rings throughout the year; a mismatch feel can be quite charming and means that each guest can recognise their napkin for subsequent meals.

LIGHT STARTERS

TWICE-BAKED CHEESE SOUFFLÉ Serves 8

Preheat the oven to 180°C/gas 4. Separate 3 eggs, and put to one side. Melt 30g unsalted butter in a pan, stir in 30g plain flour and mix to a smooth paste. Gradually add 240ml whole milk and a pinch of nutmeg, and stir until the sauce thickens. Leave to cool slightly, then beat in the 3 egg yolks, 100g grated Cheddar cheese and 2 tablespoons chopped chives. Using an electric whisk, beat the egg whites to soft peaks. Mix 1 tablespoon egg white into the sauce, then gently pour the sauce over the remaining egg whites, carefully folding everything together with a metal spoon. Spoon the mixture into 8 buttered ramekins, place them in a roasting tin and add enough hot water to come halfway up the sides. Cook in the oven for 20–25 minutes, until firm. Remove from the tin and allow to cool, then run a knife around the edge of each soufflé and carefully turn out on to a baking sheet. (At this point the soufflés can be frozen for up to 3 months and can be baked for the second time from frozen.) Increase the oven temperature to 220°C/gas 7. Combine 150ml double cream and 1 tablespoon English mustard and top each soufflé with 3 tablespoons of the mixture, sprinkle with extra cheese and bake for 15–20 minutes, until golden and risen. Serve garnished with chives.

PEAR, WALNUT AND ROQUEFORT SALAD Serves 8

Separate 4 heads each of red and white chicory and place the leaves in a large serving bowl. Add 3 peeled and thinly sliced large pears and 80g chopped walnuts, then crumble over 200g Roquefort cheese. Mix together the juice of 1 lemon, 6 tablespoons extra virgin olive oil and 2 tablespoons honey. Drizzle over the salad just before serving.

TWO WAYS WITH SEAFOOD Serves 8

Shellfish tian: mix 6 tablespoons mayonnaise, 2 tablespoons tomato ketchup, a good dash each of Worcestershire sauce, brandy, Tabasco sauce and lemon juice to taste. Season well. In a separate bowl, combine 400g fresh picked (or tinned) crabmeat, 250g small Atlantic prawns, a large bunch of chopped fresh chives and the juice of 1 lemon. Divide the crab mixture between 8 medium metal chef's rings, filling them about two-thirds full. Press down with a spoon to compress, then refrigerate. To serve, turn out each seafood 'tower' on to serving plates. Spoon a little sauce over and top with peeled king prawns and a sprig of dill.

Smoked trout pâté: mix together 350g skinless smoked trout, 2 tablespoons crème fraîche, 2 teaspoons horseradish, 4 tablespoons cream cheese and the juice of 1 lemon in a food processor until smooth. Season well and stir in 2 tablespoons chopped chives. Shape between 2 tablespoons to form quenelles. Serve 2 per person, topped with caviar and sprinkled with cayenne pepper. Delicious with Melba toast.

ROAST TURKEY

There is no doubt that carving a turkey at the table makes for an impressive display, but with so many other ingredients to serve, plating up in the kitchen will save time and keep the food warm. Because of their size, turkeys are perfect for feeding larger gatherings. If you're cooking for a small group, a roast goose or a brace of pheasant might make a welcome change.

SERVES 8

100g butter, at room temperature

zest of 1 orange

10 sprigs of thyme, 8 picked, 2 left whole

salt and freshly ground black pepper

1 x 4kg turkey at room temperature, giblets removed

3 bay leaves

olive oil

1 quantity stuffing (page 147)

1 glass of red wine, water or cider

TIMING IT RIGHT:
When the turkey is out of the oven and resting, add the potatoes (page 54) and cook for 40 minutes. Add the stuffing balls, parsnips and carrots (page 147) to the oven, and roast for 20–25 minutes.

Preheat the oven to 220°C/gas 7. In a bowl mix the butter with the orange zest and picked thyme leaves and season well. Starting from the neck end of the bird, gently push your fingers under the turkey's skin, and ease it away from the flesh. Push the flavoured butter under the skin, on top of each breast, then smooth it out evenly and replace the skin. Quarter the zested orange and place it in the turkey cavity with the bay leaves and thyme sprigs. Drizzle the turkey with a little olive oil, rub it over the skin and season well. Place some stuffing (page 147) in the neck of the bird. Roll the rest of the mixture into balls, place on a greased baking sheet and set aside (see box).

Put the prepared turkey into a large roasting tin, and add the red wine, water or cider around the base. Cover the roasting tin completely with foil, tucking it underneath to create a 'tent' over the turkey. Cook the turkey for 30 minutes at 220°C/gas 7, then turn the oven down to 180°C/gas 4 and cook for 35 minutes per kg (2 hours 20 minutes for a 4kg bird). Turn the oven up to 200°C/gas 6. Remove the foil and return the turkey to the oven for a further 30 minutes to crisp the skin.

To test if the turkey is cooked through, pierce the fattest part of a thigh with a skewer. The juices should run clear. This is an essential test to do as ovens vary. Alternatively, use a meat thermometer which should read at least 165°C. Rest the turkey, covered loosely with foil, for at least 20 minutes and up to 1 hour.

. . . AND ALL THE TRIMMINGS

The following recipes each serve 8. These are all must-have accompaniments to turkey, and most can be prepared ahead (page 111).

PERFECT GRAVY

Roughly chop the giblets from the turkey and brown them off in a little olive oil in a saucepan over a medium heat, adding 1 chopped onion, 1 chopped carrot and 1 chopped stick of celery. When the vegetables have softened, add 2 tablespoons plain flour and whisk to combine. Pour in 1 large glass of red wine or Madeira and simmer until the liquid is reduced by half. Add 1 litre fresh dark chicken stock and 1 bay leaf to the pan, bring to the boil and then reduce the heat and simmer for 30–40 minutes. Strain the broth from the giblets and vegetables. Add the juices from the resting turkey to the broth, being careful to remove the excess fat and reduce again until dark and thick. Strain into the gravy boat.

TIP: *Warm up your gravy boat by filling it with very hot water.*

BREAD SAUCE

Warm 700ml milk, 30g butter, 1 onion studded with 6 cloves, 6 peppercorns and 1 bay leaf in a pan for 10 minutes. Strain and return the liquid to the pan. Add 150g white breadcrumbs and simmer for 3–4 minutes. Add a generous pinch of nutmeg, and season with salt and pepper to taste. This freezes well for up to 6 months.

TIP: *You can stir in some of the roasting juices as a substitute for a little of the milk or to thin the sauce, if required.*

CRANBERRY SAUCE

Put 600g cranberries in a saucepan with the zest and juice of 2 oranges and 250g golden caster sugar. Add a generous splash of port and simmer for 8–10 minutes, until the sugar is dissolved, the cranberries have popped their skins and the sauce has thickened. Add more sugar if required.

PERFECT POTATOES

The recipe for roast potatoes on page 54 is an essential accompaniment to turkey. Put your potatoes into the oven as the turkey comes out to rest, and to save on washing up use disposable aluminium trays. Always make more than you think you will need!

SAGE AND ONION STUFFING

Put a large pan on a medium heat and pour in 2 glugs of olive oil. Add 2 peeled and chopped onions and 2 peeled and finely chopped cloves of fresh garlic and cook gently for 5–10 minutes, until soft and slightly golden. Add 1 bunch chopped fresh sage and 150g white breadcrumbs. Remove the pan from the heat and allow to cool. Once cold, mix in 700g good-quality sausagemeat, a handful of chopped dried apricots and a beaten egg. Season well, and set aside while you prepare the turkey. Cook according to the instructions on page 144.

BRUSSELS SPROUTS, PANCETTA AND CHESTNUTS

Bring a pan of water to the boil and parboil 500g small Brussels sprouts for 5–6 minutes until al dente. Drain them and set aside. To keep them green, plunge briefly into ice-cold water to stop them cooking. Heat 25g unsalted butter in a frying pan and add 100g diced pancetta (or chopped dry-cured bacon). Fry gently for 2 minutes until it starts to crisp. Add 80g cooked, roughly chopped chestnuts and cook for a further minute. Add the sprouts and a squeeze of orange juice and bring to a simmer. Season to taste.

TIP: *Choose small fresh sprouts for the best flavour and, when preparing them, don't peel back too much of the outer skin or make a criss-cross on the base as this can make them soggy.*

HONEYED CARROTS AND PARSNIPS

Preheat the oven to 200°C/gas 6. Peel and cut into wedges 800g each of carrots and parsnips, then place in a large roasting tin. For larger parsnips remove the core which can be bitter. Sprinkle generously with sea salt and freshly ground black pepper, then drizzle over 3 tablespoons olive oil. Toss to coat, then roast for 20–25 minutes until tender and slightly charred. Drizzle over 2 tablespoons runny honey and add a knob of butter, toss again to coat, and serve.

PIGS IN BLANKETS

Preheat the oven to 200°C/gas 6. Take 24 small sausages (allow 3 per person), such as chipolatas, and 1 packet of pancetta. Cut each rasher of pancetta in half, then stretch lightly with the back of a knife. Wrap one half-rasher around each sausage, then place on a lightly greased baking sheet, making sure the join is underneath the sausage. Roast for 10–15 minutes until the pancetta is cooked and crisp.

TIP: *My favourite Christmas side dish of all, these are also delicious as a festive canapé.*

CHRISTMAS PUDDINGS

It's a wonderful piece of theatre when the Christmas pudding (page 112) makes its grand entrance, lit with burning brandy. Serve it alongside brandy butter or cream and warm a batch of mince pies. A chocolate yule log might be a welcome alternative to Christmas pudding, decorated with woodland symbols or perhaps covered with white chocolate icing to create a snowy scene. Bring out a cheeseboard and biscuits or one large wheel of cheese to complete the feast.

BRANDY BUTTER Serves 8–10

Mix 250g softened, unsalted butter, the zest of 1 orange and 80g soft light brown sugar until thoroughly combined. Gradually add 80ml brandy while mixing, until you have a creamy, smooth paste. Once made this will keep in the fridge for up to 4 days.

CHOCOLATE YULE LOG Serves 8

Preheat the oven to 190°C/gas 5. Grease and line a 33cm x 23cm Swiss roll tin. Separate 4 eggs. Beat the egg whites with an electric whisk until stiff, then gradually add 50g caster sugar while whisking continuously. In a separate bowl, beat the egg yolks with 75g caster sugar, add 80g self-raising flour and 2 tablespoons cocoa powder, then fold in the egg whites. Pour the sponge mixture into the tin. Use a spatula to spread the mixture evenly, then bake for about 10 minutes, until the top is springy. Remove from the oven, place a damp tea towel over the top of the tray and set aside to cool. Whip 200ml double cream to stiff peaks, then add 1 teaspoon of vanilla extract.

Remove the cooled sponge from the tin and turn it upside down on a plate. Soak the sponge with 8 tablespoons of cherry liqueur (optional), then turn it back over on to the baking parchment and spread the whipped cream on top. If not using liqueur, simply spread the cream all over the sponge. Holding the baking parchment with the longer side towards you, roll the sponge up, keeping it nice and tight. To make the icing, beat 120g softened, unsalted butter until smooth and then gradually beat in 160g icing sugar and 100g cocoa powder. If using, add another splash of cherry liqueur and mix well. If the icing needs thinning, add 4 tablespoons whole milk a little at a time, then spread it over the entire cake with a palette knife, making markings to resemble bark. Sift icing sugar over the cake, then decorate with chocolate shavings (page 32) and Christmas cake decorations.

FESTIVE FUN

Christmas is still one of the few occasions when you can get everybody playing and, hopefully, enjoying games. I have picked out some traditional games and others that won't be so familiar. Charades is a classic and inclusive for all, as most people know the rules (or their own versions of them). A jigsaw puzzle can offer a welcome respite from the Christmas revelry. Pick one that has lots of colour and activity and lay it out on a table in a quiet corner so that anyone passing can add a few pieces. Have a personalised one made up from a photograph of something familiar to your family.

THE CHOCOLATE-BOX GAME

Find a tall chocolate box (or an empty cereal box) and stand it on a clear area of floor away from any furniture. Players take it in turns to lift the box using just their teeth, with only their feet touching the ground. Once everyone has had a go, tear a few centimetres off the top of the box so that it stands a little lower than before and play another round. This time, it will be harder and it's possible that some people will lose their balance or use their hands. If they do, they go out. The box continues to get smaller and smaller until it is just a flat piece of cardboard and only the most flexible and controlled players are left in the game.

PASS THE ORANGE

Players split into two teams and each team forms a line. The first person in each team tucks an orange under their chin. On 'Go!', they pass the orange to the next person in line, neck to neck. Everyone must keep their hands firmly behind their backs. The oranges make their way down their respective lines but if at any point one is dropped, the player responsible for the fall must get on to their hands and knees and retrieve the orange using only their neck and chin. The sequence of passes is then resumed and the first team to get the orange to the final player in their line is declared victorious.

OTHER CHRISTMAS GAMES

- **After Eight**: *taking it in turns, balance an After Eight on your forehead. Tilt your head back and try to shift it down to your mouth using only facial movements.*

- **Bouchon**: *you'll need corks and cards (page 59).*

- **Stop the bus**: *great for all ages (page 59).*

- **The hat game**: *Divide into two teams. Each player writes the names of famous people on small pieces of paper, scrunches them up and throws them in a 'hat'. Players take turns pulling pieces of paper and describing as many of the famous people as possible in one minute without saying their names. The team who has guessed the most names correctly when the hat is empty wins.*

BOXING DAY

This is the day for some serious downtime — a welcome and wonderful contrast to the rigours of Christmas itself. The hype, hard work and deadlines are over, and, even if you have guests, the atmosphere is likely to be lazy and laid back. Comforting, curative food is what's needed — a baked and glazed ham is inexpensive and perfect for a large gathering, along with leftovers from the Christmas feast. I like the idea of a Boxing Day ploughman's: beautifully arranged platters of cold meats and cheese (Stilton being essential), accompanied by a large green salad, apple slices, grapes, celery sticks, pâté, crunchy bread, chutney (page 404), piccalilli and pickles. Some might be tempted to build their own individually tailored, seasonal tower sandwiches.

BOXING DAY HAM Serves 8-12

The ham is completely cooked in the liquid, so can be stored for up to 3 days before you add the glaze and roast it. Put a 2kg boned ham joint in a large pan with 2 litres apple juice, 2-3 litres cider and enough water to cover. Add 1 trimmed and coarsely sliced leek, 2 coarsely sliced celery stalks, 2 bay leaves, 1 peeled and chopped onion and 2 teaspoons black peppercorns and bring to the boil. Skim off any scum. Cover the pan with a lid and simmer for 2 hours, until the ham is tender. Drain the ham and discard the vegetables and other flavourings. Set aside.

Preheat the oven to 200°C/gas 6. Mix together 4 tablespoons marmalade and 3 tablespoons soft brown sugar to form a paste. Remove the skin from the ham and score the fat. Spread on the marmalade mixture, then stud with 10 cloves and roast for 45 minutes, until golden and glistening.

 Beaujolais, soft Côtes du Rhône or leftover wines from Christmas Day.

A WHOLE STILTON

Slice the top off a whole Stilton and scoop out a little of the cheese. Pour in port, sherry, Madeira or old ale. Let the cheese absorb this for up to 3 weeks. Serve with an interesting selection of cheese biscuits, such as Italian flatbreads, grissini sticks, thin herb crackers, oat cakes and water biscuits. Add some fresh fruit, such as grapes and figs, and perhaps a little quince jelly.

TIP: *Use a Stilton scoop to dig out the soft insides of the cheese.*

MAKING USE OF LEFTOVERS

Turkey *works well as a fricassée, in a curry (page 166), Stroganoff or pie (page 67) with other leftovers.*

Stilton *is delicious in soup with broccoli. Use it to add intense flavour to cauliflower cheese (page 55) and serve with baked ham.*

Sprouts *can be stir-fried with spices and soy sauce, or used with leftover potatoes and parsnips to make bubble and squeak.*

Ring out the old, ring in the new,
Ring, happy bells, across the snow:
The year is going, let him go;
Ring out the false, ring in the true.

'Ring Out, Wild Bells',
Alfred, Lord Tennyson

NEW YEAR'S EVE

New Year's Eve looms large in the calendar due to its importance; it's one of the oldest festivals in the British Isles. It has its roots in Roman times, when people marked the occasion by feasting, dancing, singing and exchanging gifts – and is celebrated around the world. Although each country has its own traditional customs and superstitions, it's a universal experience as people wait for the first day of the new year to reach them. There is always an exhilarating feeling as the evening gathers pace – a wave of corks popping, glasses clinking and people cheering which sweeps across the world and upon the thousands who gather to eat, drink and be merry.

As a result, a New Year's Eve celebration always comes with huge expectations, which explains why it can so often be a real anticlimax and a party many dread to host. Understandably, people often panic when organising such an event, but in reality it's not so different from any other party over the course of the year. I know from past experience that it's important not to have preparations still looming over you the moment Christmas ends, otherwise you'll get in a flap and resent having volunteered to throw the celebration altogether. Fewer shops are open over this period and shelves are barer so there's even more of an incentive to have it all organised before Christmas.

My favourite New Year parties have not been the huge affairs, but the more intimate ones with close friends and family, anything between eight and twenty-five people. Whatever the numbers, the pressure is on the host to magic up all the necessary ingredients for a fantastic atmosphere. A few good cocktails and canapés early on when guests arrive will get everyone in the mood. Have some great music and (perhaps not so great!) dancing to see in the New Year. Food isn't necessarily the focus, so a simple but colourful curry buffet is the perfect meal, especially as the food can be eaten with just a fork and seating doesn't need to be confined to the table. All the dishes in this chapter can be prepared in advance, or you can make it a more collaborative affair (and less of an expense) by asking your friends to contribute to the buffet. The curries make a welcome change from traditional Christmas fare; the fragrant aromas momentarily suggest the sensory pleasures of hot and exotic climes – a far cry from the cold winter outside.

SET THE SCENE

ROOM DECORATIONS

Because the house is dressed for Christmas, New Year adornments should be quick and easy, adapted from your existing decorations. For an effervescent backdrop, hang shiny baubles (or other sparkly tree decorations) at different heights from string tied across the room. Perhaps introduce a particular colour scheme but keep silver as the dominant colour throughout. Tissue-paper pompoms (see below) are quick and easy to make, and balls of varying sizes, hung with ribbon or glittery wire, will enhance the celebratory feel. Dot white fairy lights about the room, wrapping them around silver-sprayed branches, mirrors and beams, or cluster them in tall cylindrical glass vases. If your ceiling is low, let a handful of helium balloons (tied with curling ribbon) hang freely and add in a few silver-foil number balloons showing the year you are celebrating. Alternatively, you can tie them to balloon weights, table centrepieces or to the backs of chairs to add height and drama to your table, or arrange them in empty corners of the room.

TISSUE-PAPER POMPOMS

These look beautiful hanging from the ceiling, or you can make smaller pompoms to tie around napkin rings.

I: Stack 12 sheets of tissue paper (approx 25 x 38cm sheets or double for larger ones) and accordion-fold the paper, 1.5cm wide, on the shorter side. 2: Fold in half to find the centre and tie a long piece of ribbon or sparkly wire tightly in the centre. Trim the edge of the paper in pointy or round shapes. 3: Open the fan back up and carefully separate the layers of tissue paper, pulling them away from the centre one at a time.

CELEBRATORY TABLE

Let the food provide the colour and keep your table palette relatively neutral, fresh and clean, with the focal point being beautiful flowers, twinkling candles and tea lights. Set candles in glass or etched antique silver holders (mirrored placemats and vases will double the light that they give off). Other tablecentre ideas might include small globe vases lined with a large leaf and filled with white roses, lisianthus, hyacinths, freesias, ranunculus and eucalyptus. Add sparkle to empty spaces on the table using silver or gold celebratory confetti, glitter and glass nuggets, with a few silvery party poppers and saucer crackers stacked in the centre – no need to go overboard, just go for delicate touches.

COCKTAILS FOR A CROWD

If there is ever a time to mix up cocktails, this is the occasion to do so. Set up a martini bar (page 65) for guests to make their own classic versions, or prepare the bases of the following cocktails in jugs ahead of time for ease of entertaining, then just shake over ice and strain before serving. These are refreshing enough to sip all night long, and complement the curry theme of the evening (the pear martini on page 133 is also very seasonal). Don't forget to save some bubbly for midnight toasts.

PASSION-FRUIT MARTINI Serves 4

One of my favourites. In a jug, mix together 200ml vodka and 160ml passion-fruit juice, together with 40ml pineapple juice and the juice of 1 lime. To serve, shake hard in a cocktail shaker filled with ice cubes, strain and pour into chilled martini glasses. Serve immediately to ensure a frothy top, and garnish with a few passion-fruit seeds. If you want to use very fresh passion-fruit juice, scoop the flesh out of 6 passion fruits and strain the juice through a fine sieve.

FRENCH MARTINI Serves 4

Quick and easy, the flavour is jammy and fruity. In a jug, mix together 100ml vodka, 100ml Chambord and 200ml pineapple juice. To serve, shake hard in a cocktail shaker filled with ice cubes, strain and pour into chilled martini glasses. Garnish each with a raspberry. A friend serves these in his bar in teapots, filled with ice.

MOSCOW MULE Serves 4

A drink you can enjoy all evening long, at any time of year. It's refreshing and goes particularly well with spicy food. In a jug, mix together 160ml vodka and the juice of 1 lime, 2 tablespoons demerara sugar and 4 dashes Angostura Bitters. To serve, pour into 4 tall glasses with a wedge of fresh lime and some slices of fresh ginger. Muddle together, add ice cubes and top with ginger beer. A Horse's Neck is a variation of this drink: just replace the vodka with 100ml brandy.

COSMOPOLITAN Serves 4

In a jug, mix together 200ml lemon vodka, 80ml Cointreau, 40ml fresh lime juice, 80ml cranberry juice and 10ml sugar syrup (page 104). Pour the mixture in batches into a cocktail shaker, fill with ice cubes and shake. Pour through a strainer into chilled martini glasses and garnish with a slice of orange rind, pinched together to release the oils.

COLOURFUL CURRY BANQUET

To kick off proceedings, especially if you are serving cocktails and planning to start dinner later, have a few canapés on hand – the evening is likely to be a long one. Spiced nuts (page 62) are perfect for all-night grazing and can be placed strategically for guests to munch on. Curries lend themselves to sharing and make for a bountiful and satisfying banquet to linger over. Everyone has their favourite, so a selection of main dishes served alongside fragrant rice, brightly coloured chutneys, salsas and piles of poppadoms will look appetising on the table. Label them using mini chalkboards with stands. Curries are also low maintenance (the word 'curry' comes from the Southern Indian word 'kari', which simply means 'sauce'), so each dish is self-contained and requires minimal last-minute prep, allowing you to enjoy the party with your guests.

The canapés on page 165 make for colourful small bites along a subtle curry theme; they won't clash with the fuller flavours of the main meal. Serve these on plain white plates or silvery trays to bring out the colours. Allow two of each canapé per person.

NEW YEAR'S EVE MENU

Canapés

Coronation turkey boats

Curried blinis with raita

Stuffed eggs

Mini prawn poppadoms

Spiced crab cakes

Main courses

Spicy red chicken curry

Thai green prawn curry

Side dishes

Daal and sag aloo

Basmati and jasmine rice

Mango, tomato and spring onion salsa

Desserts

Winter fruit salad

Sparkling gold-leaf jellies

Meringue kisses

CORONATION TURKEY BOATS Makes 16

Mix together 2 tablespoons mayonnaise, 1½ tablespoons mango chutney, 1 teaspoon curry powder and the juice of ½ a lime. Add 350g cooked, diced turkey breast (or chicken), season and toss until well coated. Separate the leaves of 2 baby gem lettuces and spoon a little turkey mixture into each lettuce leaf 'boat'. Cover and refrigerate. Garnish with chopped mango.

CURRIED BLINIS WITH RAITA Makes 16

Grate ¼ of a cucumber and squeeze the excess liquid from it. Mix with 200ml natural yogurt in a bowl and refrigerate until needed. Preheat the oven to 180°C/gas 4. Spread a little ready-made medium curry paste over 16 cocktail blinis, then place on a baking sheet and warm in the oven for 4–5 minutes. Spoon a little raita on to each one and garnish with mint.

STUFFED EGGS Makes 16

Place 8 eggs in a saucepan, cover with water and bring to the boil. Lower the heat to a simmer and cook for 8 minutes. When cooked, cool under cold water and peel. Submerge in fresh cold water with 2 tablespoons of natural pink food dye for 5 minutes to absorb the colour of the dye. Cut each egg in half lengthways. Remove the yolks and mash in a bowl with 4–5 tablespoons mayonnaise, a dash of Tabasco, a squeeze of lemon juice and season well. Place the yolk mixture into a piping bag and carefully pipe it into the egg whites. Garnish with a sprinkle of paprika.

MINI PRAWN POPPADOMS Makes 16

Mix together 350g small peeled and cooked Atlantic prawns with 2 tablespoons Thai green curry paste, 1 deseeded and finely diced cucumber, the juice of ½ a lime, 2 tablespoons roughly chopped coriander and ½ a deseeded and finely chopped fresh red chilli. Spoon the prawn mixture onto 16 mini poppadoms, and garnish with finely sliced red chilli.

SPICED CRAB CAKES Makes 16

Mix together 350g fresh picked or tinned white crab meat, 1 deseeded and finely chopped fresh red chilli, a 5cm piece of finely chopped fresh ginger, a small bunch of chopped coriander and the zest and juice of 1 lime with 50g breadcrumbs and 1 beaten egg. Make walnut-sized balls of paste in your hands and pat them into small cakes. Refrigerate for at least 10 minutes. At this stage the crab cakes can be frozen for up to 3 weeks (defrost thoroughly before cooking). When ready to cook, dust the cakes in flour, dip into beaten egg and lightly coat in 100g breadcrumbs. Pour 3 tablespoons vegetable oil into a frying pan or wok and heat through. Gently place the crab cakes in the pan and fry for 30 seconds to 2–3 minutes on each side until golden brown. Drain on kitchen towel, then serve warm with a sweet chilli dipping sauce.

SPICY RED CHICKEN CURRY

The chicken thighs in this curry promise tender, tasty meat, but if you prefer to use breast, make the sauce in advance and add the chicken for the last 20 minutes of cooking to stop it drying out. For more heat, add chopped chillies to the marinade. Lamb, pheasant or vegetables make lovely variations.

SERVES 8

For the marinade

8 tablespoons coconut cream

5–6 tablespoons ready-made curry paste, medium or hot

5 cloves of peeled and minced garlic

a 3cm piece of fresh ginger, peeled and grated

For the curry

20 chicken thigh fillets, chopped into large chunks

2 tablespoons vegetable oil

2–3 large onions, peeled and sliced

2 x 400g tin chopped tomatoes

100ml chicken stock

1 tablespoon caster sugar

1 x 400ml tin coconut milk

salt and freshly ground black pepper

To make the marinade, mix together the coconut cream, curry paste, garlic and ginger in a bowl. Add the chicken, mix well to combine, then cover the bowl with clingfilm and refrigerate for at least 20 minutes, or overnight if possible.

To make the sauce, heat the vegetable oil in a pan and fry the sliced onions for 5 minutes until lightly browned. Add the marinated chicken and continue to cook for a further 4 minutes until aromatic. Sprinkle in some water if the paste begins to stick.

Add the tomatoes, stock and sugar and cook without a lid for 20 minutes. Cover with the lid and continue to cook for 10 minutes. Stir in the coconut milk and warm through, then check the seasoning and adjust if necessary. (At this stage, the curry can be frozen for up to 1 month.) Squeeze over the juice of 1 lime and garnish with fresh coriander. Serve with the aromatic rice below.

 *A fruity red like an Australian Shiraz.*

AROMATIC BASMATI RICE Serves 8

To mould this colourful and fragrant rice into neat shapes, line ramekins with clingfilm, press in the rice and turn out.

Place 600g basmati rice in a sieve and rinse with cold water until the water runs clear. In a large pot, bring 3 litres vegetable stock to the boil with 2 teaspoons turmeric. Add the rice and stir once. Add 3 whole cloves, 4 cardamom pods and 2 cinnamon sticks and simmer for 12–15 minutes. Taste the rice to test if it is done, then drain and fluff up with a fork. Remove the cloves, cardamom pods and cinnamon sticks before serving.

THAI GREEN PRAWN CURRY

Fragrant, light and pale green in colour, this sauce can be made and frozen up to a month ahead, and the raw prawns (or scallops) added at the last minute to simply cook through.

SERVES 8

1 tablespoon vegetable oil

2–3 leeks, trimmed and finely chopped

3 heaped tablespoons Thai green curry paste

1 red chilli, deseeded and finely chopped

1 tablespoon palm sugar or 2 tablespoons soft light brown sugar

2 stalks of lemongrass, ends bashed

2 x 400ml tins coconut milk

2 tablespoons fish sauce

4 dried kaffir lime leaves

450g peeled and deveined raw king prawns

500g sugar snap peas

juice of 1 lime

Heat the oil in a pan and gently sauté the leeks for a couple of minutes. Add the green curry paste, chilli, sugar and lemongrass stalks and cook over a medium-high heat for 1 minute.

Pour in the coconut milk and fish sauce, add the lime leaves and simmer for 25–30 minutes. Add the prawns and the sugar snap peas and cook for approximately 3 minutes, then taste for seasoning, adding more fish sauce if needed and lime juice to taste. Remove the lime leaves and lemongrass stalks. Garnish with coriander.

An aromatic white like Riesling or Gewürztraminer.

TIP: *Baby corn and thinly sliced red pepper make nice additions to this curry — stir them in with the prawns. If using chicken, add it with the coconut milk and allow it to cook through.*

FLUFFY JASMINE RICE Serves 8

My mum has a tried-and-tested way of cooking rice: whatever vessel you are using to measure out the rice always use one and a half the amount of cold water (a little more if using brown or wild rice, as these take longer to cook).

Place 2 mugs of jasmine rice and 3 mugs of salted cold water on a high heat until the water starts to bubble. Turn the heat right down, add a lid and gently simmer for 10 minutes until all the water has been absorbed (you can test by tipping the pan on its side; you might also see small holes appearing throughout the rice). Don't touch or stir the rice until all the liquid has been absorbed. Leave to stand for 5 minutes, then fluff with a fork before serving.

SIMPLE SIDE DISHES

DAAL Serves 8

An Indian lentil dish, and a classic, healthy vegetable side. If you are asking others to help you with the catering this is a great one to delegate. For a Thai twist, substitute 200ml of the stock with coconut milk.

Pour 1 tablespoon vegetable oil into a large saucepan, and add a peeled and grated 5cm piece of fresh ginger, 1 diced green chilli, 3 tablespoons tomato purée, 1 teaspoon each of ground turmeric, cumin seeds and chilli powder and 2 cloves of finely chopped garlic. Fry the spices over a medium heat, stirring until they become fragrant.

Rinse 400g split yellow lentils (daal) under running water. Add them to the spices in the pan with 600ml vegetable stock. Bring to the boil, then reduce the heat to medium and simmer for 15–20 minutes, adding more stock if necessary, to prevent the lentils drying out. Finish with chopped coriander, a squeeze of lime juice and season to taste.

SAG ALOO Serves 8

I prefer this dish when the spinach still has a bit of bite — it's a brilliant burst of green and really tasty.

In a large saucepan, parboil 400g cubed floury potatoes (use Maris Piper or King Edward) for 7–8 minutes, then drain and set aside. Put a large frying pan over a medium heat and pour in 2 tablespoons vegetable oil. When the oil is hot, add ½ teaspoon cumin seeds and 1 large peeled and finely chopped onion and fry until the onion begins to brown.

Add the drained potato to the frying pan, with 1 teaspoon peeled and grated ginger, ½ a clove of peeled and finely chopped garlic, and 1 teaspoon garam masala. Fry until the potato softens. Add a splash of water to stop the mixture sticking to the pan. When the potato is cooked, add 400g washed leaf spinach and cook for 1 minute until it wilts. Stir in 40g unsalted butter, season to taste with salt and freshly ground black pepper and serve immediately.

MANGO, TOMATO AND SPRING ONION SALSA Serves 8

This salsa brings freshness and colour to the table. It's also great for cooling a hot and spicy curry.

In a large bowl, mix together 1 large peeled and diced mango, 3 large peeled and diced tomatoes, 1 bunch of chopped spring onions, 1 peeled, deseeded and diced cucumber, a small bunch of freshly chopped coriander, and 4 tablespoons extra virgin olive oil. Squeeze over the juice of 1 lime, and season to taste with salt and freshly ground black pepper.

ELEGANT DESSERTS

WINTER FRUIT SALAD Serves 8

An array of citrus fruits will cut through any curry flavours that might linger and cleanse palates. This fruit salad is delicious with the sparkling jelly. Serve with a sweet Muscat wine.

Slice 2 oranges, 3 blood oranges or 2 pink grapefruit, and 2 starfruit into thin rounds. Arrange the slices on a platter, alternating for a pretty effect. Scatter over the seeds of 1 pomegranate and dot with the picked leaves from ½ a small bunch of mint. Refrigerate for at least 30 minutes to allow the juices and flavours to mingle. This will create its own citrussy dressing, but a drizzle of pomegranate molasses will also work well.

MERINGUE KISSES Serves 8

Glittering meringues in a large dish topped with fizzing sparklers give a celebratory feel to the table.

Allow 2 small meringues per person. These are easily available to buy ready-made, or alternatively make your own meringue (page 346) and pipe or spoon the mixture on to a parchment-lined baking sheet and bake for 25–30 minutes at 150°C/gas 2. When cool, dust with edible silver glitter, and serve with simple whipped cream or colourful ice cream balls.

SPARKLING GOLD-LEAF JELLIES Serves 8

This is an elegant and light finish to a New Year's Eve supper. The seeds of a pomegranate work well with pink Champagne and are particularly seasonal, but blueberries, raspberries and blackberries all look pretty. The addition of gold leaf gives this a festive twinkle. Serve in stemmed glasses with the winter fruit salad.

Divide 250g blueberries or pomegranate seeds evenly between 8 glasses with 2 sheets of edible gold leaf torn into small pieces and chill. Place 8-9 sheets of leaf gelatine into a bowl with enough cold water to barely cover them. Allow to soften for a few minutes. Remove the gelatine and squeeze out any excess water. Pour 100ml elderflower or pomegranate and elderflower cordial diluted with 200ml water into a heatproof bowl and place over a pan of boiling water. Add 4 tablespoons caster sugar and allow to dissolve. Remove the bowl from the heat and add the soft gelatine. Keep stirring until the gelatine is dissolved. Pour this mixture into a large jug with 600ml chilled Champagne, pink Champagne or Prosecco and mix well. Divide between the chilled glasses and return them to the fridge for at least 2 hours, to set.

TIP: *Keeping the fruit, sparkling wine and glasses chilled until you need them ensures fizz in the jelly.*

WELCOMING THE NEW YEAR

As the clock strikes midnight, link arms with friends and family and sing in the new year to 'Auld Lang Syne'. Pop the corks and toast the year ahead. These games are great ice-breakers for earlier on in the evening, but play them at any point or save them for New Year's Day. A session of karaoke might also add to the revelry!

TIP: *If any children are still up assemble them on the sofa and get them all to 'jump' into the new year. (If they can't stay up until midnight, you could get them to do this in their pyjamas earlier in the evening to your own countdown.)*

NOSTALGIA GAMES

Collect old school reports for all your guests and make photocopies of them. On these copies, obscure the identifying details of the pupil in question. Hand around the photocopies and have different guests read extracts aloud. Players should vote on who they think the report belongs to before the real recipient is revealed. For the second game, ask all your guests to bring a photograph of themselves as babies. Fix each photo to a pinboard and number each one. On pieces of paper, against the numbers, guests should write down who they think is who.

GUESS MY RESOLUTION

Everyone writes down three of their New Year's resolutions on separate scraps of paper. The scraps are all folded up and thrown into a hat. One at a time, the resolutions are removed from the hat and read aloud. Players listen to each one and write down who they think it belongs to. At the end, everyone reveals their resolutions and then tots up how many of their own guesses were right. This is a fun way to share your hopes for the coming year.

NEW YEAR AROUND THE WORLD
In China, many traditional foods associated with luck or good fortune are served on New Year's Eve, such as a whole chicken symbolising family togetherness, noodles representing long life and spring rolls, which are supposed to indicate wealth, as their shape is similar to gold bars.

There is an old folk tradition observed throughout Spain on New Year's Eve in which twelve grapes are eaten — one for each chime of the clock as it strikes midnight. This custom is thought to protect against witches and evil spirits and ensure twelve happy and prosperous months in the year ahead.

In Scotland and elsewhere in the UK, a widespread tradition called 'first footing' — where the first friend or relative to cross the threshold after midnight brings symbolic gifts of coal, shortbread and whisky — is said to bring good fortune to the household for the coming year.

*Should auld acquaintance be forgot,
and never brought to mind?
Should auld acquaintance be forgot,
and auld lang syne?*

*For auld lang syne, my dear,
for auld lang syne,
we'll tak a cup o' kindness yet,
for auld lang syne.*

ROBERT BURNS
RARE PRINT COLLECTION

Some hae meat and canna eat,
An' some wad eat that want it,
We hae meat an' we can eat,
An' sae the Lord be thankit.

'Selkirk Grace', attributed to
Robert Burns

BURNS NIGHT

A Burns Night chapter may seem like an unusual addition to this book, but I have come to treasure Scotland, a land cloaked in nostalgia and history, as one of my favourite places. My love of the country stems from my days at Edinburgh University and is thanks to the hospitality of Scottish friends who, in the spirit of their country's traditions, encouraged my enthusiasm for practices such as eating haggis, enjoying a Scottish reel or two and listening to nerve-tingling tunes on their bagpipes and fiddles. I read Scottish literature as part of my degree, and I grew to love Burns Night and its historical significance, as well as its warming, comforting components, from the rich colours of a clan tartan to a dram of amber whisky. There is also something about the Scottish countryside that feels wild and romantic: the moors and heather, lochs and burns, long windy walks and big open skies. Burns Night provides the opportunity to honour this epic and rugged landscape that has become like a second home to me.

Burns Night is the culmination of the Scottish winter festivals, which include St Andrew's Day (celebrated on 30 November) and Hogmanay (at New Year), and a great excuse to host a Scottish-themed evening. It celebrates the life and work of Robert Burns, widely regarded as Scotland's national poet. Born in humble circumstances yet highly skilful in his art, his work resonated with people at every level of society, and his desire to keep the Scottish language alive made him a symbol of his birthplace's national identity. The poet's friends first commemorated his contribution to Scottish culture soon after his death, and today Scots around the world mark the occasion on 25 January, mostly in the form of a supper.

My first experience of a Burns Night-inspired celebration was during my days at St Andrew's prep school in Pangbourne. For lunch, meatloaf replaced the traditional haggis but we did have neeps and tatties with it, and one of the older pupils would deliver the seemingly age-old 'Selkirk Grace', attributed to Robert Burns. But it was at Edinburgh that I developed a real enthusiasm for this occasion. A few of us would arrange a Burns Night supper on an evening close to that date – it was our antidote to the winter blues and an opportunity to eat haggis to ward off the cold. Burns Night might be an institution of Scottish life, but, Scottish or not, you don't need a reason to toast the country's favourite poet and plan a Highland gathering. The format of the celebration largely depends on what you want to make of it: a black-tie affair that includes all the pomp of the night with piping, toasts, speeches and dancing, or a simple supper (perhaps a Highland tea) at home with friends and family accompanied by a few poems or anecdotes taken from the famous Scottish bard's work.

BURNS NIGHT CRAFTS

A few homemade crafts will add personality to any Highland table. Make sure the palette of your materials is rich and warm, in keeping with the Scottish theme.

POMPOM THISTLES

Children will enjoy helping you make these. Stand single stems in a mismatch of small glass bottles and vases. Old blue, brown and clear drinks bottles that have had their labels dampened and peeled off are ideal.

I: For the pompoms, cut 2 identical discs from a piece of card, 5cm in diameter with a 2cm diameter hole in the centre. Align the discs and wind wool round them, through the hole, round the edge and back through the hole again, working continuously until they are completely covered and you can hardly wind any more through the centre. 2: Snip the wool along the outer edge of the discs. Pull the discs apart very slightly. 3: Cut two 20cm lengths of leftover wool. Wind them between the discs and knot tightly to secure the wool. Remove the discs. 4: Take a twig and cover the top with PVA glue, then push it into the pompom. Stick some dried leaves to the twig at the base of the pompom.

SCENTED TARTAN BAGS

These pretty fabric bags will add an instant touch of tartan to individual place settings. Fill them with your favourite pot-pourri or a few Scottish-inspired items, such as fudge, shortbread or a miniature bottle of whisky, for going-home gifts.

I: Cut a piece of tartan fabric into a 22cm high x 16cm wide rectangle. 2: Fold over 1cm of fabric (on one of the longer sides) and sew a hem. Align the bottom edge of a 2.5cm strip of lace with the stitching of the hem and sew onto the outside of the fabric. 3: Fold the fabric in half with the lace side facing inwards, and, leaving the lace top open, sew the remaining two sides together. 4: Turn right-side out and half fill with dried lavender or cedar balls (you can buy these in hardware and general merchandise stores). Tie a ribbon around the top.

RUSTIC NAME PLACES

These are quick and easy to make and the earthy materials add a country feel to the table. You can use different coloured cards and replace the raffia string with thin tartan ribbon for variety.

I: Cut some card into a 7cm x 8cm rectangle. Fold in half lengthways. Punch a hole through the top two corners just underneath the fold. 2: Tie a twig to the top of the card using raffia, threading it through the holes, and making knots to secure it. 3: Write your guest's name on the front of the card.

A HIGHLAND TEA

For a rustic Scottish tea, a tartan blanket or rug laid over a table will add snugness and be fitting for a hearty spread for all ages: toast with marmalade, Scottish tablet (rather like fudge but with a grainier, more brittle texture), millionaire's shortbread and drop scones (page 225) dripping with butter and golden syrup. Wash these down with a hot brew or, if it's really wet and windy outside, a hot toddy with heather honey will hit the spot (page 194). Chunky, earthy china is perfect for this occasion

MILLIONAIRE'S SHORTBREAD Makes 24

This teatime morsel is a decadent three-layered treat that provides a perfect pick-me-up. For bite-size versions (great to serve as a sweet canapé), this recipe will make about 40.

Preheat the oven to 170°C/ gas 3. Lightly grease a 23cm x 32cm oblong Swiss roll tin.

For the shortbread base, place 250g plain flour, 100g caster sugar and 225g butter into a food processor and whizz together to a smooth dough. Using your fingers, press the mixture into the tin and prick all over with a fork. Chill for 15 minutes before baking in the oven for 25–30 minutes until golden and firm. Set aside to cool.

To make the topping, place 200g unsalted butter, 200g caster sugar, 3 tablespoons golden syrup and a 397g tin of condensed milk into a saucepan and stir over a low heat until the butter melts. Turn the heat up to medium, bring to the boil and then gently bubble the mixture for 5–8 minutes, stirring constantly to prevent catching, until thick and golden brown. Pour over the cold shortbread in an even layer and leave to cool. Melt 200g dark chocolate in a bowl over a pan of simmering water. Pour the chocolate over the cooled toffee and place in the fridge to set. Remove from the tin and carefully cut into squares. Store in an airtight jar for up to a week.

TIP: *To make shortbread hearts, use the above recipe for the shortbread base and roll out the dough thinly before cutting into hearts and baking for 20-25 minutes at 170°C/ gas 3. This makes about 24 biscuits.*

A SCOTTISH TABLE

For a Burns Night supper, choose a warm and romantic place for your table: a fireside spot is welcoming and the amber glow will complement the earthy components of the feast. If you're having a more informal do in your kitchen, you'll still need plenty of flickering candlelight on this cold January night to make everyone feel as if they're all tucked up inside a croft in the depths of the Scottish hills. A plaid scarf or strips of tartan fabric work well as table runners. If you're after something more subtle, use a tartan ribbon tied around a white napkin, a set of tartan napkins or a tartan lavender bag (page 178) at each place. This will set the colour scheme for the flowers and other table accessories. Thistles are emblematic of Scotland and ideal for a centrepiece, mixed with purple and white anemones (they also come in red and blue) and green foliage. Arranged in a small vase, they will add a lovely feminine touch to this rather masculine affair. Use whisky-coloured tumblers for water, burgundy candles and old bone-handled knives in keeping with the Highland theme.

A CLASSIC BURNS NIGHT

The traditional supper celebration consists of several courses: soup; then haggis; perhaps a steak pie (page 66), which is great if you are serving the haggis as a starter or canapé; followed by a dessert or cheese. You can put your own contemporary twists on the food or just choose a menu that celebrates Scottish produce, as long as haggis features at some stage. The likelihood is that you'll want your Burns Night supper to be an intimate, cosy gathering after the more sociable Christmas celebrations of the previous month, so the recipes each serve four.

BURNS NIGHT MENU

Starter
Cullen Skink

Main course
Haggis and clapshot

Dessert
Cranachan

BURNS NIGHT RUNNING ORDER

THE 'SELKIRK GRACE' This short but important prayer is read to usher in the meal.

PIPING IN THE HAGGIS The haggis is ceremonially carried to the table by the cook, accompanied by a lone bagpiper. One guest will be responsible for reading the Robert Burns poem 'Address to a Haggis'.

TOAST TO THE HAGGIS During the reading the haggis will be cut, traditionally by making a St Andrew's cross-shaped incision at its centre. At the end of the recital, toasts are made to the haggis.

TOAST TO THE LASSIES Toasts are also made to the 'lassies' to thank them for preparing the food (Burns was renowned to be fond of women). This is followed by a cheeky response from one of the lassies.

THE IMMORTAL MEMORY Often one of the central features of the evening, this is a light-hearted account of the life and works of Robert Burns (like a best man's speech).

SONGS AND DANCING Burns songs and poems, and some traditional Scottish reeling music should come after the toasts.

'AULD LANG SYNE' The evening normally concludes with a rousing rendition of this song, which was written by Burns, during which all the guests link arms and sing together.

CULLEN SKINK

Usually cock-a-leekie (chicken and leek) soup is served on Burns Night, but Cullen Skink is a delicious alternative, as a starter or light main course. Originally from the fishing village of Cullen in northeast Scotland ('skink' is the Scots word for soup), it has a delicate flavour, and the smoked haddock provides a distinctive warming scent that is just perfect on a wintry night.

SERVES 4

450g undyed smoked haddock, skin on, pinned and boned

600ml milk

20g butter

1 medium onion, peeled and chopped

1 medium leek, chopped, green parts removed

400g potatoes, peeled and diced

2 bay leaves

100g tinned sweetcorn

salt and freshly ground black pepper

2 tablespoons chopped chives or parsley

Cover the smoked haddock with the milk and butter in a saucepan, skin side down. Bring to the boil and simmer for 4–5 minutes, until cooked.

With a slotted spoon, remove the haddock from the pan and discard the skin and any bones you find. Strain the cooking liquid, and return to the pan. Break up the fish into flakes, then set aside. Add the onion, leek, potato and bay leaves to the reserved cooking liquid and simmer for 20–25 minutes.

When the potatoes are tender, remove the bay leaves and add the fish and sweetcorn to the pan. Simmer over a low heat for 2–3 minutes until the fish is warmed through, then taste and season with salt and pepper. Serve immediately, garnished with chopped chives, or parsley for a fresher taste.

 A delicate Manzanilla sherry complements this salty dish.

TIPS: *Finnan haddock is traditionally used in this soup which has a light smoky taste. Smoked haddock is a great substitute, and is more readily available. • Other hearty Scottish soups you could serve include Scotch broth, (beef, barley and vegetables) or tattie (potato) soup. • You can use quartered new potatoes, and mash them into the broth to thicken the soup. • If using parsley leaves to garnish, use the stalks in the poaching milk first to freshen the taste of the dish.*

THE HAGGIS

Fair fa' your honest, sonsie face,
Great chieftain o' the pudding-race!
Aboon them a'ye tak your place,
Painch, tripe, or thairm:
Weel are ye wordy o'a grace
As lang's my arm.

'Address to a Haggis', Robert Burns

This Scottish delicacy is the focal point of a Burns Night supper, thanks to the poet's 1786 poem 'Address to a Haggis'. It consists of a mixture of the minced heart, lungs and liver of a sheep or calf mixed with suet, onions, oatmeal and seasonings, and is traditionally encased in a sheep's stomach, but it is now more usually produced using a synthetic skin, making it more appealing. The Macsween variety is among the best and you can buy different sizes depending on how many you are feeding. Its nutty, wholesome taste is really unique, and steeping it in whisky or a rich whisky-based cream gives it that extra hearty flavour.

If haggis isn't your thing, you can find veggie alternatives or make your own vegetarian haggis using pulses, nuts and oatmeal. The traditional accompaniments to haggis are neeps and tatties. Neeps (turnips) are what are known in England as swede, and tatties are potatoes. Alternatively, serve haggis in canapé form for a Scottish drinks party.

OTHER WAYS WITH HAGGIS

- *Haggis doesn't have to be only for Burns Night; enjoy it all year round by storing it in the freezer.*

- *To save time, cook haggis by removing its casing, chopping roughly and microwaving for 6 minutes, stirring occasionally until piping hot.*

- *Fry a slice of haggis as you would black pudding, and serve it for breakfast with a poached egg on top.*

- *One of my great friends has a signature dish of chicken breast stuffed with haggis and wrapped in bacon. It keeps the chicken moist and bulks it out.*

- *Sprinkle haggis into the minced meat in a shepherd's pie or lasagne for a nutty taste.*

- *Mix haggis into sausagemeat to make haggis sausage rolls (page 360), or add haggis instead of mushrooms to the pâté in a beef Wellington (page 213).*

You could start your evening off with bite-size samples (allow 3 per person). I had some similar canapés recently at a friend's wedding and everyone, Scottish or not, loved them.

HAGGIS FILO PARCELS Makes 12

Cook 250g haggis and make 200ml whisky sauce (page 188). Cut 6 sheets of filo pastry into quarters. Melt 50g unsalted butter. Take one quarter of pastry and brush with melted butter; place another quarter on top and brush again with butter. Mix the cooked haggis with 100ml whisky sauce. Scoop a little of the haggis mixture into the centre of the pastry, brush the edges with melted butter and wrap the pastry up so that it gathers at the top, then twist gently to close. Transfer the prepared parcels to a baking sheet lined with baking parchment and cook in a preheated oven at 180°C/gas 4 for 10–12 minutes, or until golden brown and crisp. Serve with the remaining whisky sauce alongside.

HAGGIS CROUSTADES Makes 12

Cook 250g haggis and make 100ml of whisky sauce (page 188). Roll out 6 crustless slices of white bread as thinly as possible. Using a 6cm round cutter, cut the bread into 12 circles. Brush a mini muffin tin with olive oil then press the bread circles into the tin and brush each with a little olive oil. Season with salt and pepper, and bake in the oven for 8–10 minutes or until golden and crisp. Remove the baked croustades from the tin and allow to cool, then spoon a teaspoon of the cooked haggis mixture inside and garnish each with a little whisky sauce, red-onion marmalade (page 404) and chives to serve.

HAGGIS AND CLAPSHOT

SERVES 4

1kg good-quality haggis

For the clapshot

300g swede (neeps), peeled and quartered

450g potatoes (tatties), peeled and quartered

100g unsalted butter

salt and freshly ground black pepper

60ml double cream

WHISKY SAUCE

Gently heat 3 tablespoons whisky in a small pan until the alcohol evaporates. Add 400ml double cream and stir to combine. Add 2 teaspoons wholegrain mustard (optional), and then season to taste. Reduce over a medium heat until the sauce has thickened. This makes enough for 4 with the haggis recipe on this page. Halve the amounts to make enough for the haggis filo parcel canapés (page 187) and quarter them to give 100ml for the haggis croustades (page 187).

To cook the haggis, bring a large pan of water to the boil, add the haggis, then reduce the heat and allow it to simmer for 50 minutes, topping up with water if it runs low. Always check the packet instructions or with your butcher, as cooking times may vary (you can also microwave it, see page 186).

Meanwhile, bring two saucepans of salted water to the boil. Put the neeps (swede) in one pan and the tatties (potatoes) in the other. Reduce the heat and cook both for 20–25 minutes. When the neeps and tatties are tender, drain the water. Return the neeps to one pan, add half of the butter and mash until chunky. Season to taste and keep warm. In the other pan, mash the tatties with the cream and remaining butter until smooth. Season to taste and keep warm.

When the haggis is cooked, make the clapshot by mixing together the neeps and tatties. Spoon the clapshot into four chef's rings on your warmed serving plates until three-quarters full, and press down. Cut open the cooked haggis, and fill each chef's ring to the brim. Remove the rings and drizzle whisky sauce (see box) around each plate. Serve with a shot of whisky on the side. Alternatively, simply spoon a portion of haggis on each warmed serving plate, put the neeps and tatties beside the haggis, pour over a little whisky sauce, and serve.

Hearty, southern French reds such as Côtes du Rhône.

TIP: *For an indulgent twist, cover the clapshot with grated cheese and bake in the oven for what is known as 'Orkney clapshot'.*

CRANACHAN

A classic Scottish dessert, cranachan was traditionally served as several separate bowls containing each ingredient, so that each person could assemble their dessert according to their own taste. Served in layers in stemmed glasses, this is a visual treat.

SERVES 4

50g medium porridge oats

300ml double cream

2 tablespoons Scottish whisky

3 tablespoons Scottish heather honey

250g raspberries

Heat a frying pan over a medium heat and lightly toast the oats for a few minutes, shaking the pan frequently, until they have turned golden brown. Remove the oats from the pan and set aside until completely cool.

In a bowl, lightly whip the double cream with the whisky and 2 tablespoons honey until it forms soft peaks and just holds its shape.

When you are ready to serve, assemble the cranachan. Don't make this too far in advance or the oats will lose their crunch. Divide half the raspberries between 4 small serving glasses. Spoon over half the cream and then scatter with the oats, reserving a few for the topping. Make another layer of raspberries and cream, and then sprinkle the remainder of the toasted oats on top and drizzle over the last tablespoon of honey.

TIP: *'Tipsy laird' is a Scottish trifle often served on Burns Night. To make this, follow the recipe on page 258, using trifle sponges for the base and replacing the sherry with 6 tablespoons whisky.*

WHISKY COCKTAILS

With encouragement from whisky-loving friends, I have slowly come round to the taste of whisky, but for those less inclined to drink it straight, a few whisky-based cocktails wouldn't go amiss. When making these, go for a blended whisky and save special single malts for unadulterated sipping, with just a splash or two of water, if anything. Rocking glasses with balloon bases are fun and different; as they roll around on a hard surface they will release the bouquet of the whisky.

ATHOLL BROSE
Fills 1 x 75cl bottle

Somewhere between a drink and a dessert, especially when cream is added on festive occasions. Put 70g fine oatmeal and 300ml water into a bowl and stir until they form a thick paste. Allow the mixture to stand for 20 minutes, then strain to separate the liquid from the oatmeal. Discard the oatmeal. Mix the liquid with 150g clear Scottish heather honey, and stir until well blended. Pour this into a bottle, top up with Scotch whisky (approximately 400ml) and seal the bottle. Shake vigorously, then leave to stand. This can be stored for up to a week. Shake again before serving, adding a dash of single cream to the glasses if you like.

TIP: *For those with a sweeter tooth substitute Drambuie whisky liqueur for the whisky.*

FLYING SCOTSMAN Serves 1 (make to order)

A fine, delicate cocktail served in a martini glass. Pour 60ml whisky, 30ml sweet vermouth, 10ml sugar syrup (page 104) and a couple of dashes of Angostura Bitters into a cocktail shaker with cubed ice and squeeze in the juice of ¼ of a lemon. Shake well, then strain into a chilled glass. Garnish with a lemon twist (page 104). Great for after dinner, this drink was inspired by the famous *Flying Scotsman* train, which carried passengers between Edinburgh and London.

ROB ROY Serves 1 (make to order)

This is drier than the Flying Scotsman. Stir 70ml whisky, 30ml sweet vermouth and two dashes Angostura Bitters in a cocktail shaker filled with ice cubes. Shake well and strain into a chilled martini glass and garnish with a maraschino cherry in the bottom of the glass.

WHISKEY SOUR Serves 1 (make to order)

Although this is an American cocktail made with Bourbon (hence the 'e' in whiskey), and not typical for Burns Night, I have a soft spot for this one. Shake 50ml Bourbon whiskey, 50ml lemon juice, 10ml sugar syrup (page 104), a dash of Angostura Bitters and 1 egg white in a cocktail shaker filled with ice cubes. It is essential to shake well to ensure a frothy top. Serve in short glasses filled with ice cubes and garnish with lemon peel and a glacé cherry.

AFTER SUPPER

Burns Night is traditionally associated with Scottish dancing and bagpipes, but it's also known for toasts, reciting poetry and making speeches. The night is dedicated to Robert Burns after all, so a recital of his greatest poems is fitting. For the more energetic, try some Scottish reeling and, of course, a rendition of his most famous song, 'Auld Lang Syne' (see page 175 if you need a prompt). For the less lively, a quiet game of cards with a whisky will round the evening off nicely.

POETRY RECITALS

Many of Burns' poems have a lovely story behind them. 'Tam o' Shanter' tells the tale of a man who lingered too long at a public house, but 'Scotch Drink' is also ideal for an after-supper recital if you've all been imbibing the water of life! Other great poems to read aloud include 'A Red, Red Rose' or 'To a Mouse', which Burns allegedly wrote after disturbing a mouse's nest in a field he was ploughing and which inspired the title of Steinbeck's famous novel *Of Mice and Men* ('the best laid schemes o' mice an' men/gang aft agley').

Let other poets raise a fracas
'Bout vines, an' wines, an' drucken Bacchus,
An' crabbit names an' stories wrack us,
An' grate our lug:
I sing the juice Scotch bear can mak us,
In glass or jug.

O thou, my Muse! guid auld Scotch drink!
Whether thro' wimplin worms thou jink,
Or, richly brown, ream owre the brink,
In glorious faem,
Inspire me, till I lisp an' wink,
To sing thy name!

'Scotch Drink', Robert Burns

WHISKY: THE WATER OF LIFE

A whisky tasting can add another dimension to your Burns Night supper and is a great way to begin or end the evening. Scotch malt whiskies are classified by five regions: Highland, Speyside, Campbeltown, Lowland and Islay. They are so different and varied, even a sniff can be powerfully evocative. Alternatively, a hot toddy or Whisky Mac is the perfect nightcap.

For 1 hot toddy: place 50ml whisky, 1½ tablespoons runny honey and 125ml boiled water from a kettle into a saucepan. Add a slice of lemon, 1 cinnamon stick and 1 clove, and heat gently until the drink is warmed through, then remove the spices and serve immediately.

For 1 Whisky Mac: mix equal quantities of Scotch whisky and ginger wine. Serve hot or cold.

THE PARTY CUPBOARD

Store cupboards, drawers or boxes should be packed full of useful odds and ends so you always have the basics to hand for spontaneous celebrations. You can find most of what you need at large supermarkets or online from party stores; buy discounted items just after a seasonal event such as Hallowe'en, Easter or Christmas and save the items for the following year. Get in the habit of having a clear-out once in a while so they don't fill up with junk. If you keep things organised, it's amazing how many items can be stored using the minimum amount of space.

THE PRESENT DRAWER

Create a go-to place for all your wrapping essentials and last-minute gifts. Keep an eye out throughout the year for things to add to it — you might spot the ideal present for someone, which you can save until the appropriate time. Support small gift shops in towns you might be visiting and use them to source homemade produce, such as marmalades, olive oils, biscuits and regional specialities, as well as bits and pieces for the home.

TIP: *Tie a length of wide, colourful ribbon through rolls of different kinds of sticky packaging tapes so you never lose them. All you have to do is remember to put the scissors and tape right back where you found them, for the next person . . .*

PRESENT DRAWER CHECKLIST

- **Wrapping paper:** *old and new, scraps of fabric, drawer liners and assorted coloured tissue. Keep in gift-wrap storage bags, sleeves and boxes.*

- **Scissors:** *sharp-bladed scissors to cut wrapping paper in one sweeping movement.*

- **Padded envelopes and bubble wrap:** *for sending and protecting fragile gifts.*

- **Sticky tape:** *use transparent tape and a desktop (or wrist) tape dispenser, which is ideal to wrap lots of presents at a time. Double-sided sticky tape is useful for tape-free presentation and patterned printed tape to jazz up plain paper.*

- **Ribbons:** *different widths and materials, e.g. wide satin, raffia and organza. Curling ribbon and string are inexpensive.*

- **Gift boxes and bags:** *a selection of sizes, including some for bottles, are useful for odd shapes that are tricky to wrap.*

- **Gift cards and envelopes:** *have a selection of birthday cards, as well as blank cards that can be used for any occasion.*

- **Emergency gifts:** *scented candles and bath stuff; homemade jams and chutneys (pages 403-4) are lovely presents for supper parties.*

- **Gift tags:** *have a variety of themed tags, foil as well as luggage-type brown-paper ones.*

WRAPPING IT UP

A well-wrapped gift helps express how much thought you've put into it. Don't forget to remove the price tag from the gift and if the packaging isn't attractive, put it in a box with loosely scrunched-up tissue paper or shredded tissue and a sprinkling of confetti. To achieve a perfect bow on the top, ideally the present should be a box shape or have hard edges. Gift bags are useful to disguise difficult or messy wrapping.

1 : Place the present on the paper to gauge how much you will need, then cut to length.
2 : Keep the seams and folds of the paper underneath the present, and stick down neatly with tape, so the top is seamless. Fold the end flaps into a 'V' shape and stick down neatly with tape.
3 : Wrap a long piece of ribbon around the top of the present lengthwise, then turn the present over and wrap the ribbon around it widthwise to form a cross. 4 : Turn it back over again so the seamless side is facing up and tie the ribbon in a neat bow (trim the ends, if necessary; for silk or luxury ribbons make a neat 'V' and for curling ribbon pull between your thumb and scissor blade to get curls). If you don't have enough ribbon for this, simply tie the ribbon widthwise.
5 : Attach your gift tag to the bow with your ribbon.

TIP : *Other decorative wrapping ideas include coloured pompoms, feathers, charms, large buttons, bells, adhesive gift bows, fake flowers or any other items you can think of that are appropriate to the occasion or season.*

THRIFTY WRAPPING IDEAS

Sometimes you might want to get more creative with your wrapping (particularly if you've run out of gift wrap!).

- *For a personal touch, use the recipient's favourite magazine, old maps, calendar pictures, comics or newspaper as wrapping paper. For example, the pink pages of the Financial Times, tied with black ribbon, will look great.*

- *Brown parcel paper (craft paper) is cheap and chic in a minimalist way when coupled with coloured or patterned ribbon, or rickrack. You can also decorate it by potato printing, using an ink block and stamps or stickers. If you're feeling thrifty, recycle old wrapping paper (as long as it was opened carefully the first time), long pieces of ribbon, gift bags and boxes from past Christmases and birthdays, and save old jewellery boxes.*

- *Wrapping a present in a scrap of fabric using Japanese-style origami folds and tying with ribbon is both eco-friendly and pretty. Use pinking shears to cut the required size of material. Hold the fabric in place using double-sided tape and tie loose ends with ribbon. If you have a sewing machine, you can make simple drawstring bags for presents (page 179) from fabric ends and cheap material, such as ticking.*

- *Try cutting out images, coloured letters, numbers and illustrations from magazines and saving them in an envelope to make gift tags with, or to stick on to plain card. Buying a tag cutter will give a professional finish.*

PARTY CUPBOARD ESSENTIALS

These supplies are good to have on hand for celebrations, as well as more general equipment for entertaining (page 102), be it an impromptu birthday party, farewell, reunion or baby shower.

- **Bunting and banners**: homemade bunting (page 266) is charming; collect banners for all occasions: 'Happy Birthday', 'Welcome home' etc.

- **Cake accessories**: candles, indoor sparklers, cupcake cases, flags, cake decorations, doilies, fold-away cake stand, cake boxes and boards.

- **Balloons and balloon weights**: in different colours and materials (clear, foil, numbers and themed). For helium balloons, check how many balloons your canister will fill when purchasing it.

- **Curling ribbon and confetti**: ribbon is good value and useful for balloons. Themed confetti and clear gems can be sprinkled along tables.

- **Tablecloths, runners, napkins and placemats**: in both paper and linen (napkins and placemats on a roll are very useful). Stock up on blank placecards and holders with clips to fix them in.

- **Bumper packs of tea lights and candles**: battery-operated ones are good for outdoor parties, and eco-friendly sky lanterns are also fun.

- **Games and accessories**: board games, dice (Perudo), playing cards and table trivia.

- **Table favours**: saucer crackers, miniature bottles of bubbles, party poppers and streamers.

THE CRAFT TOOLBOX

Craft materials needn't be expensive. Markets are useful for cheap fabrics and car-boot sales can be treasure troves. For reliability, craft stores or art shops have the best range, and sell useful all-in-one kits.

- **Pens and pencils**: silver and gold, calligraphy and glass pens, fabric markers, crayons and coloured pencils.

- **Glue**: glue stick works quickly on most papers and card; PVA is better for tissue paper and large-scale projects.

- **Paints and paintbrushes**: acrylics, poster paints (mix with PVA and water for découpage), and at least three good-quality paintbrushes of various sizes.

- **Coloured paper, card and glitter**: for homemade cards and paper hats.

- **Sewing kit, wool, buttons and safety pins.**

- **Pinking shears and craft knife**: pinking shears will save you having to hem fabrics.

- **Hammer and nails, drawing pins, a tape measure, string, fishing and gardening wire**: for making and hanging decorations.

TIPS : *Pick up wooden stirring sticks from coffee shops and keep jam jars or saucers for mixing paints. • A glue gun can be a good investment (refills are expensive, so buy in bulk online) and a laminator can also be useful for signs and homemade placemats. • Store craft materials in clear containers to locate them at a glance and group similar items together.*

TIP: *For a fancy-dress party, get every guest to bring a dressing-up outfit and accessories in a black bin bag. Pile them all together, ask each guest to pick a bag before supper and put on the outfit they find inside. Alternatively, host a party where everyone has to come wearing some sort of hat.*

THE DRESSING-UP BOX

Dressing up is all about small details — perhaps just a simple accessory you wear or carry — but humour and plenty of imagination are essential. You can find lots of inspiration and amazing all-in-one outfits online and in fancy-dress shops but these can be expensive. Old clothes in black, white or block colours can be a base for pretty much any costume (add variety with stripes, spots and animal prints). I have a substantial collection of dressing-up items under my bed, which always comes in useful along the way. Save old clothes you no longer wear that have something authentic about them, such as uniforms or retro fashion items, and search charity shops for any bargains. Here are some ideas for a basic dressing-up box suited to a variety of occasions.

- **Old pillowcases, fabric and sheets:** *cut up to form base layers. Use a stretchy belt and safety pins to give them structure.*

- **Coloured tights, fishnets, leggings, old pyjama bottoms and tartan kilts:** *these are all useful for a variety of costumes.*

- **Wire coat hangers:** *for wings, halos and antennae (if you're really creative!).*

- **Accessories:** *sunglasses, long gloves, scarves, faux fur, waistcoats, braces, microphone, feather boa, grass skirts and lei, legwarmers, fake flowers, cape, bandanas, bow ties, fairy wings.*

- **Sparkle:** *tinsel, hair accessories, body glitter, glow-bands and stick- or clip-on jewellery.*

- **Disguises:** *masks, wigs, face paints and stencils, fake tattoos, eye-patches, moustaches and beards, animal ears, dry shampoo (for grey hair), coloured hair spray and styling gel.*

- **Cotton wool or fabric wadding:** *for snow, white beards or hair, sheep's wool.*

- **Hats:** *bowler, beret, straw boater and panama, or pirate, cowboy and other themed hats.*

SPRING

VALENTINE'S DAY
SPECIAL BREAKFASTS
EASTER
AFTERNOON TEA

Freshness cuts through the gloom. March winds blow and unpredictable April showers bring renewal and growth. Bulbs break hard ground and drifts of snowdrops with pearly heads thrust up through heavy clods of earth. Buds appear on trees, birds sing joyfully and young lambs stay close to their mothers. Cherry blossom hangs in candy-floss clouds and swathes of spring blooms scatter like colourful sweets.

Saint Valentine, who is so high aloft,
The little birds sing thus for your delight:
The winter weather you have put to flight,
And driven off the season of black night.

'The Parliament of Birds', Geoffrey Chaucer

VALENTINE'S DAY

The custom of choosing a valentine first came into existence in Europe in the fourteenth century and was inspired by the belief that birds started mating on this day, described most famously by Geoffrey Chaucer in his poem 'The Parliament of Birds'. It is referred to in parts of Sussex as the 'Birds' Wedding Day'. The romantic festival of Valentine's Day continued to grow in popularity in Victorian times. Even now, in the run-up to 14 February, every high-street window is awash with red and pink – a sea of cards, flowers, hearts and balloons, bringing colour to this cold, dark month. However, Saint Valentine is a figure lost in the mists of time and very little is known about his life, let alone why he lends his name to this day associated with romance.

Valentine's Day should be a chance to prioritise time with your loved ones without everyday distractions. Treat your family to dainty heart-shaped foods: use a mould to fry an egg, cut shapes out of your toast for breakfast in bed, or make heart-shaped biscuits (page 181). Traditionally, the custom on Valentine's Day was to exchange love notes called 'Valentines' which, by the mid-eighteenth century, were mostly in the form of handmade cards decorated with expensive materials such as lace and satin. This is still the time of year when postbags are crammed with exciting crimson envelopes, and lovingly crafted cards (page 204) are better than any shop-bought gift. Similarly, flowers are a traditional Valentine's token, and red roses are the classic symbol of romance, be it a dozen hand-tied in a beautiful bouquet or simply a single stem. However, if you're willing to experiment, there are lots of lovely spring flowers and bulbs that make sweet and thoughtful gifts and which convey a variety of messages (page 284).

As evening falls, this is a time for grown-ups to slow down and enjoy time together, whiling away a wintry night with special food and conversation. A supper for two at home is a cosy way to celebrate and gives scope for individuality and romance on a day that is no longer synonymous with spontaneity. It can also be used any other time of the year to mark something in your lives together, to convey a heartfelt message, to say thank you – or to say sorry. If it's just you two, you won't want to spend the whole evening in the kitchen slaving away – this is the time to prepare easy foods ahead of time, while keeping the ingredients luxurious and special. It might be things that you both love, but don't get to eat that often. After all, the way to a lover's heart is through the stomach, so they say . . .

MADE WITH LOVE...

Candles, hearts and lovebirds are all traditionally associated with romance. These are lovely, simple crafts to make with children in the run-up to Valentine's Day.

HEART BUTTON CARDS

If you run out of buttons, collect other bits and pieces to decorate your cards: stickers, sequins, doilies, glitter, flowers or feathers. Find loving sentiments in poems and story books to put inside and finish with a ribbon bow.

1 : Make a heart template. Place it on a piece of folded card and draw round it in pencil. 2 : Using a needle and thread, stitch from the back of the card to the front, securing the thread with a small piece of tape. 3 : Sew the buttons to the card around the outline using running stitch, with the buttons slightly overlapping. Fasten the end of your thread, as before. 4 : Using a glue stick, cover the thread inside the card with a plain piece of paper, cut to size.

LAVENDER HEARTS

Pretty fabric hearts nestled under pillows or hung on doorknobs outside bedrooms are charming.

1 : With fabric (floral or romantic designs, perhaps an old tablecloth) face-down, draw 2 heart shapes, using a template, and cut them out using pinking shears. 2 : Place front and back together (right sides out) and sew three-quarters of the way around. (If you don't have pinking shears, sew with right sides together and then turn right-side out.) 3 : Add 8 teaspoons dried lavender and continue sewing until completely sealed. Sew on a ribbon bow.

LACE-PAPER LANTERN JARS

Place these tea-light holders on side tables and in bedrooms for a pretty flickering light, or use as vases for delicate flowers.

1 : Take a selection of different-sized glass jars and a packet of paper doilies. 2 : Cut out the prettiest part of the doily, wrap it around the jar and stick down with PVA glue. 3 : Tie a ribbon around the neck of the jar and put a tea light inside.

MONKEY-NUT BIRD TREATS

According to folklore, it was thought that the first bird an unmarried woman saw on this day would provide an insight as to her future husband's character. Hang these outside for the birds to nibble on.

1 : Twist a length of thick gardening wire into a heart shape, with a few centimetres left at each end. 2 : Pierce through the middle of each nut with a skewer or thick needle. 3 : Thread the nuts on to the wire, reshape the heart and hook the ends together at the top. 4 : Tie with a string loop and add a raffia bow.

TABLE FOR TWO

Like many of the celebrations in this book, a Valentine's supper needn't be on the day itself; in fact, you could have your own romantic candlelit supper on any date throughout the year. To me, a candlelit supper at home beats jostling for elbow room in a couple-crammed restaurant over a 'romantic set menu' hands down. The main dishes serve two but can easily be doubled or trebled for dinner with friends. Prepare as much of the menu as you can in advance, so you can enjoy the evening without fussing too much in the kitchen.

If you often eat dinner at home, set the table somewhere you don't normally dine. A small table for two can be laid pretty much anywhere around your house. Fold away the extensions on your table, and take away extra chairs or use a smaller side table covered with a white cloth and have plenty of illumination in the form of tea lights, scented candles and firelight. Vary the colour of the candles from rose pink to white and red, standing them in modern glass and antique-style holders. Finish with a delicate bunch of seasonal scented flowers. As well as sweet-smelling roses, other flowers renowned for their scent are freesias and stocks, paperwhite (narcissus) and hyacinth bulbs (plant with moss and twigs for a pretty centrepiece).

OYSTERS

I always associate having oysters with special occasions, so what better time to have them than on Valentine's Day? Opening them can be quite a feat, so they are best served when there's only a couple of you to enjoy them. I like shucking them myself, but it helps if you have a good oyster knife to do this. To protect your hands and stop the knife slipping off the shell, use a mesh glove or a tea towel.

SERVES 2

6 live oysters

50ml red wine or sherry vinegar

1 shallot, finely chopped

To serve

lemon wedges

Tabasco sauce

Irish soda bread and salted butter

To shuck the oysters, put each shell on a board with a thick cloth underneath it. Push a sharp, thin knife into the hinge at the narrowest point of the shell, wiggle the knife from side to side until the hinge breaks, and discard the top shell.

Run the knife around the oyster itself, and remove the ligament that joins the meat to the shell. Remove any grit or shell. Take care to retain the wonderful juice, known as liquor, inside the shell.

Put each opened oyster on a platter on a bed of ice (make crushed ice by bashing freezer bags filled with cubed ice with a rolling pin), cover with a damp cloth and refrigerate until needed. It's best to eat these as fresh as possible, so don't prepare too far in advance.

To serve, mix together the vinegar and shallot and serve in a small bowl alongside the oysters, with lemon wedges, Tabasco sauce, some Irish soda bread and salty butter.

Light white wines like Muscadet or a richer Chablis.

TIPS: *Colchester oysters are the most common variety, with deep, craggy shells. Native oysters have shallow shells and are more delicate and expensive.* • *Make sure the shells are firmly shut or that they shut immediately when tapped.* • *Save the oyster shells, wash them thoroughly and use them as salt and pepper dishes, place-name settings or as serving dishes for canapés.*

GRAVADLAX WITH DILL MUSTARD SAUCE

A good recipe to prepare ahead because it needs to cure for 1–2 days, this is delicious with cucumber pickle and dill mustard sauce, but set out some other garnishes to sprinkle over, such as finely chopped shallots and capers. Serve with Irish soda bread or shop-bought blinis warmed in the oven.

WHOLE CURED FISH SERVES 10–12

1 x 700g organic farmed salmon fillet, skin off and pin-boned

80g coarse sea salt

65g caster sugar

1 large handful of finely chopped fresh chives, coriander and dill

peel of 1 lemon and 1 orange

1 tablespoon crushed coriander seeds

1 tablespoon crushed mixed peppercorns

2 tablespoons gin

For the dill mustard sauce

2 tablespoons Dijon mustard

2 egg yolks

2 teaspoons sugar

a pinch of salt

1 tablespoon white wine vinegar

100ml sunflower oil

1 small bunch of fresh dill, finely chopped

For the cucumber pickle

½ a cucumber, deseeded

1 tablespoon caster sugar

a splash of rice wine vinegar

sea salt and freshly ground black pepper

To cure the fish, put the salt, sugar, chives, coriander and dill, lemon peel, orange peel, coriander seeds, peppercorns and gin in a food processor and pulse to combine. Spread the mixture over the salmon, using most on the top, but covering the sides and the underneath too. Tightly wrap in clingfilm, place on a plate and apply a weight to the top of the fish. Refrigerate for 1–2 days.

To make the sauce, mix together the mustard, egg yolks, sugar, salt and vinegar. Slowly whisk in the oil until the sauce is smooth, then stir in the dill.

To make the cucumber pickle, peel and thinly slice the cucumber into strips, using a speed-peeler or mandoline. Place the sugar and vinegar in a saucepan and heat until the sugar has dissolved. Remove from the heat. When cold, add the cucumber, season with salt and pepper and leave to marinade for at least 1 hour.

When you are ready to plate up, brush off most of the curing mixture from the fish and pat it dry. With a long, sharp knife, carefully carve thin diagonal slivers off the salmon. Serve the gravadlax with slices of soda bread, capers and diced shallots, with a little cucumber pickle on top and the dill mustard sauce.

Fino sherry, white Burgundy and rosé Champagne go well with cured fish.

TIP: *There are likely to be leftovers so enjoy gravadlax for a special breakfast with scrambled eggs or as a light lunch with warm baby new potatoes dressed with the dill mustard sauce. It will keep in the fridge for a week.*

BEEF WELLINGTON

A charming twist on a classic, this parcel for two is a real luxury and can be made in advance so your clothes won't smell of cooking and you can get yourself ready safe in the knowledge that dinner just needs a quick blast in the oven. Serve simply with roasted cherry tomatoes, shop-bought French fries in the middle of the table to share, a dressed green salad and a quick Béarnaise — the steak is the star of the show here.

SERVES 2

30g unsalted butter

100g mixed mushrooms, finely chopped

salt and freshly ground black pepper

175g coarse pâté

1 x 400g piece of fillet steak

olive oil

250g puff pastry

2 slices of Parma ham

2 egg yolks, beaten

QUICK BÉARNAISE

Melt 125g butter and leave to cool slightly. In a small saucepan, simmer 3 tablespoons each of white wine vinegar and dry white wine, 2 peeled and finely chopped shallots, ground black pepper and 2 tarragon sprigs until reduced by half. Strain and add to a heatproof bowl with 2 large egg yolks. Put the bowl over a pan of simmering water, whisking for 2 minutes until thick and pale. Slowly add the melted butter, whisking constantly, until the sauce has thickened. Finish with 1 tablespoon chopped tarragon and lemon juice and seasoning to taste.

In a saucepan, melt the butter over a medium–high heat and stir in the mushrooms. Cook for 3–4 minutes until golden and any excess liquid has evaporated, then season. Once cool, add the pâté and mix well to combine.

Drizzle the steak with olive oil and season. Add to a hot frying pan and cook over a high heat for 30 seconds on each side to give a golden-brown crust. Remove the meat to a plate to cool. While the steak is cooling, roll out the pastry thinly into a square large enough to completely encase the steak. From the remaining pastry, cut out two heart shapes. Once the steak is cold, wrap it with the Parma ham slices. Mix the beaten egg yolks with a little water to make an egg wash, and lightly brush the surface of the pastry with it. Place the steak in the centre. Put the mushroom mixture on top of the steak, then bring opposite corners of pastry up to overlap in the centre, tucking in the sides as if you were wrapping a parcel. Place the two pastry hearts in the centre of the parcel and brush all over with the rest of the egg wash.

Chill for at least 30 minutes, or until you're ready to cook the parcel. Preheat the oven to 220°C/gas 7. Put the parcel on a high shelf and cook for 20–25 minutes, which will give you medium-rare steak; add another 5 minutes if you would like your meat well done. To serve, cut between the pastry hearts.

 Robust reds like American Cabernet Sauvignon, Malbec or Claret.

TIP: *In place of the Parma ham, a pancake can be used (page 224) to wrap the fillet in before encasing in the pastry.*

RASPBERRY SOUFFLÉ

These are impressive from the moment they leave the oven, but they must be eaten straight away. This recipe makes four soufflés as the mixture is easier to work with in a larger quantity. If making two and saving two for another day, use half the base mix and fold in half of the beaten egg whites. A fresh egg white mixture will need to be whisked up for making the second batch.

MAKES 4

For the raspberry coulis
300g raspberries
2 tablespoons icing or caster sugar
1 tablespoon lemon juice

For the soufflés
40g melted butter, for greasing
6 rounded tablespoons caster sugar, plus extra for the ramekins
4 tablespoons raspberry jam
90ml double cream
1 tablespoon plain flour
4 tablespoons cornflour
100ml full-fat milk
2 egg yolks
4 egg whites

To make the coulis, purée the raspberries with the sugar and lemon juice in a food processor. Push it through a sieve to remove the raspberry pips. Add more sugar to taste.

Brush the insides of 4 ramekins with the melted butter and coat with sugar, shaking out any excess. Place 1 tablespoon jam in each then chill in the fridge. Mix the cream, flour and cornflour to a smooth paste. Warm the milk over a medium heat, until just boiling, then gradually stir into the paste. Whisk until smooth then pour the mixture back into the saucepan and place over a gentle heat. Continue beating vigorously until thickened.

Place the egg yolks in a separate small bowl and add the caster sugar. Mix to a thick paste, then add to the saucepan and mix well until smooth. Return to the hob to thicken, whisking until it begins to bubble – be careful not to scramble the eggs. When the mixture looks like custard, remove from the heat and put aside to cool completely. (At this point you can chill the mixture in the fridge for up to 2 days and finish the soufflés just before serving.)

Preheat the oven to 180°C/gas 4. Put the egg whites into a large bowl and beat with an electric mixer until soft peaks form. Add 1 large spoonful of the egg whites and 6 tablespoons raspberry coulis to the cooled mixture, then beat well. Carefully fold in the remaining egg whites. Fill the ramekins to the brim and level off with a spatula. Place them on a baking sheet in the middle of the oven for about 14 minutes until risen and turning golden. Serve immediately, with the raspberry coulis and shortbread heart biscuits (page 181).

A half bottle of Sauternes to share.

ENDING THE EVENING

This should be a night distinct from your typical routine. Switch off the television to play cards or a board game for two. Backgammon is a personal favourite, but I always forget how to set up the pieces on a board, so use the photograph opposite to avoid any potential disagreements. Chocolate has long been associated with decadence and sensuality since its discovery in Mexico by Spanish conquistadors. You can buy luxury chocolate puddings for two, or impress with homemade truffles or chocolate-dipped strawberries. This is also the time to serve a delicate rose-petal martini (a signature cocktail from Table Talk, where I used to work) or a more masculine Irish coffee.

CHOCOLATE TRUFFLES Makes 12–15

Break 150g good-quality dark (70% cocoa solids) or milk chocolate into small pieces and place in a heatproof bowl. Put 150ml double cream and 75g light brown sugar in a small saucepan. Bring to the boil, stirring to dissolve the sugar, and simmer for 1 minute, then cool for about 30 seconds. Pour the cream on to the chocolate a little at a time and mix well, working quickly until smooth and glossy. Don't over-mix. Allow the ganache to cool, then put it, covered, in the fridge for at least 1 hour or until fully set. Remove from the fridge and allow to come up to room temperature – this will make it easier to handle. Sprinkle your hands with a little cocoa powder, then scoop out teaspoonfuls of the ganache and roll in your hands to make balls. Don't take too long over this, as the ganache will begin to melt. Roll the truffles in cocoa powder, chopped almonds or dessicated coconut. Refrigerate until ready to serve.

TIP: *Prepare the ganache up to 3 days in advance, or freeze it for up to a month.*

ROSE-PETAL MARTINI Serves 1 (make to order)

Fill a cocktail shaker with ice cubes and pour over 25ml vodka, 10ml rose-petal liqueur, 50ml lychee juice and 10ml lemon juice. Shake well and strain into a chilled martini glass. Garnish with a rose petal.

IRISH COFFEE Serves 1 (make to order)

Put 25ml Irish whiskey in a heatproof glass and top with freshly made coffee. Add 1–2 teaspoons brown sugar and stir until dissolved. Top with lightly whipped double cream, poured carefully on to the surface of the coffee over the back of a teaspoon – this will ensure that the cream floats. Serve sprinkled with grated chocolate, nutmeg or ground cinnamon.

'When you wake up in the morning, Pooh,'
said Piglet at last, 'what's the first thing you
say to yourself?'
'What's for breakfast?' said Pooh. 'What do
you say, Piglet?'
'I say, I wonder what's going to happen
exciting today?' said Piglet.
Pooh nodded thoughtfully. 'It's the same
thing,' he said.

Winnie-the-Pooh,
A. A. Milne

SPECIAL
BREAKFASTS

I like breakfast. A good morning meal brightens any day. Whether it's a core-warming bowl of porridge in winter, a golden-yolked egg with hot buttered toast on a bright and lazy summer morning or a lemony sugar pancake wolfed down in haste on Shrove Tuesday, breakfast is an important meal. It's the fuel for our engines, it boosts our concentration and sharpens our minds. Breakfast sets the tone and mood for the rest of the day, starting the morning off on the right foot with an added, often caffeinated, spring in the step.

Until the mid-fifteenth century, breakfast wasn't much to write home about. It was typically taken at first light and consisted of a small piece of bread and cheese and a mug of beer (a far less alcoholic drink then than it is now, and in those days safer than most drinking water). Instead, the main meal of the day was 'dinner', served as early as 10am, which marked the end of the morning's labour. Gradually, as the working day became longer and people began to work in offices, these two meals increased to three and an early breakfast became more of a necessity to see workers through to lunchtime. The invention of artificial lighting also allowed people the luxury of eating later. As new foodstuffs from all over the world became available, breakfast in the Victorian era gradually changed to become a meal full of culinary delights, many of which we still love, such as cold joints of meat, grilled mackerel, sausages, bacon and eggs, as well as muffins, toast and jams.

The rhythm and pace of our lives continues to influence how we breakfast today; our busy weekday routines make leisurely breakfasts that bit more elusive, so weekends are the time to indulge in them. The beauty of this meal is that it's flexible, with endless variations and almost no rules – it might be a preciously quiet and private ritual, a family affair to be enjoyed early in the comfort of one's pyjamas, or it might even be a social breezy brunch at midday with friends grazing right through to the afternoon.

And then there are the really special breakfasts. Many families have particular breakfast menus for Christmas, but fewer do for birthdays, anniversaries or other festive occasions – perhaps it's time to start a new family tradition. I always look forward to a birthday breakfast at my parents', unfailingly prepared with a few celebratory touches to elevate it from the everyday. This type of breakfast doesn't need to be overly fancy; it just requires a little bit more effort to assemble, but it is always worth it because it puts you in a cheery, positive mood at the beginning of the day.

BREAKFAST IN BED

Breakfast in bed can be anything from a simple pot of tea with a few digestive biscuits to a tray laden with early-morning goodies and flowers. Either way, nearly any breakfast becomes special when it's brought to you in bed. I have funny memories of creeping up the stairs with my brother and sister, carrying a breakfast tray for our parents as a surprise treat: desperately trying not to spill the tea and the orange juice or knock over the vase of flowers, stifling our giggles so that they couldn't hear us coming. Even if you've only got time to make an early-morning cuppa on a special day or birthday, it's the ideal way to surprise someone – an offering that marks a momentary pause before the rest of the day unfolds.

TIPS: *Instead of a vase of flowers, a spring bulb planted in a teacup makes a delightful change on a breakfast tray. • You can buy really comfortable 'lap' trays which have a beanbag base; some retailers will allow you to customise the surface with your own photographs. They're perfect for suppers in front of the television as well.*

FOR MUM...

Mums rarely get an excuse to have breakfast in bed, and if there's ever a time when they should, it's on Mother's Day. This is something children can get involved in, picking a bunch of flowers (such as forget-me-nots) and arranging them in a vase, lining a tray with a napkin, making a handwritten card and helping set out a few delicious dishes. It's the thought that counts, so it should be a breakfast that they can assemble, such as a granola and fruit compote sundae (page 222) or cook easily like a boiled egg with soldiers. A special-occasion porridge can be decorated with small luxuries (fresh berries and single cream, golden syrup, toasted nuts or granulated sugar). The only rule is to leave a clean kitchen afterwards, so as not to create extra work for Mum and spoil what is meant to be her treat.

FOR DAD...

Dad might not appreciate a bunch of flowers quite like Mum, but the morning newspaper or even just his favourite crossword or sudoku cut out and presented with a sharp pencil will do the trick. A pot of coffee and a crunchy piece of toast with marmalade will definitely win you brownie points, a fresh grapefruit sprinkled with brown sugar, a warm croissant straight from the oven or a bacon sandwich cooked to his liking. If you really want to spoil Dad (and his diet allows it) serve the bacon with maple syrup and pancakes (page 225).

GRANOLA AND FRUIT COMPOTE SUNDAE

Assemble homemade granola and fruit compotes in tall clear glasses with yogurt to make a sundae. As these components are sweet, stick to plain yogurt, and choose your compote flavours according to the season. Granola is easier to make in a larger quantity so there should be plenty of leftovers for the rest of the week. Store the rest in a large kilner jar for up to a month.

SERVES 4

Homemade granola: Preheat the oven to 140°C/gas 2 and grease a large roasting tin with sunflower oil. Gently warm 250ml honey and 1 teaspoon vanilla extract in a small pan. Place 250g rolled or jumbo oats, 75g raisins or sultanas, 75g chopped hazelnuts or almonds and 40g pumpkin seeds in a large bowl. Pour over the warmed honey and vanilla and mix well to coat, then tip into the prepared tin and spread out evenly. Bake for 1 hour or until golden brown and crunchy, turning the mixture every 15 minutes to prevent it burning. Remove from the oven and allow the granola to cool, then roughly break into chunks and add in 100g mixed dried fruit, such as cherries, cranberries or chopped apricots.

Spring and summer berry compote: Put 400g mixed berries into a pan and add 75g golden caster sugar, the zest and juice of ½ a lemon and the seeds from ½ a vanilla pod (or ½ teaspoon vanilla extract). Sauté the mixture for 10–15 minutes, stirring frequently, over a medium to high heat, until the berries begin to soften and release their juices. Heat for a further 2 minutes until slightly thickened.

Autumn apple and cinnamon compote: Put 4 peeled and roughly chopped Bramley apples into a pan with 100g demerara sugar and the seeds from 1 vanilla pod, 1 teaspoon ground cinnamon and ¼ of a teaspoon ground cloves. Add a small splash of water, then cook over a medium heat for 10–15 minutes, stirring frequently, until the apples have softened but still have some texture.

Winter rhubarb and ginger compote: Put 400g trimmed forced rhubarb, cut into 2cm pieces, into a pan with the juice and zest of ½ an orange, a 2cm piece of fresh ginger, peeled and finely grated, and 125g golden caster sugar. Simmer gently over a medium heat for 10–12 minutes, or until the rhubarb has softened, but still retains some texture.

TIPS: *The compotes will last for up to three days in the fridge and are delicious with ice cream. • Crunchie yogurt (bash up Crunchies in their packaging and swirl the contents into a bowl of plain yogurt) is a naughty teaspoon-dipping treat for kids.*

PANCAKE DAY

Pancakes work brilliantly at breakfast with lemon and sugar or with a fruit compote (page 222). On Shrove Tuesday, get children together for a post-school session of pancake tossing and racing, or serve up drop scones as a high tea, fresh from the pan and laced with butter. These are smaller than pancakes and easier for younger children to toss. Both recipes make 10 to 12 pancakes or drop scones.

CLASSIC PANCAKES

230g plain flour
2 free-range eggs, beaten
400ml milk
sunflower oil, for frying
To serve: lemon, caster sugar
(or Grand Marnier for grown-ups)

DROP SCONES

150g self-raising flour
2 tablespoons caster sugar
1 free-range egg, beaten
160ml milk
50g unsalted butter, melted
sunflower oil, for frying

Sift the flour into a mixing bowl (add the caster sugar for drop scones). Make a small well in the centre of the mixture and pour in the eggs and a small splash of milk. Whisk until smooth, then very gradually pour in the remaining milk (and the melted butter if making drop scones) while continuing to mix, until you have a smooth batter.

Lightly grease a non-stick frying pan with the oil and warm over a medium heat. To make classic pancakes, pour in roughly 3 tablespoons of the batter, or enough to thinly cover the bottom of the pan, and tilt it so that it is spread evenly. To make drop scones, add one generous tablespoon of batter per scone, in batches of 3 or 4 at a time. Cook until the pancakes are golden brown, then flip and cook the other side. Serve immediately.

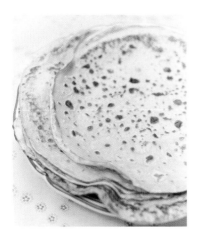

SHROVE TUESDAY AND PANCAKE RACES

Shrove Tuesday (Pancake Day) is the last opportunity for people to use up foods that were traditionally not allowed during Lent: meat and fish, fats, eggs and milk. Pancakes became associated with Shrove Tuesday as they used up most of the forbidden food in the house with just the addition of flour.

Pancake races happen all over the country these days and still have a long history. To hold your own, get all the participants at the starting line — racers hold frying pans with pancakes in them — and let them race to the finish, flipping their pancakes as they run. Ensure that participants flip their pancakes a fixed number of times.

A BIRTHDAY BREAKFAST

A birthday breakfast is a great way to gather everyone together, particularly if it falls on a weekend. To maximise your time in bed, lay and decorate the table the night before with presents piled up at the birthday boy or girl's place, cards stacked in a toast rack ready to be opened, bunting hanging as a backdrop, and perhaps a 'Happy Birthday' banner placed somewhere prominent. The following morning, add little finishing touches, such as a few balloons tied to the backs of chairs, fresh flowers and the food presented in an attractive way. Pour the milk into a jug rather than bringing out the entire carton, and decant the butter and jams in the same way. Display fresh fruit playfully: you can make mango hedgehogs by criss-crossing one side of a cut mango with a knife and turning the skin inside out so that the flesh can be eaten in cubes.

Birthdays only come once a year, so the breakfast menu has to be thoughtful, with added indulgences, like freshly squeezed orange juice (topped with sparkling wine for a Buck's Fizz). Eggs can easily be made worthy of a breakfast celebration – cover boiled eggs with homemade egg cosies (page 238) for an extra surprise, use heart moulds to fry your eggs and stamp out toast shapes, or try the ideas on page 229.

EXCELLENT EGGS

EGGS BENEDICT Serves 4

Halve 2 muffins horizontally and toast until golden. Divide between the plates, spread lightly with butter and arrange a slice of ham on each. Warm a jar of ready-prepared Hollandaise sauce. To cook the eggs, bring a deep pan of water to the boil and add a generous splash of white wine vinegar. Crack 4 eggs into separate small cups or ramekins. Use a wooden spoon to create a whirlpool and carefully drop the eggs in. Let them cook for 2–3 minutes and remove using a slotted spoon. Drain briefly on kitchen towel before placing the eggs on to the prepared muffin halves. Spoon the warm Hollandaise sauce over the eggs and ham, and finish with a pinch of cayenne or ground black pepper.

TIP : *To poach lots of eggs at the same time, line a mug with a lightly oiled piece of clingfilm so it overlaps the edges. Crack an egg inside and twist the clingfilm to create a neat parcel, repeat with more eggs, then add to a pan of boiling water.*

SALMON AND SPINACH BAKED EGGS Serves 4

Preheat the oven to 200°C/gas 6. Grease 4 ramekins with butter. Over a high heat, wilt 300g spinach in a pan for 2–3 minutes with a splash of water, then drain and squeeze out any excess liquid. Place the spinach in a bowl and season well. Add 4 tablespoons double cream, a pinch of freshly grated nutmeg, a squeeze of lemon juice and 200g flaked hot smoked salmon. Mix together well, then divide equally between the ramekins. Crack an egg inside each and top with an extra drizzle of double cream, a little more grated nutmeg and Parmesan. Bake for 10–15 minutes, until the whites are firm but the yolks soft and runny.

BOILED AND SCRAMBLED EGGS

There's a simple pleasure to be had from cracking the dome of a boiled egg with the back of a spoon as you wonder if it's been cooked perfectly, and from dunking that first soldier with the subsequent overflow of the golden yolk. To elevate them from the everyday, serve with a regiment of flavoured soldiers: spread toast with smoked mackerel (page 142) or trout pâté (page 130), make Welsh rarebit (page 142) or Croque Monsieur fingers (page 233) and, of course, a simple Marmite spread is an obvious favourite.

If I had to choose what to eat for my last breakfast, it would have to be perfectly cooked scrambled eggs with smoked salmon and toasted soda bread, but serving scrambled eggs in their shells (just wash well with hot water and dry upside down) is a fun idea – garnish with inexpensive caviar and truffle oil for a decadent treat. If the shells sit too far down, fill the egg cups with sea salt to rest them on. Serve salt and pepper in the other shell half.

A LAZY BRUNCH

A really late start warrants brunch, in lieu of lunch. This is a time for one-dish affairs that encompass both breakfast and lunch, such as a kedgeree or a full English frittata. Guests might come and go at different times, so prepare what you can in advance, and enjoy the benefits of a lazy brunch without spending all your time in the kitchen. Everyone is likely to arrive really hungry, having saved themselves for a feast, so arrange a platter of pastries for people to enjoy with their first cup of coffee – mini doughnuts and waffles nestled in cellophane or muffins wrapped in paper all look appetising.

COFFEE

A large cafetière or two of freshly brewed coffee is the easiest solution for a crowd. A stove-top percolator (moka pot) makes delicious espresso-style coffee and gives off a wonderful aroma, but also involves a rather lengthy process better suited to smaller numbers. Hot milk can make all the difference for those who like their coffee very milky so pop it in the microwave or on the hob for a few minutes to heat up (be careful not to let it boil over). If you have a small frothing device, so much the better, but you can also put warm milk into a clean cafetière and pump the plunger vigorously to aerate it. Sprinkle drinks with chocolate powder making playful shapes using stencils.

GRAND MIMOSA Serves 4

A Grand Mimosa is a variation on Buck's Fizz with the addition of Grand Marnier. Line up 4 chilled Champagne flutes and pour a tablespoon of Grand Marnier into the bottom of each one. Divide 300ml Champagne or Prosecco between them, and then use 125ml freshly squeezed orange juice to top up the glasses (approximately 2 tablespoons per glass). Serve decorated with half a squeezed kumquat or a physalis.

A JUG OF BLOODY MARY Serves 8

In a jug, mix together 8 teaspoons celery salt, 4 teaspoons freshly ground black pepper, 2 tablespoons horseradish sauce, 200ml vodka, 8 teaspoons Worcestershire sauce, 4 tablespoons Tabasco sauce, 2 litres tomato juice, 50ml sherry and a squeeze of lemon juice. Stir well with a celery stick, and adjust the spices and seasonings to taste. Serve in tall glasses with ice cubes, celery and lemon wedges.

FULL ENGLISH FRITTATA

A full English breakfast is an institution and one of the best-known national meals in the world. For larger numbers it can be tricky to get all the components ready at the same time. A quick and easy solution is an all-in-one frittata. To prepare this ahead (no more than 2 hours in advance), complete all the steps before adding the eggs. Then, when you are ready to serve, simply reheat the base ingredients, add the beaten eggs and pop it under the grill. Have favourite condiments on the side.

SERVES 8 (MAKES 2 FRITTATAS)

4 tablespoons olive oil

6 sausages, cut into chunks

12 slices streaky bacon, cut into bite-size pieces

400g baby Portobello or small flat mushrooms, halved

16 cherry tomatoes, halved

16 free-range eggs

salt and freshly ground black pepper

150g Cheddar cheese, grated

Preheat the grill to high. Divide the oil between two 26cm oven-proof frying pans and heat, then divide the sausages between the pans. Sauté for a few minutes to colour them before adding half the bacon to each pan. Continue to cook for a further 2–3 minutes. Add the mushrooms to each pan, and fry for 5–6 minutes. Divide the cherry tomatoes between the pans and cook for a further minute.

In a bowl, whisk the eggs and season generously. Pour half the egg mixture into each pan and cook over a gentle heat for 8–10 minutes to set the base. Scatter half the cheese over one frittata, then transfer the pan to the grill and cook for 4–5 minutes or until lightly golden and set. Do the same with the remaining cheese and the second frittata. When the frittatas have cooled slightly, cut each into wedges to serve.

> CROQUE MONSIEUR *If a full English is too much for younger diners, this taste of France might hit the spot with kids. Spread a slice of white bread with Dijon mustard, layer over ham and grated Gruyère cheese, season and top with another slice of buttered white bread. Fry the sandwiches for a few minutes in butter on each side, until golden. Serve with a fried egg on top for a Croque Madame.*

CLASSIC KEDGEREE

This is perfect for larger parties, because it's easy to double the quantities — if there isn't room at the kitchen table, guests can eat this standing up with just a fork. A good friend served this at her wedding, adding quails' eggs and locally caught mackerel to make it elegant and special. It goes well with a green bean salad, mango chutney and Tabasco sauce on the side.

....

SERVES 8

....

450g undyed smoked haddock

250ml full-fat milk

2 hot-smoked salmon fillets

20g butter

2 medium onions, finely diced

¾ tablespoon medium curry powder

½ teaspoon turmeric

seeds from 2 cardamom pods

1 cinnamon stick

200g mixed basmati and wild rice

175g frozen peas

6 eggs

a handful of chopped flat leaf parsley

salt and freshly ground black pepper

lemon wedges, to serve

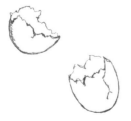

Put the haddock in a frying pan over a medium heat. Pour the milk over, cover and simmer for 4 minutes. Take off the heat, add the salmon fillets and stand, covered, for 10 minutes to finish gently cooking the fish.

Meanwhile, heat the butter in a separate frying pan. Add the onion, curry powder, turmeric, cardamom seeds and cinnamon and fry until the onion is soft and golden, about 5–6 minutes. Cook the rice according to the instructions on page 168.

Remove the fish from the milk and set it aside. Strain 150ml of the milk back into the pan. Add the cooked rice and peas and cover, cooking for 5 minutes over a low heat until the liquid is absorbed.

Meanwhile, put the eggs in a pan, cover with cold water and bring to the boil, then cook for 6 minutes. Run the eggs under the cold tap until they are cool enough to peel and quarter.

Break the fish into big flakes with a fork, removing any bones, and add to the rice. Throw in the parsley and stir gently to mix without breaking up the fish, adding the eggs at the end. Remove the cinnamon stick, season well with salt and pepper, and serve with lemon wedges.

TIPS : *Use 6 slices of back bacon chopped into small pieces instead of the fish — add it in when cooking the onions.* • *For a lighter version, heat the rice and peas in 200ml hot vegetable stock in place of the poaching milk.* • *You can add 250g cooked prawns with the hot-smoked salmon.* • *For more heat, add in 1 small finely chopped dried red chilli.*

See the land, her Easter keeping,
Rises as her Maker rose.
Seeds, so long in darkness sleeping,
Burst at last from winter snows.
Earth with heaven above rejoices;
Fields and gardens hail the spring;
Shaughs and woodlands ring with voices,
While the wild birds build and sing.

'Easter Week', Charles Kingsley

EASTER

Easter brings feelings of excitement and renewal, like the sighting of the first yellow daffodils, which provide a sense of hope and a burst of brightness. It is the first significant festival of the year, when everything that has lain dormant over the winter months awakens and life feels busy again, both inside and out: churches fill with congregations, the spicy aroma of hot cross buns pervades kitchens and butterflies emerge from hibernation. It is a celebration of the new season and the chance to be outside again: in woods for bluebell-carpeted walks or, for families with young children, visiting farms to see young lambs and parties of chicks.

Tradition, symbolism and religion lie at the heart of Easter. It is the most important festival in the Christian year, marking the death of Christ on Good Friday and celebrating his resurrection three days later on Easter Sunday. As a moveable feast, Easter follows the lunar calendar – it falls on the first Sunday after the first full moon of the spring Equinox. It is believed to derive from the Anglo-Saxon festival Eostre, which honoured Eastre, the goddess of spring and dawn, but it is also linked to the Jewish festival of Passover, or Pascha. In many churches today there is still the ceremonial lighting of a special Easter candle, known as the Paschal candle.

Many rituals come together to form Easter; the foods that we enjoy today are centred on the luxuries that were prohibited during the preceding forty days of the Lenten fast. Eggs, symbols of hope and rebirth, were forbidden, which is why they were eaten on the day before Lent began, Shrove Tuesday (Pancake Day, page 224), and then again on the day it ended, Easter Sunday, as an emblem of resurrection. Eggs also became a popular part of the festival to be decorated and handed out as gifts, often in the form of wild birds' eggs rather than the hens' eggs we use today. They still form the basis of our celebrations and offer simple, inexpensive pleasure: boiled for breakfast, hidden in flowerbeds, rolled, thrown and tapped or even raced, carefully balanced on a spoon. Another popular symbol of Easter today is the Easter Bunny, who might leave his mark outside children's bedrooms with a trail of jellybeans, a single, beautifully wrapped egg or a wicker basket embellished with brightly coloured ribbon and laden with a cluster of tiny sweets, shiny eggs and decorative chicks on a bed of straw or shredded tissue paper.

As children, the day before Easter, we would make marbled eggs by hard-boiling them, cracking the shells and leaving them in water coloured with food dye, which would seep through the cracks. It was always fun eating our creations for breakfast the next morning. We would look forward to a huge Easter egg hunt, which was (and still is) quite competitive in our household, and then have a family lunch, often with roast spring lamb, but always with plenty of chocolate before and after!

EASTER CRAFTS

Celebrations usually start a few days before Easter, so plan a craft day. It's good to give children something to do at Easter that doesn't focus on eating chocolate.

FELT EGG COSIES

These will look charming on your Easter breakfast table and can make a simple boiled egg look special.

I : Make a rectangular template (8cm wide x 11cm high) with a curved top edge. Place this on a square of pastel-coloured felt and use it to cut two identical shapes. Make a flower-shaped template (5cm diameter) and cut flowers from two other pieces of coloured felt. 2 : Cut a circle (2cm diameter) of felt with pinking shears, then cut a second circle (1cm diameter). Position the two flowers on top of each other so that both sets of petals are visible, then place the two circles on top and sew them all together through the centre using wool and a large needle. 3 : Stitch or stick these with a glue stick to the centre of one of the egg-cosy shapes. Place the two egg-cosy shapes together, right-side out, and blanket-stitch around the edge with wool. Leave the bottom edge open, but stitch around the front edge for a pretty finish.

POMPOM CHICKS

Glue these into clean eggshells stuck on pieces of card to make Easter chick place markers for the table.

I : Make pompoms as per the instructions for thistles on page 179, using yellow wool. 2 : Open up the pompom slightly. 3 : Cover the back of a pair of plastic eyes and a felt beak with PVA glue, and gently lodge them into the pompom so that they don't fall out.

EGG CRESS MEN

Cress provides children with a sense of anticipation as they wait for it to grow. Use empty shells from boiled eggs.

I : Fill an empty egg shell with damp cotton wool and sow some mustard cress seeds on it. 2 : Draw a face on the shell and let the cress sprout on a windowsill – this will take 4–5 days if kept moist. 3 : Give the cress head a 'haircut' when it's time for a cress sandwich.

EASTER BONNETS

This is a wonderful way to revive an old hat and to inject some tradition into Easter Sunday.

I : Take a length of raffia and wrap it around your fingers to form a disc. Feed the end of it into the centre, then to the outside; repeat to the centre, then the outside; and continue to weave to create a small nest shape. 2 : Glue these nests to a hat, then stick toy chicks inside the nests with PVA glue. 3 : Tie a ribbon around the hat and finish with a bow, feathers and more chicks.

MORE EASTER CRAFTS...

SPRING HATS

You will need colourful card and spring-themed accessories to make these simple Easter hats.

I: Cut two circles (18cm diameter) out of card. Cut a disc (8cm diameter) from the centre of each to make two rings, which will form the brim of the hat. Keep one of the discs and the two larger rings. 2: Cut a rectangle (14cm x 30cm) from another piece of card and roll it into a cylinder of the right size (8cm diameter) to fit through the rings. Stick it together with PVA glue. Make vertical 1cm snips around each end of the cylinder to make tabs. 3: Place one end of the cylinder through one of the rings, folding out the tabs underneath the ring to lock it in place and make a top-hat shape. Glue the tabs to the underside of the ring. 4: Attach two 50cm lengths of ribbon to the underside of the ring with PVA glue. 5: Stick the second ring to the underside of the first, sandwiching the tabs and the ends of the ribbon to hide them. 6: Fold in the tabs at the other end of the cylinder and glue the disc on top. 7: Cut a strip (5cm x 30cm) from green card, snip vertically along it to create a grass-effect trim and stick to the hat. 8: Finish off with a chick-filled raffia nest (page 238), more ribbon and egg shapes made of card.

PAPER BAGS

These are fun to make and can be used on Easter egg hunts or as party bags for children's birthdays.

I: Decorate white or coloured paper bags with any pattern you like, using potato prints or acrylic paints and brushes.

EGG DECORATING

To prepare your eggs, first add a splash of vinegar to boiling water to make sure the eggs don't crack, then hard-boil them for 7 minutes. Set up a large table covered with newspaper or a plastic cloth and lay out a range of acrylic paints, glitter, sequins and other bits and pieces that can be used for decorating. Also make sure you have plenty of PVA glue. Give every child a hard-boiled egg to decorate as brightly and attractively as possible. You might want to suggest a theme for the decoration. Animal eggs are fun, or silly faces (cotton wool and string make good hair). If you want to turn it into more of a game, you can give players two minutes for decorating and then tell them to pass their eggs to the player next to them — a bit like pass the parcel. That way, everyone gets to work on each egg and the finished products are the combined result of everyone's talents.

TIP: *To make marble eggs, hard-boil eggs, then gently crack the shells. Prepare a range of deep mixing bowls, each filled with diluted food colouring (enough to submerge the eggs). Add quite a bit of food colouring to get a dark, rich colour. Submerge the eggs and leave them for 10 minutes to 1 hour. Peel to reveal the marbled effect.*

PACE EGGS *Exquisite, beautifully decorated paste (pace) eggs were popular in Medieval Europe — the shells were pressed with flowers, foliage and scraps of material held together with a piece of linen tied to form a bundle, then boiled in water for a few hours so the colours of the material would stain the eggshells in the patterns of the petals and foliage. Often these were strung in garlands on a mantelpiece, as many as twenty at a time. Today such decorative eggs are a rarity and have been almost entirely replaced by chocolate confections.*

EGG BLOWING

To get light, hollow eggshells which you can decorate and hang up with ribbons on branches, you will need to blow out the contents of the eggs. Get a small clean bowl or ramekin and place it on the table in front of you. With a pin or needle, make a hole in each end of the egg. Carefully try to enlarge the hole at the rounded end of the egg, so that it's bigger than the hole at the pointy end. With the needle, try to pierce the yolk inside so that it's easier to blow out of the shell. Holding the egg carefully over the bowl, put your lips over the larger hole at the rounded end, and blow steadily so that the contents come out into the bowl (it's quite hard work so an adult might need to help with this). Once the shells are empty, rinse carefully under cold water and decorate when dry.

To hang, use approximately 60cm of thin ribbon and wrap the egg like a present. Place the egg at the mid-point of the ribbon and curve the ribbon lengthways around the egg, then cross the ends over and back down the opposite side, dividing the egg into four sections. At the top, tie your ribbon securely in a double knot and use the excess to tie your egg around the Easter tree.

GOOD FRIDAY SWEET TREATS

Have a few edible activities for children to make and enjoy. These are perfect for a spring tea along with hot cross buns. Serve simnel cake (page 246) for the grown-ups.

SQUASHED-FLY BUNNIES Makes 24

My granny convinced me that the currants in these biscuits were squashed flies and the name has stuck. Use cutters to shape them into bunnies and tie their necks with ribbon if you're handing them out as gifts.

Place 200g plain flour and 50g diced unsalted butter in a food processor and pulse together until the mixture resembles fine breadcrumbs. Add 70g caster sugar, 50ml milk, 1 teaspoon mixed spice and the zest of ½ an orange. Pulse briefly until the mixture comes together and tip out. Knead until smooth then wrap in clingfilm and chill for 30 minutes.

Preheat the oven to 190°C/gas 5, and grease two baking sheets. Roll the dough out on a lightly floured surface into a large square approximately 0.5cm thick, then cut it in half. Scatter one half with 50g sultanas and 50g currants and put the other half directly on top. Roll out again to 0.5cm thick, so the two pieces are sandwiched together and the currants and sultanas are showing through. Cut out the dough using a bunny cutter and transfer the biscuits to the baking sheets. Push a few extra currants on to the bunnies' faces for eyes, then brush the biscuits with 2 beaten egg yolks mixed with a little water. Sprinkle with caster sugar. Bake for 15–20 minutes, or until crisp and a light golden colour. Transfer to a wire rack to cool.

CHOCOLATE NESTS Makes 24

Kids can help make these and spoon them into colourful cupcake cases. Decorate them with chocolate eggs or mini chicks.

Lay out 24 paper cupcake cases on a tray that will fit in the fridge. Place 140g Shredded Wheat and 140g Cornflakes in a large bowl and crush them using your hands or a rolling pin. Break 225g milk chocolate and 100g dark chocolate into pieces and melt with 50g butter in a bowl over a pan of simmering water. Add 4 tablespoons golden syrup and stir. Carefully pour the melted chocolate mixture over the Shredded Wheat and Cornflakes and mix together well. Divide equally between the cases and make a small dip in the middle of each one to create a 'nest'. Arrange three mini eggs in each nest and chill until set.

TIP: *Use the same mixture to make 'birdseed', a pudding I loved to eat at school. It was always served with warm custard that would slowly turn chocolatey as it mixed with the birdseed. Make the same mixture as above but set it in a large rectangular baking tin and leave in the fridge to harden.*

SIMNEL CAKE

This fruit cake, similar to Christmas cake, has been eaten at Easter since medieval times. If, like me, you are not a huge fan of marzipan, try covering it with ready-rolled fondant icing and using edible sugar flowers, mini eggs or sugared almonds instead of the traditional decorations. Tie a ribbon around the cake.

SERVES 8–10

225g unsalted butter, softened
225g light brown soft sugar
zest of 1 lemon
zest of 1 orange
5 medium eggs
225g plain flour
1 teaspoon mixed spice
1 teaspoon ground cinnamon
1 teaspoon almond extract
150g glacé cherries, chopped
125g currants
150g sultanas
100g candied peel
75g ready-rolled marzipan
2 tablespoons apricot jam, plus a little extra
150g ready-rolled white fondant icing

Preheat the oven to 160°C/gas 3. Grease and line a 20cm round cake tin. Beat the softened butter and sugar together in a large bowl using an electric whisk until pale and fluffy. Stir in the lemon and orange zest and then gradually beat in the eggs. Add the flour, mixed spice, cinnamon, almond extract, cherries, currants, sultanas and candied peel, and fold together until well combined. Spoon half the mixture into the prepared tin, smoothing down the surface evenly.

Cut the marzipan into a neat circle (approximately 0.5cm thick), the same size as the cake tin. Place the circle on top of the cake mixture, then spoon the remaining mixture on top. Bake for between 1½ hours and 1 hour 45 minutes, until golden brown. Check after 1 hour, and cover the cake with foil if it browns too fast. Once done, remove from the oven and let it cool slightly before removing it from the tin and transferring it to a wire rack.

Once the cake is cool, brush the top with the apricot jam. Cover this with a circle of the ready-rolled fondant icing and use the trimmings to decorate. Dab a touch of apricot jam on to the bottom of the shapes to stick them around the top edge of the cake. Or see page 285 for how to make edible sugar-frosted flowers.

TIP: *Use the same recipe to make your Christmas cake, adding green holly and red berry decorations made of fondant icing.*

MARZIPAN DECORATIONS *Simnel cake traditionally contains ingredients forbidden during Lent and was distinguished by its decorative topping of marzipan balls to represent Christ's twelve apostles. There is some debate as to how many should be used, though, ranging from eleven (excluding Judas) to thirteen (to include Christ).*

CAKES FOR MUMS

Originally, simnel cakes were made for Mothering Sunday (the fourth Sunday in Lent), as people would make pilgrimages to the mother church of their parishes. Working children were given leave to visit their mothers, bringing the cake as a gift. It's a lovely tradition that could be revived on Mother's Day.

THE EASTER TABLE

Decorations should be a fusion of Easter symbols, fresh blooms and the scents of spring. Colourful bunches of tulips and daffodils are easy to come by, or choose fragrant hyacinth bulbs in a variety of pretty pastel hues. Use clusters of shiny wrapped eggs, jelly beans and sugared almonds to dot among potted plants or place in small baskets and egg cups. Easter bunnies, mini hay bales or china Beatrix Potter figurines add extra amusement to spring table displays.

PLACE SETTINGS

Tie a packet of seeds around a napkin with raffia at each place setting as a gift or perch pompom chicks cheekily inside eggshells as place names for a more playful touch (page 238).

TIP: *Bulbs planted in teacups bedded with moss will sit nicely alongside vases of cut spring flowers, and they also make great Easter presents.*

EASTER TREE

Have an Easter tree in a pot, which is not only fun for the whole family to decorate but also provides a cheery focal point on a table or mantelpiece. Luscious branches of blossom are beautiful and long stems of pussy willow will last for weeks – both can be arranged in tall vases or enamel or ceramic pitchers. Decorate the branches with hanging blown eggs, painted and glittered and tied with colourful ribbon (page 242). Even a simple bunch of green foliage set above a mantelpiece can be hung with eggs (weight the vase down inside to prevent the display toppling over).

EASTER LUNCH MENU

Canapés
Quails' eggs
Mini baked potatoes

Main courses
Salmon and prawn pillow *or*
Stuffed roast lamb

Side dishes
Potato dauphinoise
Asparagus and spring greens *or*
Peter Rabbit lettuce and peas

Dessert
Easter trifle

EASTER DRINKS AND CANAPÉS

Depending on what you're serving for your main course, offer a few of these at your Easter gathering. Serve sparkling soft drinks with primrose ice cubes (page 295).

QUAILS' EGGS WITH CELERY SALT Makes 16

Boil 16 quails' eggs (allow 2 per person) for 4 minutes, then rinse under cold water and leave to cool. Remove half of each shell and serve with a sprinkling of cayenne pepper and celery salt for dipping. These are also great served with a Bloody Mary (page 234).

MINI BAKED POTATOES WITH CRÈME FRAÎCHE AND CAVIAR Makes 24

Preheat the oven to 190°C/gas 5. Place 24 baby new potatoes (allow 3 per person) on to a baking tray and drizzle with a little olive oil. Season with salt and white pepper and roast for 20–25 minutes. Remove from the oven and, once cool enough to handle, cut a small cross into the top of each potato and press the sides together to reveal the flesh.

Mix 100g crème fraîche, 2 tablespoons horseradish, 1 tablespoon finely chopped parsley, 2 finely chopped spring onions and the zest of ½ a lemon in a bowl and season to taste. Top the potatoes with a teaspoonful of the crème fraîche mixture, some Sevruga caviar (or hot-smoked salmon), and garnish with chopped chives. Serve on a bed of straw.

RHUBARB COCKTAIL Serves 1 (make to order)

An Easter martini, using seasonal rhubarb. Fill a cocktail shaker with ice cubes and pour over 40ml vodka, 15ml pomegranate (or cranberry) juice and 50ml rhubarb purée (see below). Shake well and pour into a chilled martini glass. Garnish with a thin strip of rhubarb tied in a knot.

TIP: *To make rhubarb purée, cut 250g rhubarb into chunks and place in a saucepan with 115ml water and 110g caster sugar. Bring to the boil, then reduce the heat and simmer gently for approximately 15 minutes until the fruit is soft and the liquid has thickened. Purée until smooth. Makes approximately 400ml.*

WHITE LADY Serves 1 (make to order)

An elegant drink. Fill a cocktail shaker with ice cubes and pour over 40ml dry gin, 20ml Cointreau, 10ml sugar syrup (page 104), the juice of ½ a lemon and 1 egg white. Shake well and pour into a chilled martini glass or Champagne coupe. Garnish with a disc of lemon peel (page 104).

SALMON AND PRAWN PILLOW

The practice of eating fish on Good Friday stems from the early Christians, who believed that meat should be forbidden on the day that Christ was crucified. This is a welcome Easter bundle — serve with Peter Rabbit lettuce and peas (page 256) and a warm, shop-bought Hollandaise sauce. The uncooked pillow can be frozen for up to a month. If baked from frozen, add another 15 minutes to the cooking time.

SERVES 8

30g unsalted butter

1 small onion, peeled and finely chopped

1 leek, cleaned and finely sliced

4 tablespoons plain flour, plus extra for dusting

2 teaspoons mustard powder

200ml fish stock

350ml double cream

salt and freshly ground black pepper

200g baby spinach, picked

zest and juice of 1 lemon

4 tablespoons chopped dill

750g puff pastry

4 x 125g salmon (or other fish) fillets, skinned

225g raw tiger or large prawns, peeled

2 egg yolks, beaten

Preheat the oven to 190°C/gas 5. Melt the butter in a large pan and sauté the onion for 4–5 minutes to soften. Add the leek and cook for 2 minutes. Stirring all the time, add the flour and mustard powder and cook for 1 minute. Add the stock and allow this to reduce by half. Add the cream, reduce the heat and cook for 6–8 minutes until the sauce has thickened. Season well, stir in the spinach and cook until the sauce becomes thick and creamy. Remove from the heat and cool, then stir in the lemon zest and juice and chopped dill.

Cut the pastry in half and roll each half out on a floured surface to a rectangle, one approximately 20cm x 32cm and 0.5cm thick and the other slightly larger and thinner. Cut the salmon into 2cm chunks, season well and add to the sauce with the prawns. Mix well to coat. Lay the thicker pastry rectangle on a non-stick baking sheet, then spoon the mixture down the centre, piling it up high. Mix the beaten egg yolks with a little water to make an egg wash and brush the edges of the pastry with it. Place the other piece of pastry on top, trimming and crimping the edges to make a 'pillow'. Use leftover pastry to decorate the top. Brush all over with the rest of the egg wash and bake in the preheated oven for 25–30 minutes. Remove from the oven and allow to stand for a few minutes before slicing.

 White Burgundy or good-quality New World Chardonnay.

STUFFED ROAST LAMB

Throughout Europe there is a tradition of eating the new season's lamb at Easter. The stuffing is really tasty, but give yourself enough time to carefully tie up the lamb to create a neat parcel. If you are roasting lamb on the bone (see timings opposite), roll the stuffing into small balls and bake on a greased baking sheet for 30–35 minutes until crisp and golden.

SERVES 8–12

For the stuffing
150g dried apricots, finely chopped
150g prunes, finely chopped
200g white breadcrumbs
zest and juice of 2 oranges
4 garlic cloves, peeled and finely chopped
8 tablespoons chopped flat-leaf parsley
1 egg, beaten
salt and freshly ground black pepper

For the lamb
2 x 1.5kg legs of spring lamb, deboned (boneless weight)
4 tablespoons olive oil
2 garlic bulbs, cut in half horizontally
8 sprigs of rosemary

For the gravy
4 tablespoons plain flour
1 litre lamb stock
400ml red wine
4 tablespoons redcurrant jelly
salt and freshly ground black pepper

Preheat the oven to 200°C/gas 6. To make the stuffing, mix the apricots, prunes, breadcrumbs, orange zest and juice, garlic and parsley together in a large bowl with the beaten egg to combine. Season well with salt and pepper.

Lay the lamb legs out on a chopping board, skin side down; season, and place the stuffing down the middle of each. Roll up the lamb, tying in four to six places on each leg using butcher's string. Heat the oil in a large roasting tin and, once hot, add both legs and brown all over until nicely golden. Roast in the oven for approximately 1 hour 20 minutes until pink. After 15 minutes of cooking, add the halved garlic bulbs and the rosemary sprigs to the tin. Continue to roast for the remaining cooking time. Remove from the oven, transfer the lamb to plates and cover with foil. Let the meat rest for at least 20 minutes.

For the gravy, heat the meat juices in the roasting tin over a high heat. Whisk in the flour to combine, and cook for one minute, then gradually pour in the stock and wine, whisking constantly. Bring to the boil, then reduce the heat and allow to simmer and reduce for 8–10 minutes, or until thickened. Stir in the redcurrant jelly and season to taste. Strain the gravy into a small pan and warm it to serve.

Carve the lamb and arrange on serving plates. Serve with the gravy, asparagus and spring greens and potato dauphinoise (page 257).

 A velvety rich red wine, such as Ribero del Duero or Claret.

ROAST LAMB ON THE BONE *Calculate the roasting time for lamb on the bone at 30 minutes per 450g. For pink lamb, reduce the overall cooking time by 30 minutes. Check and baste the meat frequently and adjust the timings for your particular oven.*

POTATO DAUPHINOISE Serves 8

A rich and indulgent potato dish that can be made up to a day in advance and which goes well with any roast, particularly lamb. Peel and slice the potatoes ahead of time and keep fresh in cold water to prevent them going brown — just pat dry before using them.

Preheat the oven to 180°C/gas 4. Grease a 30cm x 20cm baking dish with a little butter. Heat 30g butter in a large non-stick frying pan over a medium heat. Place 2 medium peeled and finely sliced onions in the pan and cook for 6–8 minutes until soft but not coloured. Add 3 cloves of peeled and finely chopped garlic and cook for a further 1–2 minutes. Season with salt and freshly ground black pepper and turn off the heat.

Peel and finely slice 1kg Maris Piper or King Edward potatoes, preferably using a mandoline or a thin slicer fitting in a food processor. Layer the potatoes in the dish, overlapping slightly. Scatter a small amount of the cooked onion mixture between each layer and season well. Repeat until all the potato slices have been used up. Place the dish on a baking sheet.

Place 225ml milk and 350ml double cream or crème fraîche in a pan over a low heat and bring to a simmer. Pour the liquid over the potatoes — it should come just to the base of the top layer of potato. Bake for 1 hour, sprinkling 30g grated Gruyère, Parmesan or Cheddar cheese over the top for the final 15 minutes. Remove from the oven and let it stand for a few minutes before serving straight from the dish, or use a round chef's ring to stamp out elegant individual portions.

ASPARAGUS AND SPRING GREENS Serves 8

You can serve these together or separately, adding Parmesan shavings and a drizzle of good-quality olive oil to the asparagus (a platter of these work well as spring canapés with Hollandaise sauce as a dip).

Steam 1kg spring greens and 600g asparagus for 2–3 minutes until soft, or alternatively fry in a pan with 1 tablespoon oil for a few minutes. Add 50ml water and a knob of butter and simmer gently with the lid on for 2–3 minutes. Season well before serving.

PETER RABBIT LETTUCE AND PEAS Serves 8

These are delicious with the salmon on page 253 and can be made using either fresh or frozen peas.

Melt 30g unsalted butter in a pan and add 1 peeled and finely chopped small onion. Soften over a low heat for 4–5 minutes. Increase the heat, then stir in 400g garden peas or petits pois and the finely shredded leaves of 2 little gem lettuces, and sauté for 2 minutes. Add 100ml chicken stock and allow to reduce by half. Pour in 75ml double cream and season well.

EASTER TRIFLE

This is an Easter twist on the classic version. Using toasted hot cross buns as a base gives this trifle a beautifully intense flavour, but to guard against them becoming soggy, the trifle should be assembled no more than 1 hour before serving. If you need to make this in advance, use 8 normal trifle sponges instead. You could use a small toasted panettone as the base for a Christmas trifle.

SERVES 8

4 hot cross buns, halved, toasted and cut into bite-sized cubes

9 tablespoons dry sherry

2 x 298g tins of mandarin segments, drained

1 x 135g packet of orange jelly, made and set in advance, according to packet instructions

500ml good-quality thick vanilla custard

600ml double cream

50g icing sugar, sifted

4 tablespoons flaked almonds, toasted

2 tablespoons mini eggs

Arrange the hot-cross-bun pieces in the base of a large trifle dish and drizzle over 3 tablespoons sherry. Scatter the mandarin segments on top. Cut the orange jelly into thin slices or cubes and arrange on top of the fruit. Pour the custard over and place in the fridge for 1 hour.

Whip the cream, icing sugar and the rest of the sherry (to taste) in a large bowl until you have soft peaks and the cream just about holds its shape. Spoon the cream on top of the custard, making sure it reaches the edges of the bowl, and finish it with attractive peaks on the top using the back of the spoon. Scatter with the flaked almonds and mini eggs to serve.

 An Italian slightly sparkling dessert wine, such as Moscato d'Asti.

HOT CROSS BUNS

Hot cross buns!
Hot cross buns!
One a penny, two a penny,
Hot cross buns!

If you have no daughters
Give them to your sons
One a penny, two a penny,
Hot cross buns!

English nursery rhyme, c.1798

Hot cross buns are typically eaten on Good Friday and are marked on top with a cross, either cut in the dough or composed of strips of pastry. They can be toasted over an open fire with a long fork (or these days, under the grill). Many cultures have a similar tradition of preparing Easter bread or sweet cakes studded with raisins, honey and other dried fruits — these are often beautifully shaped into rings or even plaited.

ACTIVITIES AND GAMES

With Easter so often a family affair, play these games with both grown-ups and children. As well as the ceremonial and all-important egg hunt, there are plenty of other egg-inspired games to get everyone involved in, or you could play a seasonal twist on pin the tail on the donkey (page 315) by pinning a tail on the Easter Bunny instead. Mix up the teams, putting enthusiastic younger players with their more measured elders – the different age groups will bring their own skills and dynamics. For prizes, award bags of bunny biscuits (page 245) or cheaper branded eggs. They can be made to look more appealing by wrapping them in pastel tissue paper, tied with a spring-coloured ribbon.

EASTER EGG HUNT

The traditional Easter egg hunt is one of the simplest but most enjoyable Easter games. This is one of those precious activities that is part game, part ritual. It's hugely enjoyable for a large gathering and can be played almost anywhere. For young children, keep it fairly simple. An adult hides a selection of eggs (they should be low down within easy reach of the children). I recommend using small eggs or painted hard-boiled ones that can be exchanged for chocolate ones at the end of the game. That way, your young players won't be too distracted by eating their eggs during the hunt, and you can make sure that everyone gets a fair share of the goodies once the game has finished. For older children, you can make the eggs harder to find and give clues to help them track them down – picture clues are good. For instance: take a photo on your phone of the kind of flower or shrub that the eggs are near. Show the picture to the children and then send them off to find the eggs. Written clues for older players can be as complicated or subtle as you like. I know some families who devise clues that form part of a crossword and others who compose poems. Most people, though, are happy to make up something more straightforward, such as 'What rhymes with bath?' for looking on a path. It is almost as much fun composing the clues as it is going on the hunt.

EGG TAPPING OR EGG JARPING

This is a simple and traditional Easter game along the lines of a conker tournament. Players split into pairs. Each player holds a hard-boiled egg and attempts to tap and break their opponent's egg without their own breaking. The winner then moves on to play the winner from another pair. The overall winner is the player who succeeds in cracking the greatest number of eggs while keeping their own egg untarnished.

EGG AND SPOON RACE

This is an old Easter favourite – and if there's a crowd of you, introduce some team spirit and organise a relay race. Everyone is given a spoon and players are split into teams, arranging themselves in single file behind a starting line. Opposite each team is a flag (a stick with a handkerchief tied to it will do fine) stuck into the ground. The first person in each line places an egg on their spoon. On 'Go!' they must move as quickly as they can around their flag and back again, without letting their egg fall. Once they have made it back to the starting line, they must transfer their egg to the next player's spoon. If at any point an egg is dropped or anyone is caught holding the egg in place with their hands, the player responsible must head back to the beginning and start their leg of the race again. The first team to have all their players back home wins. It's fun to play this with raw eggs but it depends on how much mess you are willing to put up with – hard-boiled eggs work just as well. Or try making it harder – ask everyone to hold the spoons in their mouths instead of their hands.

EGG TOSS

Players split into pairs. Each pair receives a fresh egg. To start, partners stand 2m away from each other (but reduce the distance for children as appropriate). Across this distance, one player throws their egg gently, to be caught by the other. If it breaks or touches the ground, the pair goes out. Pairs who manage to throw and catch their egg successfully then take a few steps further away from each other. The person who caught the egg last time round becomes the thrower for this round, and so on. The game continues, with partners moving further and further apart after each throw and catch. The team that manages to keep their egg intact for longest, successfully tossing it across the greatest distance, wins the game.

*There are few hours in life more agreeable
than the hour dedicated to the ceremony
known as afternoon tea.*

The Portrait of a Lady, Henry James

AFTERNOON TEA

There is something very British about tea. This ritual has prevailed for centuries, and even today there is still great enthusiasm for indulging in all the ceremony and pomp that goes with it. Afternoon tea is wonderfully versatile: it might be enjoyed early or late, as a quick cuppa, with a biscuit or two, as a hearty, warming high tea, or as a more formal cream tea with a batch of scones and thick yellow clotted cream. It can be shared with grandparents and favourite great aunts in the garden at home or wolfed down alone in the kitchen after a wet and muddy day outside, with a thick doorstep of bread and hot crumpets dripping with butter. Tea can also be a celebratory event; it's an increasingly popular way to commemorate birthdays, baby showers and even hen parties. Whichever way you have it, it always feels like a treat, and a nostalgic, British one at that.

Teatime is an experience most of us remember fondly from our childhoods. One of my most treasured associations with it is in the form of our school match teas. Eaten at half-time or after a sports game, it was welcome refreshment for players and spectators alike. It always tasted much better after a sporting success! Tea and cake seem sweeter when you've done the exercise to earn them.

Afternoon tea developed in the late 1800s as a small extra meal to fill the gap between lunch and dinner, one that continued to widen as people took their evening meal ever later in the day. Nowadays, changes in our social customs and working hours mean that most of us rarely take a proper, ceremonial afternoon tea, which makes it all the more special if you decide to make an occasion of it. A lazy summer day is the perfect time for this celebration: as the afternoon stretches before you, there is nothing more glorious than sharing a full teatime spread complete with pots of tea and dainty confections arranged next to a variety of finger sandwiches made with cotton-soft bread.

Afternoon tea certainly makes for a less stressful form of entertaining than lunch or dinner – you can easily set up a spread at home or in the garden, and everything can be baked in good time, and stored well or frozen undecorated days before. Then you can sit back and enjoy the company, letting the late afternoon drift by in a leisurely fashion, and relax to the sound of spoons tinkling against china cups and saucers. How civilised!

AFTERNOON TEA CRAFTS

A few homemade and inexpensive crafts can make all the difference to your teatime spread and will bring a personal touch. Make quick invitations and pretty envelopes, and get a creative friend to help design some labels and make vintage-style cake stands and bunting which can be reused throughout the year.

BROWN-PAPER TAGS

For a 'bring your own bake' tea party, send guests a couple of plain tags in decorative envelopes and ask them to personalise their produce. These are also useful for labelling foods on a buffet table or as gift tags.

1: Buy a selection of plain paper tags. 2: Using pens, watercolour paints and ink stamps, illustrate them with your own designs. 3: Thread some string through the hole and secure with a knot.

DECORATIVE ENVELOPES AND INVITATIONS

A creative way to decorate plain envelopes and cards. Use a calligraphy pen or fine paintbrush to write details.

1: To make your own lined envelopes, unfold a standard envelope. 2: Use it as a template to cut out your chosen paper, such as pretty drawer liner or wrapping paper. 3: Line the insides and reseal with glue stick. 4: For decorative invitations use a selection of watercolours on cards and illustrate with tea-themed symbols. Use a craft punch to cut pretty shapes.

HOMEMADE BUNTING

Make vintage-look bunting using leftover fabric scraps. It's useful decoration for all celebratory occasions.

1: Make a triangle template out of card. 2: Place the template on to cotton fabric and cut around it with pinking shears. Repeat as required. 3: Sew the triangles on to the back of a ribbon, pattern side out. Leave 25cm at both ends to tie around a pole or branch.

CAKE STANDS

This is a fun way to make your own mismatched cake stands. Handle carefully, as these are very fragile.

1: Using a large plate as the base of the stand, stick down a glass or teacup in the centre using epoxy glue (available in hardware shops). 2: Continue the sequence for as many layers as desired, using smaller plates as you go along and finishing with either a plate or a cup. 3: Leave to dry in a safe place for 24 hours before use. Clean with care, using a damp cloth.

SETTING THE TEA TABLE

Decide whether you are going to have a buffet-style spread laid out on a table so that your guests will be helping themselves, or whether you're after a smaller, more intimate affair with beautifully set places at a table. Cover tables with delicate floral

or pastel coloured tablecloths. Use small side plates and little napkins (pretty paper cocktail ones are easy) with mismatched china — you can seek out interesting crockery at antique or charity shops to create a tea set. Add comfort to wrought-iron chairs with pretty cushions and drape sweeping bunting as a celebratory backdrop. Old-fashioned birdcages can be found at garden centres or antique shops and work well as features on a central table. Weave ivy through the bars of the cage and fill it with a bunch of mixed flowers, such as roses, stocks, peonies and sweet peas. Old tea caddies look authentic as 'aged' vases to hold extra flowers, and stack teaspoons, which can easily be overlooked, in jam jars decorated with ribbons.

AFTERNOON TEA MENU

Teas and infusions

One or two pots of classic teas (page 270)
A selection of herbal or fruit teas
Lemon and mint iced tea (page 271)

Finger sandwiches

Allow one round per person, with two
or three different fillings (page 273)

Bite-size fancies

Allow a couple per person:
Nutella madeleines (page 281),
mini fruit tarts (page 274), or macaroons

Traditional scones

Allow one per person (page 274):
serve with jam and clotted cream

Whole cakes

Offer two varieties:
carrot and walnut cake (page 277),
coffee cake (page 278), Victoria sponge
(page 273), lemon drizzle loaf (page 274)

Fresh fruit

Bowls of cherries or berries, or glasses
of sparkling fruit jellies (page 173)

A TIME FOR TEA

Tea is the second most popular drink in the world, after water. In the eighteenth century it was so popular that supply couldn't meet demand and it also carried a heavy import duty, which many people couldn't afford. As a result it was bulked out with substitutions, such as leaves from various native trees, as well as other things like used tea leaves. It's easy to see why tea was so admired: it's endlessly varied, with a remarkable array of subtly different flavours. Earl Grey, with its delicate and fragrant aroma, is a favourite afternoon tea in the Western world — its sales far outstrip any other tea variety. It makes for a refreshing, light summer tea, although in the winter I enjoy a good English Breakfast tea.

At a proper tea party, the tea bags should go in a teapot, rather than individually in mugs. That said, it can be fun for guests to choose their own flavoured tea bag from a range of several types set out in baskets or tea chests. Loose-leaf tea in pots makes for excellent, fuller and fresher flavoured tea, and it can be fun to experiment with different varieties, but on a larger scale it might be less practical and not everyone (except for connoisseurs, like my tea-loving brother) will appreciate the difference.

Fresh herbal and flower-based teas are cleansing, elegant and look great in clear glass teapots (jasmine tea with dried flowers looks pretty as the flowers unfurl). Serve a refreshing, chilled iced tea in the warm summer months from teapots filled with ice (great for children). Cocktails poured into tea cups and served with saucers are a fun idea for a hen party or baby shower.

TEAS TO TRY

- *Fragrant tea (such as Earl Grey or Lady Grey).*

- *Lapsang Souchong (its smoky and refreshing flavour is an acquired taste — a favourite of my father); mix with English Breakfast for a more subtle flavour.*

- *Black tea with or without milk (try Darjeeling, Assam or Ceylon); offer slices of lemon, or sugar or honey to sweeten.*

- *Fruit or flower-based tea (such as lemon and ginger, berries, jasmine or rose); try adding slices of lemon studded with cloves.*

- *Herbal tea (both dried teas and infusions of fresh mint, ginger slices or rooibos/redbush tea are popular).*

- *Green tea (plain or a flavoured variety).*

LEMON AND MINT ICED TEA Serves 4

Place 1 litre water, the juice of 2 lemons, 4 tablespoons caster sugar and a handful of mint leaves in a large pan and bring to the boil. Turn off the heat and add 3 lemon and ginger tea bags to the liquid. Let the tea bags infuse for 10 minutes. Strain the liquid into a large jug and allow to cool completely. Divide crushed or cubed ice between 4 serving glasses and pour the cold tea mixture over. Garnish each glass with a sprig of mint and half a slice of lemon.

TEATIME CLASSICS

A celebratory afternoon tea calls for plump rounds of springy cakes iced high and fanciful tarts filled to the brim. Choose a variety of sweet treats of differing shapes, textures and flavours, both homebaked and shop-bought. Display finger sandwiches, scones and delicate individual bites, such as madeleines, retro Bakewell tarts or fondant fancies on tiered stands, and plate up cakes to complement their icing and decorations on simple-stemmed pastel, white and glass stands. Colourful paper doilies will lift plain white plates. If setting up a buffet table, arrange one end for food, with the tea service, crockery and cutlery at the other end. Have plenty of cake knives to cut slices, small plates with forks for stickier cakes, sugar bowls filled with cubed or shaped sugar and milk jugs. And don't underestimate the number of pots of tea required. You can buy giant tea pots that serve 8–12 people, or just make sure that you have extra pots of boiling water to top up as required.

FINGER SANDWICHES

An essential savoury addition to a teatime spread. Remove the crusts using a large chef's knife and cut them into fingers or triangles with a single up-and-down cutting motion to create plump-looking sandwiches. Thinly sliced cucumber is a classic filling, or try the fillings in the box. Cover them with a damp tea towel or kitchen towel to keep them from drying out, or wrap them tightly in clingfilm.

TIP: *Make sandwich flags, so that guests can see fillings at a glance. Cut pretty paper and card into 6cm x 2cm strips. Cover the card strip with glue stick and attach a cocktail stick to one end, then stick the paper strip over the top to cover it. When dry, cut out a 'v'-shape to make a flag, and write on the sandwich filling.*

FILLINGS

- *Homemade egg mayonnaise with cress.*
- *Mature Cheddar with homemade marrow chutney (page 404).*
- *Chicken, avocado and watercress.*
- *Baked ham (page 154) with salad.*
- *Brie, ripe tomato and basil.*
- *Smoked salmon, cream cheese and rocket.*
- *Prawn mayonnaise.*
- *Smoked trout pâté (page 142), cucumber and lambs lettuce.*

VICTORIA SPONGE Serves 8–10

An all-time classic sponge cake, and quintessentially British. Grease and line two round 20cm tins with baking parchment. Evenly divide the basic sponge mixture on page 311 between them. Bake in a preheated oven for 35 minutes at 180°C/gas 4, then cool on a wire rack. Fill with jam (page 403) and cream, buttercream (page 311) and fresh berries, or whatever takes your fancy. Decorate the top with sifted icing sugar.

MINI FRUIT TARTS Makes 24

Fill 24 mini ready-made shortcrust pastry tart cases with simple fruit jams (page 403) or lemon curd, and bake on a lined tray at 180°C/gas 4 for 6–8 minutes until the filling melts. Leave to cool. As an alternative, you could also fill with thick shop-bought vanilla custard or sweetened cream topped with ripe fresh fruit and glaze with warmed apricot jam.

TIP: *To make sweetened cream, whisk 150ml double cream with 1 tablespoon sifted icing sugar and ½ teaspoon vanilla extract until it forms soft peaks. Add more sugar to taste. Makes enough for 24 mini pastry cases.*

LEMON DRIZZLE LOAF Serves 8–10

Grease and line a 900g loaf tin. Preheat the oven to 165°C/gas 3. In a bowl, cream 175g softened, unsalted butter and 175g caster sugar together until light and fluffy. Gradually beat 3 medium eggs into the mixture one at a time. Carefully fold in 100g self-raising flour, 100g ground almonds, 3 tablespoons milk, the zest of 2 lemons and 1 teaspoon vanilla extract using a large metal spoon. Pour the batter into the tin and level the surface with a palette knife. Bake in the centre of the oven for 45–50 minutes until firm and a skewer comes out clean. Let the cake stand in the tin for 5 minutes before turning out on to a wire rack. In a bowl, mix together the juice of 2 lemons and 50g caster sugar until combined. Prick the warm cake all over with a fork and brush the mixture over it. For a thick lemon icing, beat 200g icing sugar with the juice of ½ a lemon and 1 tablespoon water. Spread over the cake. Garnish with candied lemon peel.

TIP: *For candied lemon peel, add the zest of 2 lemons in strips to a small saucepan with 150ml water and 100g caster sugar. Bring to the boil, simmer for 10 minutes until the peel is translucent and crinkles at the edge, and drain.*

TRADITIONAL SCONES Makes 12

Preheat the oven to 200°C/gas 6. In a bowl, mix together 225g self-raising flour and a pinch of salt, and rub in 40g unsalted butter, cut into cubes. Stir in 2 tablespoons caster sugar, then slowly add 50ml milk and 70ml water until you have a soft dough. Turn the dough out on to a floured work surface and bring together gently with your hands; to ensure a light scone do not overwork. Pat out the dough to 2cm thickness and, using a 5cm cutter, stamp out rounds and place them on a baking sheet. Repeat until you have used up all the dough. Brush the tops with beaten egg yolk, sprinkle with demerara sugar and bake for 15 minutes until well risen and golden. Serve with jam (page 403) and clotted cream.

> MACAROONS *Add a touch of Parisian chic to the table and offer macaroons in an assortment of sizes and gem-like colours. They are quite a fiddle to make so I'd recommend buying them from a good bakery. Experiment with different flavours; their vivid shades will really vamp up the tea spread.*

CARROT AND WALNUT CAKE

Decadent and moist, this cake is best eaten from a plate with a fork, as it can get quite gooey using your fingers. A glass or net food cover can be useful to protect sticky cakes like this from flies.

SERVES 8–10

250ml vegetable oil

175g light brown sugar

3 medium eggs

175g self-raising flour

1 teaspoon baking powder

a good pinch of nutmeg

a good pinch of cinnamon

a good pinch of ground ginger

a small pinch of salt

115g walnuts, roughly chopped

50g raisins, soaked in water and drained

225g carrots, grated

For the cream-cheese icing

25g unsalted butter, softened

150g icing sugar

300g cream cheese

75g whole walnuts

Grease and line two 20cm round cake tins with baking parchment. Preheat the oven to 170°C/gas 3.

Beat the oil and sugar together until combined, then add the eggs and mix well. Sift in the flour, baking powder, spices and salt, then add the walnuts, raisins and carrots and beat well.

Divide the batter between the tins. Bake for 25–30 minutes until the cakes are well risen and spring back when lightly touched. Transfer to a wire rack to cool completely.

To make the icing, beat the butter and icing sugar together until light and fluffy then mix in the cream cheese. Thickly spread half the icing on one of the cake layers, sandwich the two together and spread the remaining icing on top. Place the whole walnuts on top of the cake before serving.

TIPS : *There is always cake left over at tea parties. Cakes and biscuits do store well for up to 5 days (if kept in a cool, dry place) so you can keep any untouched slices in airtight cake tins or plastic containers. Alternatively, buy a selection of cake boxes and send guests home with the leftovers. • You can freeze the cooled cakes before the icing stage for up to 1 month. Defrost fully and ice as above.*

 CUPCAKES *To make cupcake versions, grease and line 2 bun tins with 16 paper cases and divide the mixture between each. Bake for 18–20 minutes.*

COFFEE CAKE

One of my favourite cakes; the rich, deep flavour of the coffee sponge makes a slice perfectly satisfying. This cake is a lovely contrast to lighter-coloured sponge cakes on a tea table.

SERVES 8–10

120g caster sugar

240ml golden syrup

170g unsalted butter

2 tablespoons instant coffee powder or granules

2 large eggs

30ml milk

240g self-raising flour, sifted

1 teaspoon baking powder

For the buttercream icing

100g unsalted butter, softened

200g icing sugar

3 teaspoons coffee essence (such as Camp)

cocoa powder

chocolate-coated coffee beans

Preheat the oven to 180°C/gas 4. Grease and line a 20cm round cake tin with baking parchment.

Melt the sugar and syrup in a pan, together with the butter, over a gentle heat. Stir in the instant coffee until dissolved.

Allow to cool completely (you could put the pan into a large bowl of ice-cold water to speed this process up), then gradually stir in the eggs and milk.

Pour this mixture with the sifted flour and baking powder into a large bowl. Beat until smooth, then pour into the tin and bake for 30–35 minutes, until well risen and the cake springs back when lightly touched. Transfer to a wire rack to cool completely.

For the buttercream icing, mix together the butter and icing sugar in a bowl, then stir in the coffee essence. Spread the icing over the cooled cake, dust with sifted cocoa powder and decorate with chocolate-coated coffee beans.

CHOCOLATE-COATED COFFEE BEANS *Line a tray with baking parchment. Melt 100g dark or milk chocolate in a bowl over a medium heat. Add 50g roasted coffee beans and stir to coat. Turn out on to the tray and leave to cool, dusting with cocoa powder, if required, just before the chocolate has set.*

NUTELLA MADELEINES

These are irresistible to both adults and children and so easy to make. Nutella isn't just for spreading on toast! You can also try using white or plain chocolate spread instead.

MAKES 24

75g unsalted butter, melted and cooled slightly, plus extra for greasing

2 tablespoons plain flour, for dusting

75g caster sugar

3 medium eggs

1 teaspoon vanilla extract

60g self-raising flour

15g good-quality cocoa powder

For the topping

125g Nutella

60g icing sugar

30g hazelnuts, toasted and chopped

Preheat the oven to 180°C/gas 4. Brush two madeleine tins with melted butter. Dust with plain flour, invert the tins and tap out the excess.

Place the sugar, eggs and vanilla extract in a large bowl and whisk together for at least 5 minutes or until pale, thick and able to hold a trail on the surface. Carefully sift the self-raising flour and cocoa powder over the mixture, then fold in with a large metal spoon. Pour the melted butter down the edge of the bowl and fold it in quickly and gently.

Spoon 1 tablespoon of the mix into each of the madeleine moulds. Bake for 10 minutes. Remove from the oven, transfer to a wire rack using a palette knife and leave to cool completely.

To make the topping, mix together the Nutella, icing sugar and a touch of hot water to loosen the mixture slightly. Spread over the tops of the madeleines, and sprinkle over the chopped hazelnuts to serve.

TIPS : *If you are worried about those with nut allergies, supermarkets stock nut-free chocolate spreads. Check the label for nut content.*
• To make plain madeleines, leave out the cocoa powder from the recipe above and increase the flour to 75g. Add the finely grated zest of ½ a lemon, and bake as directed. Dust with a little icing sugar before serving.
• The sponges will freeze un-iced for up to 1 month.

FABULOUS FLOWERS

Flowers add the finishing touch to any celebration. You don't need to spend a lot on elaborate arrangements — even a bunch of fresh herbs or a few stems picked from the garden in a small glass jar, pottery pitcher or vintage tin can look good.

SIMPLE FLOWER ARRANGEMENTS

There's no 'right' way to arrange flowers, but the following steps give a few basic tips for displaying flowers in a vase or as a more formal arrangement; adapt to suit the occasion and your personal taste.

VASE ARRANGEMENTS:

1: Choose your vase according to the flowers you are working with — tall fluted or convex vases for long stems, square or globe vases for shorter arrangements. Fill with clean water and flower food. 2: Begin by adding a mix of greenery. The foliage will act as a base to support your blooms. Place your flowers in between. 3: For a large vase arrangement with tall flowers, place crumpled chicken wire into the bottom of the vase and use it as a support, placing the stems into the holes in the wire to stop them from moving.

FORMAL ARRANGEMENTS OR TABLE CENTREPIECES:

1: Cut florists' foam to fit your container and soak it in water. 2: Secure the foam to the container with pot tape and begin to create the shape of your arrangement using foliage or aromatic herbs. Start with the largest and longest pieces of foliage in the centre, and work outwards. 3: Intersperse the foliage with flowers, starting with the largest, and finishing with the more delicate flowers for texture.

TIP: *If arranging long stems, such as amaryllis, use a garden cane (and ties) to support the weight of the flowers.*

TABLE ARRANGEMENT DOS AND DON'TS

- Do use ordinary jars or jugs for flowers if you've run out of vases.

- Do choose round globe vases, which are low and can be filled with a little water and a few flowerheads, such as hydrangeas, or decorated by wrapping calla lillies and grass stems around the insides.

- Do form clusters or rows of potted flowers or bud vases to suit the size of your table.

- Don't use strongly scented flowers on a dining table.

- Don't clutter the table or interfere with the eyeline — ensure tall arrangements sit above eye level, or move them aside when guests are seated.

- Don't leave the stamens on lilies as they will stain furniture, tablecloths and clothes: pull them off with your fingers.

CUT-FLOWER CARE

Make your flowers last longer with these simple tips:

- Cut flowers or herbs in the morning or evening, when they are holding water, rather than in the heat of the day.

- When buying flowers, choose ones that are not yet in full bloom. If using flowers from the garden, to avoid them wilting, condition them prior to use by stripping the stems of leaves, cutting the stems at an angle and giving them a good drink. This is especially important if putting them into a florist's foam arrangement.

- If you receive a hand-tied bouquet as a gift, it will stay fresh until you're ready to put it into a vase. Carefully remove the packaging and re-cut the stems about 3cm up at an angle, before putting into a vase filled with fresh lukewarm water. You don't need to untie the bouquet unless you want to rearrange the flowers or split them up. Do snip off any leaves and foliage below the water line.

- Flowers will last much longer if you use flower-food sachets (usually supplied with bouquets), make sure the vase is clean and change the water every couple of days. Re-cut the stems every few days and remove any dying flowers.

- Keep vases of flowers out of direct sunlight and away from ripening fruit, in a cool, well-ventilated place.

- If flowers, such as hydrangeas or roses, wilt, re-cut the stems and submerge them in deep water up to the base of the flowerheads to revive them.

- For flowers arranged in florists' foam, water the foam every couple of days to keep it from drying out.

WORKING WITH THE SEASONS

All kinds of imported flowers are available year-round, but the cheapest and greenest option is to go for seasonal, locally grown flowers and plants:

- **All year:** alstroemeria, carnations, freesia, gerbera, gypsophilia, lilies, roses.

- **Spring:** anemones, blossom (such as cherry blossom), bluebells, daffodils, forget-me-nots, hyacinths, primroses, pussy willow, tulips.

- **Summer:** alchemilla mollis (lady's mantle), cornflowers, daisies, delphiniums, elderflowers, herbs, hydrangeas, lavender, lilac, peonies, stocks, sunflowers, sweetpeas.

- **Autumn:** calla lilies, dahlia, delphiniums, gladioli, hydrangeas, phlox.

- **Winter:** amaryllis, bulbs, cyclamen, evergreens, holly, ivy, mistletoe, poinsettia.

DRYING AND PRESSING FLOWERS

Dried flowers, particularly lavender, are lovely for making scented bags as gifts (page 179) or as 'confetti' for scattering along tables (but you can buy biodegradable dried-flower confetti packs if you don't have the time or patience to make your own). Pressed flowers look lovely stuck on cards or on the outside of pillar candles. For enthusiasts, a flower press makes a lovely present.

To dry flowers, pick them in the heat of a dry day, strip the stems of their leaves and hang them upside down in small bunches secured with a rubber band in an airy, dark place. Leave them for about a fortnight. Some flowers, like hydrangeas, need to be dried upright in about 2cm of water.

To press flowers, place them between sheets of absorbent paper inside a heavy book, and weigh it down with a stack of other books. Leave for a few weeks.

MEANINGFUL BLOOMS

- Freesias: lasting friendship.
- Pansies: 'think of me'.
- Gypsophila: everlasting love.
- Lilies: majesty and great beauty.
- Ranunculus: radiant with charms.
- Snowdrops: lift the spirits, bringing hope and consolation.
- Orchids: refined beauty, elegance and grace.
- Roses: the stronger the affection, the deeper the colour; white roses for a heart unacquainted with love, pink for grace and red for a full emblem of love.
- Carnations: a pink carnation for pure love, a red carnation for an avowal of love and a white carnation as an affectionate gesture.
- Myrtle: this fragrant shrub with delicate white flowers symbolises love.

FLORIST'S TOOLKIT

- *Floristry scissors/shears.*
- *Assortment of vases, both tall and short (tank, fluted, convex, column, globe and bud vases) in glass and china.*
- *Enamel jugs, terracotta pots, metal buckets, old decanters and jam jars.*
- *Florists' foam and floristry wire.*
- *Fine gravel to weigh pots and vases down.*

EDIBLE FLOWERS

Here are a few decorative ways to use flowers in food. It's important to identify them correctly, and use only unsprayed flowers.

- **Salads and garnishes:** nasturtiums or dandelions add a splash of fresh colour.

- **Ice cubes:** when borage is in flower, freeze the pretty blue blossoms in ice cubes. These are amazing with Pimm's. Primrose heads are wonderful in spring-time cocktails (page 250).

- **Cake decorations:** crystallised flowers and leaves, such as violets, primroses, cowslips and mint, are easy to make and are fabulous for decorating cakes or garnishing drinks. If using rose petals, remove the white part as it is bitter.

MAKING CRYSTALLISED FLOWERS OR LEAVES

Brush each petal or leaf carefully with lightly whisked egg white and dip gently into a dish of caster sugar. Shake off the excess sugar and dry on a wire rack in a warm place for a few hours or overnight, until the petal or leaf has hardened.

GARDEN SHED MUST-HAVES

Keep these items handy when you're entertaining outdoors.

- *Plastic sheeting for a slip and slide, waterpistols and sprinklers.*

- *Wheelbarrow (to chill drinks in).*

- *Gazebo, tent and hammock.*

- *Fold-away chairs and trestle tables.*

- *Firepits, braziers and firelighters.*

- *Garden torches, storm lanterns, citronella candles.*

- *Kite, Frisbee, sun canopy and beach kit.*

- *Hessian cloth and table clips for outdoor dining tables.*

- *Wooden crates, buckets and bamboo sticks.*

- *Croquet, badminton and boules sets.*

- *Cricket and rounders bats and stumps.*

- *Balls: football, rugby and tennis.*

- *Giant games: Jenga, pick-up sticks and Connect Four.*

- *Cones for party games.*

SUMMER

CHILDREN'S PARTIES
BARBECUES
PICNICS
CAMPING

Days stretch long into violet dusks where swallows dip and swoop. Borders of sweet-scented flowers buzz with industrious bees and butterflies flutter. Outside lawnmowers hum and smoky barbecues sizzle. People gather together, soaking up the sun or cooling off in dappled shade. A distant roll of thunder echoes through the muggy, heat-charged afternoon — a close promise of rain. It clears and turns into a balmy, pink-skied evening.

'We do not stop playing because we grow old,
we grow old because we stop playing.'

Benjamin Franklin

CHILDREN'S PARTIES

This chapter is all about creating a colourful children's party that is fun, achievable and traditional. The key to any successful party is not how much you spend on it, but that you approach it creatively and thoughtfully – making it special and magical for your children and their friends. Some of my fondest childhood memories are of birthday parties at home or at friends' houses, playing all our favourite games (many of which are included here, and all of them are very easy), enjoying party treats . . . and, of course, judging the greatness of the event by the size of the birthday cake and the contents of the party bags. I used to love helping Mum prepare for my birthdays at home: writing the invitations, helping fill the party bags the day before and blowing up balloons to decorate the house. Choosing a favourite dress to wear and being involved in the decisions and the preparations was all part of the excitement – rather like the anticipation I felt in the build-up to Christmas.

What should always be at the forefront of your mind while you're planning a celebration like this is that children's birthday parties should be happy occasions, full of fun and enjoyment, with the children at the centre of it – and that you're not doing this, as can often be the case, to impress other mums or dads. Birthdays are really important to little ones; I recall being so excited about being a whole year older and having a day to revel in things I wouldn't normally be allowed to do or eat. This is not to say that every birthday party should be an expensive extravaganza. You can still organise a successful party at home or in a nearby venue affordably and simply, even if it means getting a friend to help you. Doing things within your means and to a budget can bring an immense sense of satisfaction. You may even decide that you want to dedicate the majority of your budget to an entertainer who can generate a few seamless hours of amusement and games to keep the children happily occupied.

The amount of time you dedicate to planning the party all depends on what you can manage, but it's worth remembering that these occasions do not need to be very different year on year – the main components can remain the same. Subtle changes can be brought about with a topical theme, and food and drink labelled accordingly or a novelty cake, for instance – small details that help make these parties so special and memorable.

PLANNING AND PREPARING

PARTY TIMELINE

The following guide will help you start planning your party, keep things on track and avoid any last-minute panic. Keep a party diary or journal and make notes of useful tips, games and ideas you used. Jot down reminders of what worked and what didn't to refer to next year.

8 WEEKS AHEAD Set a date and time. Decide on the number of children, the location and theme. Book a venue and entertainer, if necessary.

3 WEEKS AHEAD Send out invitations with an RSVP date and arrange helpers.

1—2 WEEKS AHEAD Shop for party supplies when you know how many children are coming. Prepare and plan games. Check guests' food allergies with parents. Order non-perishable party food and drink (individually packed foods are better than larger packs to avoid waste) and prepare freezable foods. Confirm bookings.

2 DAYS AHEAD Make the cake, and any food that can be stored in plastic containers. Fill and assemble party bags. Charge your camera battery and get last-minute foods and any extra accessories for the cake.

1 DAY AHEAD Decorate the cake, and prepare other food (if hot food, cook and reheat the following day). Discuss the next day's plans with the birthday girl/boy. Decorate your house in the evening and clear the games area. Check the weather forecast if the party is outside.

DAY OF THE PARTY Prepare fresh food: sandwiches (cover with damp tea towels to stop them drying out), fruit and drinks. Blow up balloons. Decorate your front door or driveway. Play music, put up a sign for the bathroom, set the table and lay out food. Get the birthday child ready and clear a space for birthday presents (have a pen and paper handy to note who they are from).

ORDER OF THE DAY

- *Welcome guests with balloons tied outside the front door or garden gate.*

- *Calm ice-breaker or quiet game (page 314).*

- *Lively games (page 320).*

- *Birthday tea and cake (page 303).*

- *Quieter games or activities (page 314).*

- *A few musical games (page 318).*

- *Party bags or lucky dip (page 324).*

- *Wave goodbye.*

- *Settle your own children in front of a film.*

- *Have a glass of wine!*

OUTDOOR PARTIES

It's always easier to host children's parties outside, but remember to have a contingency plan in case the weather turns bad. If you live near the sea, a fun idea could be a trip to the beach with seaside activities, such as building sandcastles, kite-flying or shell crafts (page 359). You could host a sports party in a nearby park with relays, egg and spoon races (page 262) and obstacle courses, or a game of rounders (page 350). Bring mini bottles of water and orange jelly segments (page 308) for half-time. Let parents know if their children need to dress for messy or outdoor activities.

TIMING

Assuming the party is held at home, restrict its length to 2–3 hours in an afternoon, so that your guests leave in high spirits before they become tired and grumpy (for older children it could stretch a little longer or later). For toddler parties, mid-morning works well, although bear in mind that they can get tired after an hour and a half. Make sure you let parents know what meal you will be providing for their children.

NUMBERS

With your child's input, plan how many guests you want to invite – and, more importantly, how many you can manage. For toddlers or children under five years old, keep numbers limited and expect parents to come along too (and perhaps extra siblings). For children aged five or above, any number between eight and twelve guests should be about right, although budget and space will be the deciding factor. Don't feel pressurised into inviting the whole class, particularly if it's a large one, and remind your child to keep it low-key in front of those who aren't invited. One option is to have a joint party and team up with another family – this is particularly good if a child has a friend in the same class with a birthday around the same time. Alternatively, you might consider inviting just the boys or just the girls for a gender-specific party. This will help to avoid any class upset as well. You can always ask the teacher if your child can bring in a birthday treat, such as cupcakes, for the whole class to make everyone feel included.

HELPERS

Enlist friends, family members or babysitters to act as assistants at the party. Older siblings can also help out. Get them to be responsible for specific elements of the party, such as looking after other parents, running a few games, manning the music station during musical games, making cups of tea or taking children to the bathroom. Have a list of things they can help with beforehand, too, such as preparing sandwiches and laying out the party food, looking after guests' coats and shoes, taking photos or doing face painting.

TIP: *Have plenty of wet wipes for sticky fingers. A first-aid kit might be useful, too.*

CRAFTS AND ACTIVITIES

Children love to use their imagination, whether it's creating crafts or making food such as mini pizzas (page 307). You can also get them to help make a few decorations or plan some inexpensive craft activities during the party, like decorating plain paper hats, masks, place mats or party boxes with sequins, glitter and pasta shapes.

ORIGAMI PLATTER

These are a colourful way to serve children's favourite things. Fill each of the four cones with different sweets.

I: Cut a 50cm square out of thin card. Fold in all four corners to the centre. Turn over and again fold in the four corners. 2: Turn back over and stick numbers on each square, and decorate. 3: Fold in half between the squares in both directions. Place thumbs and forefingers into each square and bring together so that all the points meet. Turn over and fill the holes with snacks and sweets.

DIY T-SHIRTS

A fun activity for early on so that the decorations have time to dry, ready to take home at the end of the party.

Let children design their own T-shirts using fabric markers or fabric paints. You can customise new white T-shirts or revive old ones.

DECORATING BISCUITS AND CUPCAKES

Get children to design fun cookie characters or cupcakes to match the theme of the birthday party.

Bake shaped biscuits (pages 23 and 244) or plain cupcakes (page 311), then let children decorate them. Have different coloured icing and a variety of edible decorations: hundreds and thousands, silver balls, sugar flowers, glitter, glacé cherries and icing pens.

TISSUE TEA LIGHTS

These look beautiful hung out of reach on trees or shrubs. For a children's party, use battery-operated tea lights.

I: Loop wire around the neck of a jam jar, twisting the ends to secure. Attach a second loop of wire to hang the jar from. 2: Cut up pieces of coloured tissue. 3: Paint the inside or outside of the jam jar with PVA glue and stick on the tissue. Place a lit tea light inside.

TIP: *Decorate jam jars or glass tea-light holders with glass paint for a stained-glass effect and as a gift to take home.*

BUTTERFLY LANTERNS

Buy inexpensive plain paper lanterns, then spruce them up with tissue-paper butterflies to hang indoors and out.

I: Make a template and cut out two butterflies from coloured tissue paper and one from coloured card. 2: Stack the three pieces together and crease down the centre. 3: Use PVA glue along the fold of the card, then place a tissue butterfly on top. Add another line of glue down the fold, and place the last tissue butterfly on top. 4: Glue the butterflies on to the paper lantern, card side down. 5: Repeat as required.

HOMEMADE MAYPOLE

Make your own maypole using a long stick and colourful ribbons. Children will love dancing around it and weaving their own colour in and out. You could combine this with a game of musical statues.

1: Attach five ribbons (each approximately 2.5m in length) to the tip of a long, thick piece of wooden dowling using a hammer and nails or a professional staple gun. 2: Wrap heavy-duty masking tape around the top of the pole, then stick on ribbons and felt flowers using a glue stick to decorate the top. 2: Make a hole in the lawn, stick in the pole and tap it gently with

MAYPOLE DANCING *This custom stems from a celebration of the end of winter. Historically, in spring, young branches were cut from trees and stuck into the ground, and became a focus for festivities. Over the years these tree poles became maypoles. They were reused each year on May Day, and danced around by children who made pretty patterns by plaiting colourful ribbons around the poles as they danced.*

PARTY DECORATIONS

Mix and match what you already have at home with shop-bought disposable decorations and a few that you might make. There's always plenty of choice for children's parties so it's the perfect opportunity to go all out with colour. Stock up on fun accessories, such as party poppers, streamers, confetti and party hats. Have helium balloons hanging freely from the ceiling with bright curling ribbons cascading down or tied in clusters to the backs of chairs (write names on single balloons as place cards).

BANNERS, BUNTING AND STREAMERS

You can find all sorts of decorations from party shops and online, especially if you have a theme and want matching banners. Hang banners and bunting in the main party room or, if the party's outside, tie them between trees or use them to festoon hedges. Make the most of windows by sticking cut-out shapes and stencils on them (page 16), and hang garlands and paper lanterns from light fixtures or tree branches. Non-marking Blu-tack and sticky tape, as well as a hammer and nails, are useful for fixing decorations.

THE PARTY TABLE

Make your table the centre of attention but don't go overboard with clutter. A plain-coloured or white tablecloth is a good base (and paper or plastic ones are a practical option) to which you can add a few block colours or one prominent theme with your choice of tableware. Fill brightly coloured tin buckets with cutlery wrapped in napkins, or use a fun table runner: you can buy paper versions in rolls that can be cut to size or used as over-sized placemats (white ones can be used to doodle on with crayons). To avoid things being knocked over, attach larger bowls, plates and cake stands to the table using Blu-tack. If you have limited space or don't have enough chairs, plan a party picnic on a rug or groundsheet on the floor with cushions and beanbags scattered around. When setting your party table outside, make sure it's out of the wind and in the shade, and that the tablecloth is fastened with table clips or drawing pins. Individual cartons of juice and water bottles act as useful weights to keep paper plates and napkins from flying away. You could also place tubes of bubbles in paper cups – a practical solution that doubles up as presents.

Make the tablecentre an eye-catching one with origami platters (page 294) or large jars filled with sweets (tuck-shop style), jugs filled with colourful punches or tiered cupcake stands laden with sweet or savoury snacks. A birthday cake makes a good centrepiece but set this on a pedestal (a box covered with foil, for example) to enhance its magic. As a finishing touch, fill the empty spaces on the table with handfuls of confetti, sequins or curls of ribbon.

THE BIRTHDAY TEA

Feeding children is often tricky, as there will always be some fussy eaters, so keep the party menu simple and don't prepare anything too exotic or spicy. Children tend to eat a little less than usual when they are excited so it's best not to go overboard. Avoid putting all the sweet and savoury foods out at the same time, as children will inevitably reach for the sweeter options first. Remember that children love things imaginatively presented — sandwiches cut into shapes, veggies in party cones and fruit juices turned into colourful ice cubes.

CASUAL PARTY PICNIC *For a more informal party set-up in a nearby park or garden, lay out a rug in the shade and bring a tray filled with individually-labelled picnic party boxes for each child. Good, portable, packed-lunch-type items include mini filled rolls (easier than sandwiches, which can fall apart), pots of yogurt or jelly with plastic spoons, individually wrapped cheeses, cartons of juice, fruit crisps or plain popcorn, boxes of raisins or handfuls of grapes. If there's room, include pretty napkins, party blowers and hats.*

PARTY DRINKS AND FUN ICE CUBES

Offer a selection of soft drinks: squash, diluted cordials or milkshakes are all popular. Remember to fill cups only once everyone is sitting around the table to avoid spillages. Straws, paper umbrellas and, for older kids, edible garnishes on cocktail sticks are nice celebratory touches. Make fizzy cordial drinks and plain juices more fun by adding colourful fruit juice ice cubes. To make these, simply freeze fruit juice (or puréed fruit for a stronger flavour) in ice-cube trays, which you can buy in all different shapes.

STRAWBERRY MILKSHAKE Serves 4

For a strawberry milkshake, put 400g washed strawberries into a blender and blend until smooth. Add 600ml milk, 2 tablespoons caster sugar and 2 scoops of strawberry or vanilla ice cream and blend again for 1–2 minutes. Divide between 4 tall glasses and serve immediately. Almost all fruits work well — make classic single flavours, try tropical fruits or make up combinations such as peanut butter and banana. For a dairy-free option, replace the milk with almond milk and omit the ice cream. Straws are essential.

OLD-FASHIONED ST CLEMENT'S Serves 4 (makes 1 litre)

This classic drink is simple to prepare for a crowd and popular with most children. Mix together 500ml good-quality orange juice and 500ml old-fashioned lemonade (for a homemade recipe see page 375). Orange-juice ice cubes are best for this drink.

TIP: *Have a few chilled bottles of wine, or pots of tea and coffee, to offer parents who are staying to help out.*

A SAVOURY SPREAD

FUN SANDWICHES

Turn basic sandwiches into something more appealing for your party. For ease, use thinly sliced bread and spreadable butter. Have up to three different sandwich fillings and use paper flags (page 272) as labels to identify each filling, or arrange on tiered cupcake stands.

Snail Pinwheels: Spread crustless bread slices or tortilla wraps evenly with a creamy filling, such as tuna or egg mayonnaise. Roll the bread (or wraps) up tightly in clingfilm and chill. To serve cut into 2cm pieces and decorate using a cocktail stick cut in half for the antennae, and peas or sweetcorn for the eyes.

Shaped Sandwiches: Cut sandwiches using cookie cutters, such as flowers, hearts or stars. Spreads, such as Marmite, jam or cream cheese, or sliced ham are good for these. Take out the middles with a small cutter to let the filling show through, or use gingerbread-people cutters and decorate them with food.

Sandwich Boats: Cut sandwiches into triangles (crusts off) and use cocktail sticks to thread on cherry tomatoes, little gem lettuce leaves, slices of cucumber or salami as sails.

VEGGIE CONES AND DIPS Serves 8

Present an assembly of crunchy vegetable sticks in paper cones for kids to dip.

Hummus: Blend together until smooth 400g rinsed, tinned chickpeas, 1 teaspoon ground cumin, 6 tablespoons olive oil, 1 teaspoon salt, 1 clove of garlic, 3 tablespoons tahini paste and the zest and juice of 1½ lemons, then season to taste.

Cheese Dip: Melt 30g unsalted butter in a saucepan and stir in 30g plain flour to make a smooth paste, then cook gently for 1–2 minutes before gradually pouring in 300ml milk. Stir for a few minutes more until it thickens, then add 200g grated Cheddar or Red Leicester cheese and stir until completely melted. Season to taste.

THINGS ON STICKS

- **Cheese 'n' Tomato Balls:** *Thread cherry tomatoes and mozzarella balls on to toothpicks and stick into a wedge of watermelon. Do the same with other chunky vegetables.*

- **Skewered Sandwiches:** *Shape your bread with a small cookie cutter and 'sandwich' together on a skewer whatever your chosen filling is — baby gem lettuce leaves, rolled ham, cheese and half a cherry tomato.*

MINI BURGERS Serves 8

Use kid-size mini baps or warm mini pittas which are flatter and easier to handle.

Place 400g lean beef mince into a large bowl with 2 teaspoons Dijon mustard, 1–2 teaspoons Worcestershire sauce, a tablespoon tomato ketchup, 1 small peeled and grated red onion and 1 egg yolk. Season and mix well. Using damp hands, shape into 8 mini patties and flatten into burgers. Transfer to a tray, cover with clingfilm and chill for 1 hour.

When ready to cook, preheat the grill to medium–high. Heat 2 tablespoons olive oil in a non-stick ovenproof frying pan over a medium heat and pan-fry the burgers for 3–4 minutes on each side, or until cooked through and nicely coloured. Lay a slice of cheese on top of each burger and place under the grill until the cheese has melted. Spread a little mayonnaise or ketchup on the bottom half of 8 buns, arrange tomato slices and lettuce on top, followed by the burgers, place the lids on and skewer with cocktail-stick flags.

HOMEMADE PIZZA DOUGH Serves 8

Get children to help shape and decorate mini pizzas for a fun party activity. Use passata for the sauce, grate lots of cheese and lay out a variety of toppings for everyone to create their own combinations.

Mix together a 7g sachet of fast-action dried yeast, 2 teaspoons sugar and 250ml warm water in a jug and leave to stand for 5 minutes. Place 400g '00' or strong white bread flour and 1 teaspoon salt into a large bowl. Make a well in the centre and pour in the yeast mixture. Add 2 tablespoons olive oil and mix together to a soft dough. Add more flour if necessary.

Turn out on to a lightly floured surface and knead well with floured hands for at least 5 minutes, until the dough is smooth and springy to the touch. Place it in a large, lightly oiled bowl, cover with clingfilm or a damp cloth, and leave it in a warm place for approximately 1 hour, until doubled in size. Knead it on a floured surface.

Divide into 8 and roll each piece out to 8cm diameter circles about 1cm thick. Place on a lightly floured baking tray and add toppings. To cook, drizzle them with extra virgin olive oil and bake in a preheated oven for 10–15 minutes at 220°C/gas 7 or until the pizzas are golden, the cheese has melted and the crust is crisp.

TIP: *If you don't have time to make your own dough, buy plain pizza bases, or use English muffin halves instead.*

SWEET THINGS

This is always a popular part of the birthday tea. Buy cake pops (or invest in a machine to make your own), butter bread and cover with hundreds and thousands for fairy bread, swirl breadsticks into melted chocolate and sprinkles to make sparklers, or dip strawberries in chocolate and leave to set in the fridge.

KNICKERBOCKER GLORY Make to order

Set out a variety of ice-cream flavours, shop-bought chocolate sauces or a homemade fruit coulis (page 214) and toppings, such as fresh fruit, crushed Maltesers or popping candy, and get children to create personal concoctions in sundae glasses. Add wafers for a finishing touch.

CHOCOLATE BROWNIES Makes 16

Lightly grease a 20cm square tin and line with baking parchment. Preheat the oven to 180°C/ gas 4. Melt 200g good-quality dark chocolate and 150g unsalted butter in a pan. In a large bowl, beat together 150g light brown soft sugar and 3 large eggs with an electric whisk until light and fluffy, then pour in the melted chocolate. Sift 60g self-raising flour into the bowl with 1 teaspoon salt and fold it in, retaining as much air as possible. Add 100g mini marshmallows, 100g chopped pecan nuts (optional) and 100g chopped white chocolate. Pour the mixture into the tin and bake for 25–30 minutes, until a skewer comes out sticky, but not with raw mixture attached. Let it cool in the tin completely then serve in squares.

RICE KRISPIE SQUARES Makes 16

Lightly grease a 20cm square tin and line it with baking parchment. Melt 50g unsalted butter in a large pan over a gentle heat, then add 2 tablespoons golden syrup (run the spoon under hot water first for ease) and 250g pink and white marshmallows. Once melted, stir and remove from the heat, add 200g Rice Krispies to the pan and mix well to combine. Press the mixture into the tin well and refrigerate until set. Arrange in a chequerboard pattern with the brownies.

ORANGE JUICE JELLY Serves 8

To make orange-juice jelly, soak 11 sheets of gelatine in cold water to soften. Dissolve 50g caster sugar in 800ml orange juice in a saucepan over a low heat. Let it cool slightly, then add the gelatine and allow it to dissolve. Before pouring into individual jelly moulds, add some tinned mandarin segments, then refrigerate until set. Serve with vanilla ice cream.

TIP: *To make orange jelly segments, make the jelly according to the packet instructions, pour into scooped-out skins of halved oranges and allow to set firmly. To serve, cut into wedges.*

BIRTHDAY CAKES

The highlight of any children's party is usually the birthday cake, smothered in lots of icing and decorations. The recipe opposite can be used as a handy base not only for a plain sponge cake but for little cupcakes and fairy cakes, too. These can be a visual spectacle, particularly if arranged on tiered cupcake stands as a centrepiece and decorated with mouth-watering delights. If you aren't confident making your own or don't have time, there are lots of quick and easy solutions to help you cheat. Buy plain sponge cakes, such as Madeira cakes or Swiss rolls (these are also good and firm for carving into novelty cakes), or assemble a shop-bought cake mix and ice and decorate it yourself. You can also buy photo cupcakes, customising the photos according to the birthday boy or girl's tastes or using their picture on the top. Buttercream icing is best for large cakes or you can buy ready-rolled fondant icing in different colours. When you are ready to bring in the cake, close the curtains or dim the lights and make a grand entrance with the candles alight – the 'magic' ones that continually re-light once you've blown them out were always my favourite.

BASIC SPONGE MIXTURE

Makes enough for 1 x deep 20cm round or 18cm square cake tin. Cream 200g softened unsalted butter, 200g caster sugar and 1 teaspoon vanilla extract in a large bowl with an electric whisk, or add the ingredients to the bowl of a food processor and beat until light and fluffy. Gradually beat in 4 eggs, one at a time, mixing well after each addition, then carefully fold in 200g sifted self-raising flour with a large metal spoon. Follow the baking instructions for fairy cakes (below), Victoria sponge (page 273) or rainbow cake (page 312).

FAIRY CAKES Makes 12

Line a 12-hole bun tin with paper cases and make up a batch of the basic sponge mixture (as above). Divide the mixture between the cases. Bake in a preheated oven for 20 minutes at 180°C/gas 4. To decorate, use a simple glacé icing (icing sugar and water, mixed thickly to avoid drips), or use buttercream (below) and add a few edible sugar decorations.

TIP: *Make butterfly fairy cakes by cutting a round disc out of the top of each cake and filling the hole with buttercream icing. Cut the sponge disc in half and stick the pieces at angles into the icing to create 'wings'.*

BUTTERCREAM ICING

Makes enough to ice 12 fairy cakes or 1 large sponge cake. Beat 125g softened unsalted butter until light and fluffy. Sift in 250g icing sugar and add 2 teaspoons freshly boiled water, then beat well until combined. Spread over your cake using a palette knife.

RAINBOW CAKE

A great friend of mine always had a rainbow cake like this one at her birthday parties and they were the best. The food colouring in this recipe might make you gasp, but you can get natural versions — and, remember, it is a treat and not something your kids will have every day!

SERVES 10–12

unsalted butter, for greasing

3 egg whites

2 batches basic sponge mixture (page 311)

2 tablespoons milk

1 teaspoon each of food colourings in red, yellow, orange, green, blue, purple and pink, adding more if required

For the filling

1 quantity buttercream icing (page 311)

Preheat the oven to 180°C/gas 4. Grease and line the bottom of 2 x shallow 20cm round cake tins with greaseproof paper.

Using an electric whisk, beat the egg whites in a large bowl until they form soft peaks. Add the basic sponge mixture and fold together. Add the milk and continue to fold for 1–2 minutes to combine.

Divide the mixture into seven separate bowls. Put a few drops of red food colouring into the first bowl and stir, adding more as necessary to get to the desired intensity. Repeat with the remaining colours and bowls until you have seven bowls of coloured cake mixture.

Divide spoonfuls of cake mixture between the prepared tins, alternating the colours as you go and keeping each separate in the tin until all the mixture is used up.

Bake for 35–40 minutes or until risen and a skewer inserted into each cake comes out clean. Allow to cool in the tins for a few minutes before turning out on to a wire rack and cooling completely.

Turn one cake over on to a plate and spread with buttercream icing before placing the other cake on top.

TIPS: *For a marbled version of this cake, use 1 deep 20cm cake tin and layer the coloured batter, gently swirling as you go. To decorate, cover with buttercream icing and dot with Smarties. • Rather than cutting a round cake into wedges, try cutting it in long slices all the way across, then divide it into finger-sized portions. These will be easier for small people to manage and the cake will go much further.*

TRADITIONAL PARTY GAMES

Have a long list of games you are familiar with or have tried out beforehand and keep to a schedule when planning them – excited children get bored easily. For a two-hour party, you will need at least four to six games and activities. Outdoor games will be weather dependent, and you should have more lined up than you think you'll need; some will go down better than others. Play a selection before the birthday tea and a few after. Remember to buy enough prizes (that will fit into party bags) for all the games. Children under the age of four might not understand games in which a child is eliminated and may be upset at having to sit out, so give each participant a prize (a badge, sweet or toy) at the end of the game, keeping everyone happy. Ask a helper to look after those who don't want to join in or those who are out. Most of the bits and pieces you'll need for these party games are very easy to find in corner shops, large supermarkets and online. To avoid over-excitement, alternate between lively and quiet games.

QUIETER GAMES AND ACTIVITIES

SLEEPING LIONS

Two players (or grown-ups) are chosen to be the hunters. All the other children are lions and must lie down with their eyes closed. Once the lions are sleeping, the hunters move among them, trying to 'wake' them. They can move close and whisper in the lions' ears to make them move or giggle, but they cannot touch them. Any lion who moves or makes a sound becomes a hunter until there is just one triumphant sleeping lion left.

ANGELS

This is a lovely game for younger children and requires real concentration from everybody involved. If you're playing with boys, replace the angels with ghosts. If you're playing indoors, ask everyone to take their shoes off, so that the room is as quiet as possible. Two angels are selected, and the rest of the group become mortals, who must space out across the room, stand still and close their eyes (use blindfolds to ensure no peeking). The angels then walk among the mortals as quietly as they can, each choosing a mortal to stand behind. If a mortal thinks that they sense an angel, they ask 'Is there an angel with me?' The adult in charge replies yes or no. If the mortal is correct, they too become an angel. If they are wrong, or if an angel stands behind a mortal and counts to five (silently!) and then taps them on the shoulder, they must go out. The game ends when everyone is either out or an angel.

PIN THE TAIL...

Draw a tail-less donkey on a large piece of paper and stick it up on a wall or a tree. Ask a child to come forward and stand in front of the picture. Place a neat clump of raffia with sticky tape at the end into the child's hand and then blindfold them. Spin them around a few times and bring them to a stop facing the picture. Ask the child to 'pin' the tail on the donkey, then remove their blindfold so they can see where they placed the tail. Initial the point they chose. Award a prize to the player who came the closest.

TIP: *Replace the donkey with another animal to fit the theme of your party.*

THE FLOUR GAME

Prepare the game in advance by filling a medium-sized bowl with flour right up to the brim, and press down firmly until the flour is compact. Place a large chopping board over the top of the bowl and then turn it all upside down so that the board forms a base. Leave the bowl and board to stand for a few hours, giving the flour time to settle. When everyone is ready to play, bring out the board, place it on a low surface (use a table covered with newspaper if you're playing indoors) and remove the bowl to reveal a smooth, perfectly formed flour mound. This will invariably earn gasps of admiration from everyone. Gently place a square of chocolate on top of the mound. Choose a large knife (a dinner knife or ruler will be safer for younger children) and ask each player to step forward in turn to cut a slice from the flour mound. The aim is to keep the mound from collapsing for as long as possible. You'll be surprised by how many slices the flour can withstand before it finally caves in. When the mound does fall, the piece of chocolate on top will go with it. The player responsible for the collapse must then put their hands behind their back and retrieve the chocolate using just their mouth. They will emerge white-faced but happy.

TRAY MEMORY GAME

Before everyone arrives, cover a tray or table with around 20 small objects. These can vary from the mundane to the maverick. Everyday items, such as stationery and cutlery, are good, and so are more unusual knick-knacks and trinkets. Variety is key. Once your tray is ready, cover it with a large cloth.

Ask the children to stand around the tray, then remove the cover with a flourish. Allow everyone one minute to remember as many objects as they can. Once the time is up, replace the cloth and give everyone a piece of paper and a pen. Now everyone has five minutes to jot down all they can recall. The person with the longest list of correctly remembered items wins.

Everyone will have a different way of remembering. Some will have a photographic memory, allowing them to recall the items simply by visualising them, others might remember them alphabetically. One fun way to jog their memories is to create a story that incorporates as many of the objects as possible.

MUSICAL GAMES

These simple games test the speed of your guests' reactions. You'll need plenty of space or a room cleared of furniture. Wireless speakers are useful if you're outside.

MUSICAL STATUES AND MUSICAL BUMPS

Ask players to spread out, then turn on some music and get them to dance. Whenever the music stops, players must either stay completely still, like statues, or fall down on their bottoms with a bump (depending on which version of the game you're playing). In statues, anyone moving after the music stops is out. In bumps, the last person to sit down goes out. Vary the amount of time that the music plays for — a couple of long bursts punctuated by a very short one will often catch people out. When players are out, get them to help you identify the moving statues or the last person to hit the floor until you have a winner.

NEWSPAPER ISLANDS

Give every player a sheet of newspaper and ask them to put their paper down somewhere on the floor. Then turn on some music and get them to dance around the room, taking care not to step on the sheets of newspaper. When the music stops, it means that there is a shark attack: players must find a newspaper island to stand on to avoid being eaten. After each shark attack, take a few pieces of newspaper away and continue playing. Islands can only hold one person at a time, so the next time the music stops there will be a mad dash for safety and some players will find themselves eaten by sharks and out of the game. Repeat until you have a winner.

TIP: *To play musical chairs, set up a circle of chairs, seats facing outwards, one fewer than the number of players. While music plays, the children walk around the circle, and, when it stops, they race to find a chair and sit on it. The person left standing goes out, one chair is removed and the game begins again. Repeat until you have a winner.*

PASS THE PARCEL

This takes a bit of preparation before the party, but is worth it and is an excellent way to calm things down. Wrap a small gift in many layers of paper — use newspaper or brown paper instead of wrapping paper on the outer layers, but try to make the layers closest to the prize a bit more interesting. Between every layer include a sweet or another tiny prize. You could also include a question on a piece of paper, so that the person unwrapping the parcel must ask it, and the first person to give the correct answer gets the sweet. To play, sit everyone in a large circle and ask them to pass the parcel around as the music plays. Every time the music stops, the person holding the parcel gets to unwrap a layer. Make sure that everyone gets to unwrap a layer and find a sweet so the whole party will really enjoy the game.

LIVELY GAMES

As well as the games below, Simon Says is a great time-filler and easy to play between other games. Call out commands, with accompanying actions, using the phrase 'Simon says', for example, 'Simon says pat your head'. Everyone must do as Simon says until the next direction is called. Occasionally, the leader gives an instruction *without* the words 'Simon says' and then players should do absolutely nothing. Anyone who follows the order goes out – you'll be suprised by how easy it is to fool them! To make things more difficult, give your orders in very quick succession. Another good activity is to fill an empty piñata with goodies and get children to take turns trying to break it with a stick.

CORNERS

This game is perfect for large groups of children and works best in bigger venues like a village or sports hall. Number the four corners of the room one, two, three and four (or colour code each with balloons). Give a quick guided tour, pointing out the numbers. Choose someone to be 'it' and blindfold them. They stand in the middle of the room while everyone else scatters, with each player deciding on a corner to move to. Once everybody is in their corner of choice, the blindfolded player calls out a number: one, two, three or four. All the children at that corner are then out. Everyone left in the game scatters again and the whole process is repeated. When there are four or fewer players left, they must all choose different corners. The final player left in the game is blindfolded for the next round. Although it's total chance, the winner can congratulate themselves for excellent guesswork!

GRANDMOTHER'S FOOTSTEPS

Someone is chosen to be Grandmother. This person stands at the end of the room or the garden with their back to the other players. Everyone else arranges themselves along a starting line. On 'Go', players begin to make their way towards Grandmother. She can turn around at any point in the game and when she does the other players must freeze for as long as she is looking at them. If she catches anyone moving, they are sent back to the starting line. The aim is to reach Grandmother first and tag her on the shoulder. The player who successfully tags her becomes Grandmother in the next round. There are a number of fun variations on this game. You can lay out a set of chairs and demand that players climb over one of them before they can tag Grandmother. If she turns around mid-climb, players will inevitably struggle to maintain their balance. The more obstacles the better!

THE CHOCOLATE GAME

For this game, you'll need a large chocolate bar, a knife and fork, some winter layers (hat, gloves and scarf) and a dice. The chocolate bar is unwrapped and placed on a chopping board. Players form a circle around the chocolate and take it in turns to roll the dice. When a six is thrown, the player who rolled it shouts 'SIX!' and puts on the layers as fast as they can. If you want to make things harder, add extra layers, such as legwarmers, fake moustaches or sunglasses. Once the player who threw the six is dressed, they must pick up the knife and fork and attempt to cut and eat a square of the chocolate bar. This is much easier said than done. All the while, other players continue to pass the dice around the circle and when another six is rolled, the person in the centre must stop what they're doing – whatever stage of dressing or cutting they have reached – and hand over the clothes and cutlery. The chocolate is remarkably difficult to cut through, especially when the knife is held through woolly winter gloves; for younger children, use giant chocolate buttons that they can pick up with their fingers instead.

OTHER LIVELY GAMES FOR CHILDREN'S PARTIES

- *Doughnut tree (page 43)*
- *Egg and spoon races (page 262)*
- *Pass the orange (page 152)*
- *Kick the can (page 307)*

- *Three-legged race (page 352)*
- *Wheelbarrow races (page 366)*
- *Cup and ball (page 352)*
- *Tug of war (page 352)*

- *Bowling (page 39)*
- *British bulldogs (page 366)*
- *Limbo (page 352)*
- *Capture the flag (page 307)*

SACK RACE

The sack race tends to join the egg and spoon race at fêtes and school sports days. Players put both their legs inside a sack or pillowcase. The higher the sack reaches on the players' bodies, the harder the game becomes. Beginners might want to start with sacks that reach waist-height, but for the more ambitious and experienced sack-racers you can provide ones that come all the way up to the neck to keep their arms inside. Everyone stands along a starting line and, on 'Go', players start jumping in their sacks towards the finish line. Over-enthusiastic racers will most likely get themselves in a tangle and fall. Watching them try to get up again inside their small sacks is especially amusing for spectators. The first person to cross the finish line is declared the winner.

GOODBYES

PARTY BAGS

Assemble party bags in advance and keep them in a large tray or basket, well hidden to avoid any peeking. Personalise them with stickers or labels to avoid confusion and to make sure you haven't forgotten anyone. Keep the contents the same to prevent squabbling over who gets what, unless you differentiate between boys' and girls' bags. The best party bags are often those that have been well thought about, with fillers chosen to fit a particular theme, age group or gender – they needn't be expensive.

There are lots of cheap present ideas that are great for younger children. Older ones might prefer an individual keepsake gift, such as a plant, story book, craft or baking kit. 'Loot' or paper bags are the most practical and popular (pre-filled ones can save the day), but you can use all sorts of other bags and even containers: fill plastic cups or mugs with treats, wrap them in cellophane and tie them with ribbon; fabric bags or organza bags are useful as they can be kept afterwards; even party picnic boxes can be used, with tissue paper and confetti to make it more of a surprise. Another option for going-home presents is to have a lucky dip, a box or container filled with shredded paper or straw into which children can dive and pick out a colourfully wrapped present to take home. Have a few spare bags or prizes handy for siblings.

GOOD FILLERS

- *Pocket-size gadgets, puzzles, badges or medals.*

- *Foam gliders, pull-back cars and spinning tops.*

- *Soft toys, slinky snakes, finger puppets or fortune-teller fish.*

- *Bubbles, bouncy balls, yo-yos and biff bats.*

- *Stationery sets, notepads, activity books and stickers.*

- *Modelling clay, play dough or magic slates.*

- *A cupcake or piece of birthday cake in an organza bag.*

- *Jewellery sets, hairclips, sunglasses, paper fans.*

- *Sweets, such as popping candy, marshmallows, Smarties, gummy bears, sherbet sticks or flying saucers.*

I question not if thrushes sing,
If roses load the air;
Beyond my heart I need not reach,
When all is summer there.

'Love's World', John Vance Cheney

BARBECUES

Nothing says summer quite like a barbecue. People all over the world have been grilling pieces of meat over fire for thousands of years, but barbecues as we recognise them today are thought to have originated in the Caribbean, a region that is still passionate about outdoor cooking. Grilling food outdoors and sharing it with others has become an essential part of modern living and a way to enjoy and celebrate the warm summer months.

It's true that the British climate is not ideally suited to cooking outdoors: the weather is often a gamble, making a day of soaring temperatures, unbroken blue skies and a balmy evening a thrilling rarity. But even with cloud-ridden skies, there is always good British cheer that the weather has held and – most importantly – it's not raining! Cancelling a barbecue celebration is unheard of, unless it's actually forecast to thunder all day and night – most guests will, without doubt, still relish the chance of eating outside wrapped up in blankets and coats. Optimism never wavers, even if, in the end, you have to eat indoors.

Cooking on a barbecue offers those who prefer more casual entertaining an opportunity to host something without the pressures of formal courses or culinary etiquette. No one expects to sit down at the table – a bench, garden chair or even standing will do. It's a meal that no one really seems to mind waiting for. The billows of smoke set the atmosphere, wafting over garden fences, hedges and walls and whetting the taste buds. A glass of something cold – a pale pink rosé or a heady punch – and a few outdoor games that can be played barefoot in the grass will keep everyone happy on this most laid-back of occasions.

Whether it's a planned affair or a more spontaneous shindig, the joy of cooking outside is that you don't have to slave away and overheat in the kitchen. That's not to say no preparations are needed, but it's how and what you choose to barbecue that is the key here, where possible making and marinating in good time to lock in the juicy flavours. Side dishes can be ready-assembled in bowls, made up of all the fresh, seasonal and colourful ingredients you have missed in the winter, and pudding might be just a combination of ripe berries and cream, Britain's signature summer dessert. Whatever the menu or occasion, everyone can enjoy a barbecue, making it one of the most all-embracing celebrations.

SUMMER FLOWERS

Bring bursts of colour to your setting with delicate scented blooms such as sweetpeas. Bright hydrangea heads look lovely floating in a globe vase with a little water, and peonies come in all shades of pink, white and coral. Dahlias grow in more vibrant tints, and stocks, delphiniums and gladioli add height, creating a country-garden feel wherever you are. For more celebratory occasions, line pathways with shepherd's crooks and hang them with jam jars filled with posies, or thread colourful flower heads such as gerberas on fine floristry wire to make garlands (these will probably only last the day so spritz them with water to prevent them wilting). If your gathering goes on into the evening, fill storm lanterns with a few centimetres of water, add pillar candles and decorate with sprigs of fresh herbs or flowers; rosemary and lavender both smell wonderful.

GARDEN TABLES

There is no real need for decorations when throwing a barbecue party – let the summer garden, in all its vibrant and luscious splendour, speak for itself. For garden parties at home, we often bring one of our indoor tables outside so we can seat more people. Arrange extra benches and seats close by for children and youngsters to sit on if you don't have enough places at the table. Use tablecloths or runners in fresh colours (overlap a few if need be) to bring out the natural surroundings. A hessian runner will look suitably rustic. If it's a long table, line the centre with vases and a variety of inexpensive flowers; white and green meadow flowers, such as daisies or achillea, are perfect base colours for a summer party paired with soft green foliage, such as alchemilla mollis (lady's mantle) or cow parsley, picked from the wild.

For place settings, write names on dried bay leaves and skewer them with cocktail sticks into lemons or other fruits. Tie napkins folded around individual sets of cutlery with hessian string, and decorate with sprigs of fresh herbs or flowers, for a practical yet 'from-the-garden' touch. Use table clips or drawing pins to keep the tablecloth from flying away and make sure any decorations are firmly secured against the wind (fill the bottoms of smaller vases with handfuls of stones to keep them sturdy). Coloured glasses, patterned bowls and tableware will create a Mediterranean feel, and a parasol will provide much-needed shade on a hot day. For later in the afternoon, have tea lights, lanterns, garden torches, braziers or fire pits ready for warmth as the light fades. Use citronella candles and anti-mosquito coils to keep bugs away.

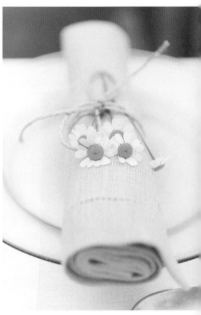

STARTERS AND SNACKS

CRUDITÉS WITH ANCHOVY DIP Serves 8–12

A selection of fresh vegetables makes for a stunning and colourful centrepiece. Use miniature vegetables that can be served whole, such as baby carrots, radishes (scrubbed but with the tops left on), blanched tenderstem broccoli and asparagus, yellow and red pepper strips, baby sweetcorn and a few grissini sticks (wrapped in Parma ham). Keep prepared crudités cold and crisp in a bowl of iced salted water.

To make the dip, put 4 garlic cloves and 200g drained tinned anchovies in a small blender, and blend until you have a rough paste. Stir in 2 tablespoons olive oil and 8–12 tablespoons crème fraîche. Season well. Arrange prepared vegetables on a large platter or in a large bowl and serve alongside.

GAZPACHO Serves 8

This fresh soup is really refreshing on a hot summer's day and makes a wonderful starter.

Place 1.2kg chopped ripe plum or vine tomatoes, 1 peeled and chopped small red onion, 2 peeled and chopped cloves of garlic, 1 deseeded and chopped red pepper and ½ a peeled and deseeded cucumber into a blender and blitz until smooth. Add 250–300ml tomato juice, 2 tablespoons sherry vinegar, 4 tablespoons dry sherry, 1 tablespoon caster sugar and a pinch of cayenne pepper. Season well with salt and freshly ground black pepper. Blend again until well combined and smooth (in two batches if necessary). Pass the mixture through a sieve into a large jug or bowl, pushing through the sieve to make sure you get all the juices from the pulp. Chill in the fridge for at least 1 hour. Serve in bowls and garnish with finely diced hard-boiled eggs, yellow, green and red peppers, cucumber and spring onions.

BARBECUED CAMEMBERT Serves 8–12

Delicious cooked straight on the barbecue or in the oven and served as a starter with red-onion marmalade (page 404).

Light a barbecue and allow the flames to settle until the charcoal has turned white and is piping hot. Remove 2 x 250g Camemberts from their boxes and paper wrappings and make incisions in the top of the cheeses. Stud with rosemary sprigs and 2 peeled and finely sliced cloves of garlic. Place the cheeses back in their boxes and on to a sheet of foil. Drizzle with olive oil and season with salt and freshly ground pepper. Wrap the foil around both boxes to make a secure parcel. Place on the barbecue and cook for 10–15 minutes until the centre is melted and oozing.

A chilled Provençal rosé or a Chilean Sauvignon Blanc are lovely with Mediterranean-style summer starters.

MEATS AND MARINADES

During summer, food preparation should reflect the mood of the season. Everything should be easy to assemble, as the last thing anyone wants to do is slave away inside on a hot, lazy day. Sausages and burgers are staples of most barbecues, while marinated chicken thighs are inexpensive and probably my favourite. Marinate meats in the fridge for at least 1–2 hours, but preferably overnight so the flavours develop. For a hungry crowd a marinated leg of lamb is always a popular choice, sliced and served in wraps with a variety of salads.

PRACTICAL TIPS FOR BARBECUING

- *A charcoal barbecue is traditional and provides the unique, hands-on satisfaction of building and starting a fire, but a gas grill is quick, clean and convenient — better for catering on a larger scale.*

- *Useful kit includes tongs, skewers to cook food on (always soak wooden ones in water beforehand so they don't burn), aluminium trays and disposable foil platters to keep food warm on (don't use the same plate or board for uncooked and cooked foods). Always cook meat from room temperature rather than fridge cold.*

- *When cooking over coals, allow the flames to settle on the barbecue and wait until the charcoal has turned white.*

- *An oven can be useful to start cooking larger pieces of meat and is another place to keep food warm.*

- *Cook on a clean grill each time. Use a wire brush while the grill is still hot so the food comes off easily.*

MEDITERRANEAN MARINADE Serves 8

These flavours are wonderful with butterflied leg of lamb. Cook for roughly 6–8 minutes per 450g, plus an extra 20 minutes. Allow the lamb to rest to give you juicy pink meat. As a guide, a 1.8kg leg will feed 8 people.

Mix together 100ml olive oil, the zest and juice of 2 lemons, 2 tablespoons anchovy sauce (or 30g finely chopped anchovies), 4 tablespoons chopped fresh rosemary, 4 peeled and crushed cloves of garlic, and season well.

SPICY YOGURT MARINADE Serves 8

This is a lovely marinade for up to 16 chicken thighs or drumsticks. As a guide, bone-in chicken thighs will need about 15 minutes on each side to cook through, and boneless ones around half that time.

Mix together 800ml Greek or natural yogurt, 4 peeled and crushed cloves of garlic, 4 tablespoons mango chutney, the zest and juice of 2 oranges, 4 tablespoons mild curry powder, 4 tablespoons chopped fresh coriander, and season well.

HOMEMADE BURGERS

Homemade burgers are very easy to make in advance using good-quality mince with lots of seasoning. Classic beef burgers (page 306) are a safe choice, especially mini ones for children, but adults will appreciate more interesting flavour combinations. Avoid turning your burgers too often on the barbecue, otherwise they will fall apart. For an extra surprise, cram a chunk of your favourite cheese into the middle of the patty and let it melt as the burger cooks. Yum!

SERVES 8 (MAKES 8–10 OF EACH)

LAMB AND MINT

1kg lamb mince

1 small red onion, peeled and finely chopped

2 garlic cloves, peeled and finely chopped

2 tablespoons mint sauce

a small handful of chopped fresh mint

1 egg yolk, to bind

salt and freshly ground black pepper

PORK AND HERB

1kg pork mince

1 small onion, peeled and finely chopped

2 garlic cloves, peeled and finely chopped

3 tablespoons apple sauce

2 tablespoons wholegrain mustard

4 tablespoons chopped sage leaves

2 egg yolks, to bind

salt and freshly ground black pepper

To make the burgers, put all the ingredients into a large bowl, season well with salt and freshly ground black pepper, and mix together well to combine. Using clean, wet hands, shape the mixture into 8 equal patties, pressing down to make burger shapes. Place on a baking sheet, cover with clingfilm and chill in the fridge for 1 hour. Light a barbecue and allow the flames to settle until the charcoal has turned white and is piping hot. Drizzle the burgers with a touch of olive oil and then grill on the barbecue for 6–8 minutes on each side, until cooked through.

 Red wines, such as Australian Shiraz or Cabernet Merlot.

BUILD YOUR OWN BURGER *The joy of a well-made burger is in being able to customise it to your particular taste. Make sure you buy a good selection of bread: white, brown and seeded rolls, as well as ciabatta, pitta and wholemeal wraps. This can make or break a really good burger (remember, the buns need to be the right size for the burgers). Offer a wide selection of fillings: different cheeses, such as Cheddar, Emmenthal, mozzarella and blue cheeses, sliced tomatoes, avocados, gherkins and lettuce. As well as standard condiments, offer other garnishes such as fresh pesto, chilli sauce and garlic mayonnaise, or for ease, mix up an all-in-one combo sauce of equal parts mayonnaise, ketchup and mustard.*

FOIL-WRAPPED FISH

Wrapping and steaming in foil is a great way to cook delicate fish on the barbecue, as you seal them up like tasty presents. These neat parcels serve 8 as part of a barbecue spread, or 4 as a main course. Light the barbecue and allow the flames to settle until the charcoal has turned white hot. To prepare any of the fish parcels below, arrange two large sheets of foil on a flat surface in a double layer. Brush the top layer with olive oil to prevent the fish from sticking as it cooks.

A dry white Bordeaux is a good choice for barbecued fish.

SEABASS WITH FENNEL, LEMON AND CAPERBERRIES

Finely slice 1 fennel bulb, 2 celery sticks and 1 lemon and spread half the slices over the centre of the foil in a layer. Place 1 x 1kg whole seabass, scaled and gutted, on top and fill the cavity with the rest of the fennel, celery and lemon. Scatter 75g caperberries and 2 teaspoons fennel seeds in and around the fish. Fold the edges of the foil inwards to ensure no juices escape. Pour in 200ml dry white wine, 4 tablespoons vermouth and 100ml fish stock. Season well, dot with butter and wrap securely. Barbecue for 30–35 minutes until the flesh is opaque, the skin comes off easily and the flesh flakes away from the bones.

TIP: *Follow the method above, but replace the seabass with 2 rainbow trout, flavoured with lemon and herbs.*

MACKEREL WITH LIME, GINGER AND CHILLI

Score 8 pin-boned mackerel fillets and place in a shallow dish. For the marinade, whisk 2 tablespoons each of runny honey, fish sauce and soy sauce with 4 tablespoons sesame oil, 2 peeled and crushed cloves of garlic, and the zest and juice of 2 limes in a bowl, and season well. Peel and finely grate a 2.5cm piece of fresh ginger and add to the marinade with 1 deseeded and finely sliced red chilli. Pour over the fish and allow to marinate for 3–5 minutes. Transfer the fillets to the centre of the foil. Fold the edges of the foil inwards to ensure no juices escape. Pour over the remaining marinade and wrap securely. Barbecue for 4–5 minutes until cooked through. Alternatively, barbecue the mackerel fillets directly on a well-oiled grill for 3–4 minutes on each side until nicely charred for crispy skin.

TIP: *As an alternative, wrap salmon fillets with sunblush tomatoes, black olives, capers, lemon juice and parsley.*

VEGETARIAN SIDES

Asparagus is delicious cooked straight on the barbecue grill for 5–7 minutes. Corn on the cob (page 392) can also be cooked on the grill until its outsides are nicely charred, and is wonderful dripping with melted flavoured butter.

TOMATO, RED ONION AND BASIL TART Serves 8

This tart is quick and easy to prepare; it's also tasty sprinkled with crumbled feta cheese. Eat it hot or cold.

Unroll 1 x 320g sheet of ready-rolled puff pastry, score a 1cm border around the inside and prick all over. Chill it while you prepare the filling. Preheat the oven to 200°C/gas 6 and place a baking sheet in the oven to heat up. Heat 2 tablespoons olive oil in a large frying pan. Add 3 peeled and sliced red onions, season well and fry over a medium heat, stirring frequently, for 10 minutes or until the onions have softened. Add 3 cloves of peeled and finely chopped garlic and fry for another 2 minutes. Remove from the heat and leave to cool slightly while you prepare the rest of the ingredients.

Thinly slice 400g plump ripe tomatoes. Spread 2 tablespoons sun-dried tomato paste evenly over the chilled base, followed by the onions, then place the tomato slices on top in rows. Drizzle with 1 tablespoon basil oil, season well and bake for 15–20 minutes or until the pastry is golden brown and well risen. Scatter 50g soft goat's cheese over the top and bake for another 5 minutes. Sprinkle over a handful of basil leaves and drizzle with balsamic vinegar. Cut into slices before serving warm.

RATATOUILLE VEGETABLE SKEWERS Serves 8

Soak 8 wooden skewers in water for 30 minutes, or use metal skewers. Light the barbecue and allow the flames to settle until the charcoal has turned white and piping hot. Chop and deseed 4 mixed peppers into bite-sized pieces, along with 1 courgette and 1 large red onion cut into wedges. Mix together in a large bowl 4 tablespoons olive oil, 2 tablespoons red wine vinegar, 2 peeled and crushed cloves of garlic, 1 tablespoon herbes de Provence or dried oregano and season until combined. Add 16 whole cherry tomatoes, the peppers, courgette and onion and toss together to coat. Allow to marinate for 30 minutes. Thread the marinated vegetables on to the skewers, and cook directly on the barbecue for 3–4 minutes on each side, until they are nicely charred and the vegetables have softened.

TIP: *For a quick ratatouille, heat 2 tablespoons olive oil in a large pan and sauté the vegetables for 4–5 minutes until soft. Season, add a little vegetable stock and a dash of sherry vinegar. Simmer for 15–20 minutes, then add a handful of shredded basil and cook for a further minute before serving.*

COLOURFUL SALADS

A selection of vibrant salads complements the caramelised smoky foods at a barbecue. Try the suggestions below, or toss fine ribbons of carrot and toasted cumin seeds with orange juice and a mustard vinaigrette. Keep your dishes covered until needed to deter insects (beaded net food covers are useful), and dress salads lightly just before serving, otherwise the leaves will wilt.

LENTIL AND GRILLED PEPPER SALAD Serves 8

The base of this salad can be made well in advance. Use dried Puy lentils for a nutty bite, or buy good-quality ready-prepared lentils. Peeling the skins off the peppers isn't essential but will make all the difference; as soon as they are cooked put them in a freezer bag and seal for a few minutes — then open and peel off the skin.

Preheat the grill or griddle or wait until the barbecue coals are red hot. Deseed and quarter 1 red, 1 green, 1 yellow and 1 orange pepper, drizzle with a little olive oil and season. Grill or barbecue for 6–8 minutes on each side until nicely charred and softened. Once cool, cut into strips or bite-size pieces.

Heat 1.2 litres vegetable stock in a large pan and add 300g Puy lentils and 2 bay leaves. Boil for 10 minutes, then simmer for 15 minutes or until tender. Drain and rinse the lentils in cold water, discard the bay leaves and transfer to a large serving bowl. Add the peppers and a small handful of chopped herbs, such as basil, parsley and chives. Season to taste and mix together with 150g cubed soft goat's cheese and 3 tablespoons olive oil.

PEA, MINT, BROAD BEAN AND RADISH SALAD Serves 8

Combine sweet emerald peas and fresh, slightly bitter broad beans (shell them by gently squeezing the cooked pods between your finger and thumb).

Boil a large pan of salted water and cook 600g (unpodded weight) fresh broad beans for 2 minutes, then add 300g garden peas and cook for a further 1–2 minutes until tender. Drain and rinse under cold water, pod the broad beans, then place the beans and peas in a large bowl. Add a small bunch of fresh chopped mint, 150g crumbled feta cheese and 150g radishes cut into quarters.

For the dressing, whisk together the juice and zest of ½ a lemon, 1 peeled and crushed clove of garlic, 2 teaspoons Dijon mustard, 1 teaspoon runny honey, 6 tablespoons extra virgin olive oil and salt and freshly ground black pepper to make a light vinaigrette. Add more oil, if necessary, until you achieve the desired consistency. Pour the dressing over the salad and toss to combine. Serve scattered with baby mint leaves and a little lemon zest.

SUMMER BERRIES

Nothing could be more symbolic of British summer afternoons than strawberries and cream. Eton Mess, a delicious combination of meringues, strawberries and whipped cream, is always popular. For a twist, freeze the mixture for 5–6 hours in a loaf tin and allow to soften slightly before serving as an ice-cream slice (see picture opposite).

SUMMER PUDDING Serves 8

Place 800g mixed summer berries into a large saucepan, add 100g caster sugar, 4 tablespoons fruit liqueur (Framboise or Cassis) and 4 tablespoons water. Bring to a simmer and add sugar to taste. Cook for a few minutes until the fruit has slightly softened and the sugar has melted. Allow to cool and strain, keeping the juices from the fruit.

Remove the crusts from 8 slices of thick white bread. Cut one slice into a circle to fit the base of a 1-litre pudding basin and another two slices to fit the top of the basin. Cut the remaining slices in half lengthways. Dip the smaller bread circle into the fruit juice so it absorbs the juice (use this to line the pudding basin). Dip the bread into the juice, lining the sides of the basin, overlapping as you go and pressing the edges together until all the bread is used up. Spoon the fruit into the centre. Dip the bread for the top of the pudding into the juice and use it to cover the top. Place a small plate over the pudding, top with a heavy weight and refrigerate overnight. Turn the pudding out and serve with double cream.

GOOSEBERRY FOOL Serves 8

This pudding is simple, elegant and light. The origins of its name derive from the French term 'fouler', meaning 'to mash'. If using frozen gooseberries, you will need to drain off any excess liquid.

Place 800g fresh or frozen gooseberries (reserving a few for a garnish) in a saucepan with 250g caster sugar and the seeds from 2 vanilla pods. Heat gently for 4–5 minutes until softened (allow 10–15 minutes if using frozen fruit). Transfer to a food processor and blend to a smooth purée, then pour into a large bowl and cool. Lightly mix 400ml Greek yogurt with 400ml shop-bought vanilla custard, then gently fold into the gooseberry purée to give a rippled effect. Spoon into serving glasses, drizzle with 2 tablespoons runny honey and garnish with gooseberries and lime zest.

STRAWBERRY AND ORANGE GRANITA Serves 8

The tangy flavours in this deep-orange-hued granita are almost too good to be true. Each mouthful tastes like a sherbet sweet and makes a cool palate cleanser after eating charred, barbecued foods.

Place 300g washed and hulled strawberries, the zest and juice of 2 oranges, 125g caster sugar and 100ml water in a food processor and blend until smooth. Transfer to a freezer-proof box with a lid and freeze for 2 hours. Stir, using a fork to break up the ice crystals, and return to the freezer for a further 2–3 hours or until completely frozen.

Remove from the freezer and allow to stand for 5–10 minutes at room temperature. Stir using a fork to fluff up the mixture and spoon into serving glasses (you could also use an ice-cream scoop to create perfect balls). Garnish with mint leaves.

HAZELNUT ROULADE

This was one of my granny's signature puddings, which she would always serve with a homemade berry compote (page 222) with fruits from her garden. I always think of her when I eat it. It's a great buffet-type pudding that can be made in advance. Serve alongside a jug of passion-fruit coulis to add a burst of colour.

SERVES 8

4 medium egg whites

200g caster sugar

2 teaspoons vanilla extract

½ teaspoon cornflour

I teaspoon white wine vinegar

75g toasted hazelnuts, chopped

80g Dulce de Leche

½ teaspoon sea salt

125ml double cream, softly whipped

For the coulis

8 passion fruit

150g icing sugar, sifted

Preheat the oven to 160°C/ gas 3. Cover a lightly buttered 32cm x 23cm Swiss roll tin with baking parchment. Whisk the egg whites in a large bowl until they form soft peaks, then gradually add the sugar, continuing to whisk as you do so. Add the vanilla extract, cornflour and vinegar and whisk until the mixture is stiff. Spread the meringue mix evenly over the tin. Scatter with the hazelnuts, reserving some for the filling and garnish. Cook in the oven for 25 minutes, then remove from the oven and allow to cool.

To create the roulade, place a sheet of baking parchment on a work surface and put the meringue face down on it. Using a palette knife, spread over an even layer of the caramel, allowing space along the sides for the filling to spread out, and sprinkle with sea salt. Spread with whipped cream and finally scatter over more hazelnuts.

Starting with the longer side closest to you, roll the roulade up, using the baking parchment to help you. Once completely rolled, turn it so that the join is on the bottom. Wrap in foil until ready to serve, then sprinkle with the remaining hazelnuts.

To make the coulis, scoop the passion-fruit contents into a blender. Pulse a few times to loosen the pulp from the seeds, then press through a sieve to extract all the juice. Add the icing sugar a little at a time and whisk until smooth, adding more sugar to taste.

SUMMER DRINKS

Summer drinks should be refreshing and packed with plenty of ice. Nothing celebrates the start of summer better than Pimm's. There are lots of variations but the basic recipe is on the bottles (one part Pimm's No.1 to three parts lemonade). I prefer the vodka-based No.6 Cup. If you find the mix too sweet, replace some or all of the lemonade with ginger ale. For a Pimm's Royale add a splash of Pimm's to a glass and top with Champagne. Ice cubes (page 285) made with borage are a fun garnish.

THE WIMBLEDON Serves 8

A fruity white-wine spritzer. Pour 16 tablespoons strawberry cordial into a large jug or bowl. Add 1.5 litres of chilled dry white wine, 800ml soda water, a handful of fresh mint leaves and the juice of 2 lemons. Mix together well. Serve over ice cubes in tall glasses.

MUSTIQUE RUM PUNCH Serves 8

This recipe is so good it has been renamed Pum Runch in my family due to its after-effects, probably because the typical rum used in Mustique is an 80%-proof Sunset rum. For this slightly less potent version, mix together 75cl white rum and 75cl dark rum with 1 litre of both orange juice and pineapple juice. Add 500ml passion-fruit juice and the juice of 4 limes (adjusting quantities to taste). Add a dash of Angostura Bitters and grenadine syrup to achieve the desired colour along with a generous grating of nutmeg. This will keep for 1 month if refrigerated, so make a batch in advance and store in large plastic water bottles.

SUMMER PUNCH Serves 8

A light, refreshing drink for a summer's day, that can easily be doubled if you're serving
a thirsty crowd. Pour 200ml elderflower cordial (page 405) into a large jug or bowl and
add 200ml vodka, 1.5 litres of chilled Prosecco and 800ml soda water. Stir to combine.
Garnish with slices of lime and cucumber. Serve over ice cubes in tall glasses.

'ONE OF SOUR . . .' *Punch is a mixed drink that usually contains fruit juice. The name is derived from
the Hindi word 'panch', meaning 'five', a reference to the number of original ingredients — spirits, water, lemon
juice, sugar and spices. Employees of the British East India Company introduced punch to England from India
during the early seventeenth century. For homemade concoctions, stick with the rhyme 'one of sour, two of sweet,
three of strong and four of weak'. This should get everyone nicely in the mood!*

SUMMER SPORTS

Choose games that are suited to the space you have around you: play boules on gravel driveways while croquet, short tennis and badminton can be set up temporarily for a few weeks on grassy patches in the garden. Skipping games with giant ropes, hopscotch, tug of war and three-legged races can be enjoyed absolutely anywhere, on any surface, providing there's plenty of space, and if you are lucky enough to have one of those big trampolines, they are fun for young and old alike.

WATER, WATER EVERYWHERE ...

For children, water-fuelled games can save the day in hot, muggy weather. Provide a wide selection of water pistols and water guns in various sizes, which offer the possibility for both sustained and staccato squirting. The water bomb is also a firm favourite and can be used as a defence in water fights, with the potential for soaking multiple players in one go. Finally, the garden hose or sprinkler are not to be underestimated. If your venue allows it, turn a slope into a slippery slide using a sheet of plastic and a running hosepipe.

BALLOON DASH

Split everyone into pairs. Ask partners to arrange themselves along a starting line, standing back to back with their arms interlocking. Place a large water balloon in the small space between each pair's backs and when everyone is ready, call 'Go!' The pairs must then make their way to the finish line without dropping or breaking the balloon between them. If a balloon does break, then the pair responsible must head back to the start line – a little wetter than before – to get a new balloon and start again. The first pair to complete the race with their balloon still intact wins.

ROUNDERS

Rounders dates back to Tudor times and is enjoyable for kids and adults alike. I feel nostalgic whenever I think about this childhood game and it's great to play in the park or on the beach on sunny Sunday afternoons. Grab a rounders or baseball bat and ball, divide into teams and set up four 'bases' in a large open space (ideally these should be tall wooden poles pushed into the ground but shoes and clothing will do just as well). Look online to brush up on the rules, and let the competition commence.

TRADITIONAL FAVOURITES

THREE-LEGGED RACE

This is an old favourite from primary-school sports days but it can be enjoyed by all age groups. Ask everyone to get into pairs and give each pair a scarf or old pair of tights. Tie one player's left leg to the other player's right leg. Give everyone a few minutes to practise walking together, then line them up at the starting line. On 'Go!' everyone has to run to the finishing line. The first pair over the line are the winners. Make the race more difficult by forcing the pairs to walk sideways, like crabs. With adults you can make them face one another and tie the scarf around their waists. One person will be walking forward while the other has to walk backwards.

TUG OF WAR

Lots of English villages used to have a tug of war every year as a ritual to bring the community together. Divide your group into two evenly matched teams. Each member of the team stands in a line, one behind the other, with the two teams facing each other, about 3m apart. Draw a horizontal line or leave a length of ribbon at the midpoint between the teams and pass a long length of thick rope between them. On the starter's signal the two teams should begin to pull as hard as they can on their side of the rope. The object of the game is to pull the opposing team over the line. Make the contest the best of five.

CUP AND BALL

This is a variation on the ever-popular egg and spoon race. Give each player a plastic or paper cup and a tennis ball. Ask them to put the ball inside the cup and to balance it on their head. The weight of the tennis ball should hold the beaker in place but you have to keep your back very straight and move very smoothly to stop it slipping off. Line your players up, and on 'Go!' they must make their way to the finishing line without the beaker falling off their head. Every time they drop the ball they have to go back to the beginning. To make this game more 'refreshing', you can replace the tennis ball with water.

LIMBO

You'll need something to act as your limbo stick, such as a piece of bamboo, a kitchen broom or simply a length of string pulled taut. Everyone takes it in turns to pass underneath, leaning their shoulders backwards and turning their face up towards the limbo stick, without falling or putting their hands on the ground for balance. At head height, everyone should make it to the other side. The bar is then lowered a few centimetres and players take another shot at limboing under it. Anyone who touches the stick or the ground goes out. It gets harder as the bar continues to lower: the person who can limbo lowest is declared the winner.

'Hold hard a minute, then!' said the Rat. He looped the painter through a ring in his landing-stage, climbed up into his hole above, and after a short interval reappeared staggering under a fat, wicker luncheon-basket.

'What's inside it?' asked the Mole, wriggling with curiosity.

'There's cold chicken inside it,' replied the Rat briefly; 'coldtonguecoldhamcoldbeefpickledgherkinssaladfrenchrollscress-sandwichespottedmeatgingerbeerlemonadesodawater—'

'O stop, stop,' cried the Mole in ecstasies: 'This is too much!'

The Wind in the Willows, Kenneth Grahame

PICNICS

Being outside in the open air, lazily picking at foods while surrounded by nature, is what I love about picnics. Eating *al fresco* seems to heighten the senses; food tastes better, air smells cleaner, birds sing louder and you notice little things like the wildlife passing close by. The earliest picnics were in the form of medieval hunting feasts where people ate pastries, hams and other cooked meats, but the practice became popular during Victorian times. The development of the railways encouraged rambling in the countryside, and the decline of coaching inns – until then relied upon for a decent meal – meant people had to cater for themselves. Today, the possibilities of picnicking are endless, and it has become a more accessible activity than ever before; be it close to home, faraway or abroad, each picnic spot is unique and evocative in its own way. Perhaps the best locations for these moveable feasts are those that are unexpected and random – maybe reached by bike, or stumbled across on a walk: little pieces of previously undiscovered paradise.

You can picnic almost anywhere and in any scenario; a favourite secret place in a local park under the shade of intertwining tree branches; a spot in a wild meadow hidden among lush long grass, surrounded by dandelion clocks and visited by wayward insects; or perhaps on the beach alongside bats and balls, sandcastles and swimming – the seaside in all its glory with seagulls swooping down on crumbs after you've left. Picnics can also be part of a sociable and celebratory occasion: at the side of a cricket pitch, at an outdoor concert or after a school sports day.

Some of my fondest family memories are of picnics while on walks in the Lake District, perched on the brow of a hill with strikingly beautiful views, miles from anywhere, the landscape punctuated by mountains, tarns and the speckle of Cumbrian villages. There was always a flurry of activity before we set off, as we prepared the picnic as efficiently as possible so as not to lose the best of the day. One would butter the bread slices, another would fill them and someone else would gather bits and pieces, such as chocolate bars, fruit and drinks, making sure nothing was forgotten. The challenge was to be able to fit everything neatly into a few rucksacks so that it would travel well on our backs and in such a way that an essential reward – such as Kendal Mint Cake or flapjacks – might be savoured towards the end of our expedition to fuel the last steps home.

OUTDOOR EXCURSIONS

Choosing the perfect spot always takes time if you're anything like me, but it's primarily about finding the flattest ground possible. The type of excursion will also determine what you can bring; if you are transporting the food on your back you need your picnic to be practical and minimal, but if you are driving to, say, the beach and are planning to settle in for the afternoon, you can bring plenty of food, utensils, wicker baskets and bags, as well as items to give shelter, shade and comfort.

Picnics are by nature casual affairs and the key is to reflect that when it comes to the contents of your hamper, bag or rucksack. The food needn't be elaborate; somehow the simplest food looks mouthwatering and delicious when spread on a rug and eaten outside in the elements. Figure out in advance how long you plan to picnic for – be it an excursion where you'll have half an hour to refuel (while admiring the view), or a more lazy, casual affair that often turns into an afternoon's grazing, as you while away the time exploring the surroundings or gently dozing off in the heat of the day.

A COMMUNAL FEAST

Foods that don't need cooking and only require a knife to divvy up are the best, or those that come in their own packaging will guarantee minimal fuss. Get fellow picnickers to contribute something special to the spread, be it homemade or grabbed from their local market. Each exciting parcel can be carefully laid on the rug and unveiled – a parade of treats and surprises, each simple component a wonder in itself. Washed down with chilled white or rosé wine, or a cold beer, this is the way to stop for lunch.

PICNIC ESSENTIALS

- **A rug**: *the focal point of any picnic; everything centres on this.*

- **A wicker hamper**: *complete with creaking hinges, the perfect accessory for a fancy picnic.*

- **A cool bag with chiller packs**: *ideal for drinks and perishable foods. Cool drinks in streams or rockpools and freeze fruit juices beforehand so they become slushes by the time you want to drink them. Store homemade drinks in stoppered bottles and flasks.*

- **Containers and crockery**: *Tupperware and tins (good for stacking), melamine plates and cups that can take being bashed about, or eco-friendly bamboo picnic-ware. Use party boxes for kids.*

- **Utensils**: *bottle opener, cutlery, napkins, mini chopping board with pocket knife, rubbish bags.*

- **Beach luxuries**: *deck chair, beach cushions, parasols and wind breakers, beach bag with games kit and towels or sarongs.*

BEACH PICNICS

There is something about the seaside — the salty air, the sand and sea between your toes and the liberating feeling of wide open space under big blue skies — that conjures up a sense of holiday and adventure. It provides the perfect location for picnicking, either hidden away between the rolling dunes or set back in a sandy inlet. Make paper windmills in advance to mark out your picnic spot or bring a bit of the beach back home with you in the form of a handful of pretty shells to make things with.

BEACH CRAFTS

PAPER WINDMILLS

In the run-up to your trip, build the excitement for children by making these windmills to take to the beach.

I : Stick two sheets of brightly coloured paper together using a glue stick. 2 : From each corner, cut a 10cm incision towards the centre of the paper. Gently bend every second point into the centre of the paper. 3 : When all four corners are folded, secure them at the centre by pushing a dressmaking pin through them. Use superglue to attach the pin to a cork. 4 : Glue a thin, short bamboo cane to the cork on the back of the windmill.

SEASIDE JEWELLERY

Rockpools and shorelines are treasure troves for discovering interesting objects to make keepsake jewellery out of.

I : Buy a friendship bracelet kit that includes coloured yarns and mixed beads or collect lengths of ribbon, raffia and leather. 2 : Using a thick darning needle, or the point of a pair of scissors, make a hole in the shells or other seaside objects. 3 : Thread on to lengths of yarn and other materials to make bracelets and necklaces.

SHELL SKEWERS

These are ideal for serving prawns, scallops or other seaside-themed foods on, and as a fun canapé-serving idea.

I : Wash any shells collected from the beach to thoroughly remove any sand, grit or salt from the surfaces. 2 : Using superglue or a glue gun, stick each shell to the top of a skewer.

PICNIC HAMPER FARE

Pasties and sausage rolls make ideal portable picnic snacks; the sausage rolls are pre-spread inside with condiments and the pasties are mini versions, so less likely to fall apart. Uncooked they can be frozen for up to 3 months (add to the cooking time until piping hot). Serve with real ale, lager shandy or lager top.

CORNISH PASTIES Makes 8

To make the filling, place 2 tablespoons Worcestershire sauce, 2 teaspoons English mustard (optional), 2–3 tablespoons cornflour, 2 teaspoons caster sugar and 300ml beef stock in a saucepan, then bring to the boil and simmer, stirring continuously, until thickened. Peel and dice I small potato, I small onion and ¼ of a swede and mix in a bowl with 200g beef stewing steak, trimmed of fat and finely chopped, and season well. Pour the sauce over and stir to combine. Leave to cool completely.

Preheat the oven to 220°C/gas 7. Roll 2 x 320g packs shortcrust pastry out until each is about 0.5cm thick and 20cm in diameter. Cut into 8 circles (approximately 12cm) using a pastry cutter. Spoon the filling into the centre of each pastry circle and spread it out, leaving a Icm gap at the edges. Brush the edges with a beaten egg yolk mixed with a little water and draw up the sides so they join at the top. Using your fingers, crimp together to seal. Transfer to a baking sheet, making sure to space them out. Brush all over with the rest of the egg yolk mixture. Chill for at least 20 minutes. Bake in the oven for 10 minutes at 220°C/gas 7, then reduce the heat to 180°C/gas 4 and cook for a further 15 minutes, or until golden.

SAUSAGE ROLLS Makes 8

Preheat the oven to 200°C/gas 6. Unroll one 320g ready-rolled puff pastry sheet on to a lightly floured surface and roll out to make it slightly bigger. Cut into 8 equal rectangles, each a little longer than the sausages you are using. Lightly spread each rectangle with ½ teaspoon mustard. Place a sausage in the centre of each rectangle and top with a tablespoon of tomato chutney or red onion marmalade (page 404). Brush the edge of the pastry square with a beaten egg yolk mixed with a little water.

Roll out a second puff pastry sheet to the same size as the first. Cut into 8 equal rectangles, placing one on top of each sausage. Press around the sausage firmly to make sure it is well sealed and then trim the edges (leaving a 0.5–Icm border) with a sharp knife. Place on a baking sheet lined with baking parchment. Using a fork, crimp the edges of each sausage roll and prick the top. Brush all over with the rest of the egg-yolk mixture and chill for at least 20 minutes. Bake for 20–25 minutes, until the pastry is golden brown.

THE CORNISH PASTY *This traditional British pie has attained iconic and protected status and is instantly recognisable by the distinctive shape of its pastry casing. By the end of the eighteenth century it had become a staple lunch for farmers and miners in Cornwall because it was nutritious (the traditional filling is beef, potato, swede and onion seasoned with salt and pepper) and portable. Some accounts say that the crimping across the top acted as a convenient handle that could be discarded without being eaten to ensure that dirty hands didn't touch the food.*

WATERCRESS AND GOAT'S CHEESE QUICHE Serves 8

For more civilised picnics, transport this quiche whole in its tin. Pre-slicing it will make it easier to dish out, or make individual versions in mini tart tins and store in a large plastic container layered with baking parchment. You can make this up to 3 days in advance.

Roll 375g shortcrust pastry out on a floured surface and use to line a 26cm loose-bottomed fluted flan tin. Press the pastry into the tin, allowing an overhang. Prick with a fork and chill in the fridge for 30 minutes. Preheat the oven to 200°C/gas 6. Line the pastry with baking parchment or foil and fill with ceramic baking beans. Bake blind for 20 minutes. Remove from the oven and brush with beaten egg. Return to the oven to cook for a further 5 minutes, until golden. Allow to cool and then carefully remove the pastry overhang using a small, serrated knife. Reduce the oven temperature to 170°C/gas 3.

For the filling, heat 2 tablespoons olive oil in a pan and gently sweat 2 trimmed and sliced leeks (approximately 150g) for 10 minutes until softened. Stir in 150g trimmed and roughly chopped watercress, stalks and allow to wilt. Remove from the heat to cool. In a large bowl, beat 6 medium eggs and 300ml double cream together until combined. Stir in 1 teaspoon freshly grated nutmeg and 4 tablespoons green pesto and season well with salt and freshly ground black pepper. Stir in the cooked watercress mixture. Place the tin on a baking sheet and pour in the filling. Arrange 150g thinly sliced or crumbled goat's cheese on top and bake in the oven for 30 minutes, until light golden and set. Remove from the oven and allow to cool slightly if removing from the tin.

TIPS: *The uncooked pastry case can be blind-baked from frozen. Add a few more minutes to the cooking time until golden brown and crisp. • You can replace the watercress with cooked, drained spinach.*

SMOKED MACKEREL PÂTÉ Serves 8 (makes 400g)

This provides an authentic taste of the sea and can be made in a flash. Decant into a sealable plastic tub for dipping or spread straight on to mini buns with a few lettuce leaves and wrap in clingfilm to keep fresh. It makes a delicious starter, served in quenelles with red-onion marmalade (page 404).

Place 4 fillets (approximately 250g) smoked mackerel, the zest and juice of ½ a lemon, 1 tablespoon creamed horseradish sauce and 125ml crème fraîche or light cream cheese into a food processor. Add a generous pinch of cayenne pepper and season with salt and freshly ground black pepper. Blend until smooth and transfer to a serving dish. Place in the fridge and chill for at least an hour. Sprinkle with 1–2 tablespoons chopped chives, cayenne and cracked black pepper to serve. This will keep in the fridge for 3 days.

A SHELLFISH FEAST

There's something wonderfully satisfying about cooking fish or shellfish fresh off the boat. Peeling the shells, dipping the sweet flesh into garlic mayonnaise (just add crushed garlic to your favourite brand and combine) using only your fingers brings out a hunter-gatherer feeling. Live, freshly caught lobster, crab and langoustines should all be cooked in rapidly boiling, salted water. Cook lobster for 6 minutes per 450g, crab for 10–15 minutes until they float, and langoustines for 2–3 minutes.

POTTED SHRIMPS Serves 8

These tiny shrimps set in butter have a sweet, distinctive flavour and are delicious spread on bread or oatcakes. Alternatively, serve these as a starter with Melba toast. Picked white crabmeat can also be used in place of the shrimps.

Clarify 300g salted butter by melting it in a pan over a gentle heat. Allow it to simmer very gently until foam forms on the surface, then use a spoon to skim off the foam, until you are left with a clear butter. Once it has settled, pour it into a jug, discarding any sediment left behind. Place 500g cooked and peeled brown shrimps in a large bowl and add ½ teaspoon ground blade mace, ½ teaspoon freshly grated nutmeg, 1 teaspoon Gentleman's Relish, the zest and juice of 1 lemon, salt and freshly ground black pepper and a generous pinch of cayenne pepper. Stir together to combine. Spoon the shrimps into eight ramekins. Pour the clarified butter over the shrimps so they are just covered. Chill in the fridge for 1 hour or until set. These will keep in the fridge for 3–4 days.

MUSSELS IN WHITE WINE Serves 4 (or 8 as a starter)

When we have mussels at home, you'll always find my dad in the kitchen. Aside from time spent cleaning them up (debearding them), they are quick to cook and can even be wrapped in foil and steamed on the barbecue.

Melt 30g butter in a large, deep saucepan that is big enough to hold all the mussels, then add 6 peeled and finely chopped round shallots and 4 crushed garlic cloves. Cook for a few minutes until softened but not coloured. Add 2kg cleaned mussels to the pan with 300ml white wine and cover with a lid. Cook for 4–5 minutes over a high heat, shaking the pan occasionally, until the mussels have opened. Discard any that do not open. Spoon out the mussels keeping them warm in another pan and reduce the liquor a little. Add a squeeze of lemon juice, 200ml double cream, some chopped flat-leaf parsley, and season. Heat for a further 2–3 minutes to thicken slightly. Serve in bowls with the sauce poured over, with a French baguette.

A cold Meursault, Muscadet or Champagne goes well with shellfish.

BEACH GAMES

There's a whole host of fun to be had on a wide open beach with a cricket bat and ball, a kite to fly, traditional quoits or diablo juggling.

WHEELBARROW RACES

Divide players into pairs. One in each pair needs to get on all fours, to be the 'wheelbarrow', while the other holds their legs and is the 'driver'. You can devise a huge variety of races. An obstacle race involves more skill and can include negotiating sandcastles, spades stuck in the sand and cricket stumps. The average beach bag is bound to contain everything you need for props.

BRITISH BULLDOGS

Two 'home' areas are marked out at either end of the space, and one or two people are chosen as bulldogs. They stand in the middle of the space; everyone else lines up in a home area. When the bulldogs shout 'British Bulldogs!' the players must run across the pitch to the opposite home area. If they are caught by a bulldog who manages to hang on to them long enough to shout 'British Bulldog – one, two, three', they must become a bulldog too in the next round, and so it goes on. The last player to be caught is the winner.

ULTIMATE FRISBEE

Split into two teams of between four and ten people. Mark out two 'endzones', or goals, at either end of a large, rectangular playing space. To start, teams line up within the endzone they are defending. A player on the starting team throws the Frisbee to someone on the other team in the opposite endzone. This first catch marks the beginning of play and everyone is now free to run into the middle of the pitch to attack and defend, intercepting the Frisbee when it comes their way. A goal is scored when a team completes a pass to a player standing in the endzone that they are attacking. Players cannot run with the Frisbee; they can only pass it. If the team not in possession intercepts the Frisbee by catching it or knocking it to the ground, they can start heading towards their endzone. Agree a number of goals to aim for to decide the winning team.

ROUNDING OFF THE DAY

When the heat has gone from the sun and the light turns golden, mix up some seaside-inspired sundowners. Once home, with sand still sticking to your hands and feet, a sandcastle cake is the perfect solution to flagging spirits, especially if you happen to have missed the passing ice cream van.

ICE CREAM SANDCASTLE CAKE

To recreate your day at the beach, buy a tub of vanilla ice cream on your way home. Just before serving, run a knife around the ice cream and cut the tub with scissors before turning it out on a serving plate. Scatter with crushed digestive biscuits.

TIP: *Use mini ice cream tubs for individual servings, varying the flavours and biscuit type.*

SEA BREEZE Serves 4

Pour 100ml vodka, 200ml cranberry juice, 200ml grapefruit juice and the juice of 1 lime into a cocktail shaker, flask or jug. Shake or mix together well to combine. Divide ice cubes between four glasses and pour the cocktail over. Stir well and garnish with lime wedges.

TIP: *Keep drinks really cold in flasks or cool bags and bring along a few salted nuts as nibbles to go with them.*

DARK AND STORMY Serves 4

Mix 100ml dark rum with the juice of 1 lime in a cocktail shaker, flask or jug and shake or mix well to combine. Pour into four glasses over ice cubes and top each with ginger beer. Stir well and garnish with lime wedges.

TIP: *A rum punch is another classic sunset cocktail (page 348).*

COUNTRYSIDE PICNICS

Walking or cycling to a picnic spot brings a real sense of achievement and satisfaction; the food is more enjoyable eaten in the fresh air, mid-expedition. However limited the space is in your backpack, include a few luxuries to make the excursion worthwhile.

PACKING ESSENTIALS

- **A rucksack**: *practical for longer expeditions. Pack a couple of picnic rugs and wrap foods well to avoid leaks, spillages and things getting squashed.*

- **Snacks**: *scrubbed radishes, a bunch of carrots, tomatoes on the vine, hard-boiled eggs, Scotch eggs, pork pies, cheese sealed in its rind and energy-rich treats (page 378).*

- **Drinks**: *homemade infusions in stoppered bottles (page 375), cans of beer, individual juice cartons and miniature screwtop wine bottles (easy to open and practical to pack and chill quickly).*

- **Sandwiches**: *wrap tightly in baking parchment, clingfilm or foil so they don't fall apart. Rolls are good because they are squashable and are less likely than slices of bread to fall apart. See page 272 for some filling ideas.*

- **Fruit**: *shiny cherries still in their brown-paper bag, bunches of grapes, watermelon slices, whole strawberries, plums, apples and bananas. Store soft fruit in hard plastic containers to avoid bruising and squashing.*

COUNTRYSIDE PICNIC FOOD

When I think of idyllic picnics in the countryside, the sorts of foods I enjoy have a Mediterranean feel to them. If you're on an excursion, then of course sandwiches are practical, but elevate them from the ordinary by making a giant filled picnic loaf that can be cut into hearty slices (page 374). Let your menu be dictated by what's in season: take a trip to a farmer's market for fresh fruits and vegetables, and choose interesting local cheeses and wines. If the picnic spread is for a summer sports day or a cricket match tea and you're catering for a crowd, homemade foods, such as a prepare-ahead roulade, a vegetarian quiche (page 363) or a pork terrine (page 377) are always appreciated. Make your picnic food as exciting as the action on the pitch.

Keep it light, with Beaujolais and cool, crisp whites, such as Pinot Grigio, Gavi and Sancerre.

SPINACH ROULADE Serves 8

This looks really impressive, but tastes surprisingly light. Make it the day before or freeze the unfilled roulade up to one month ahead (defrosting it fully before filling it). Transport it tightly wrapped in clingfilm or in a loaf tin.

Preheat the oven to 220°C/gas 7. Lightly butter a 23cm x 32cm Swiss roll tin and line with baking parchment greased with butter. Wash 500g baby spinach, stalks removed, and put into a pan without draining. Cook over a gentle heat for 1–2 minutes until the spinach has just wilted. Drain well, squeezing out any excess water, then coarsely chop it in a food processor. Separate 4 eggs. Tip the spinach into a large bowl and beat in 30g butter, the egg yolks and a generous grating of nutmeg. Season with salt and pepper. In another bowl, whisk the egg whites until firm but not dry, then fold gently into the spinach mixture. Pour into the prepared tin and bake for 10–12 minutes.

For the filling, mix together 200g ricotta, 20g grated Parmesan, the zest and juice of 1 lemon and a small handful of chopped basil, and season well. Spread in an even layer over the roulade. Scatter over 75g chopped sunblush tomatoes and then roll up from one long side. Cover and chill for 30 minutes. Allow the roulade to come up to room temperature and sprinkle with a little grated Parmesan before cutting into slices to serve.

TIP: *Experiment with different fillings depending on what's in your fridge at the time, such as sundried tomatoes, a combination of crème fraîche with mushrooms, smoked salmon, prawns, blue cheese or a garlic and herb cheese.*

PICNIC LOAF Serves 8

The best way of feeding a crowd on a picnic, this loaf packs everything in and has a special-occasion feel about it. You can make this the night before and refrigerate it to let the flavours develop. Combine 2 tablespoons grainy mustard and 6 tablespoons good-quality mayonnaise in a small bowl with a squeeze of lemon juice. Mix together 80g sliced artichoke hearts, 75g finely chopped sunblush tomatoes and 3 tablespoons chopped basil and season well. Cut a 'lid' off a medium round cobb loaf, then scoop out the bread from the inside to make room for the filling. Spread the mustard mayonnaise around the inside of the bread, then start to layer up the fillings with the artichoke and tomato mix, 200g thickly sliced cooked ham, 200g Somerset Brie and 75g picked watercress leaves. Press together gently, put the lid back on the bread, secure with string like a parcel and wrap it tightly in clingfilm to pack in your rucksack.

PEA AND MINT SOUP Serves 8

Gently heat 1 tablespoon olive oil in a large saucepan, then add 1 bunch spring onions, trimmed and roughly chopped, and cook over a gentle heat for 3–4 minutes, until they are soft. Add 1 crushed garlic clove and cook for a further minute. Add 1kg frozen peas, 1 bunch fresh mint leaves, 1½ tablespoons caster sugar (optional) and 850ml vegetable or chicken stock. Cover the saucepan with a lid and simmer for 5–6 minutes, then put to one side to cool slightly. Remove the mint from the pan, transfer the soup to a food processor and blend. (It can be frozen at this stage for up to 3 months. Defrost before reheating and adding the crème fraîche.) Return to the pan, and stir in 50g crème fraîche. Warm through for a further 4–5 minutes, add a squeeze of lemon juice and season to taste. Serve hot or cold with crusty fresh bread.

REFRESHERS

OLD-FASHIONED LEMONADE Makes 2 litres

Put 200g caster sugar, 300ml water and the zest of 1 lemon into a large saucepan. Stir over a medium heat for 4 minutes until the sugar dissolves. Remove from the heat. Stir in the juice of 6 lemons and 1.7 litres of water. Strain into a jug and chill. This will keep for 3 days in the fridge.

HOMEMADE GINGER BEER Makes 2 litres

Finely chop 500g peeled root ginger in a food processor. Place in a large saucepan with 400g brown sugar and 2 litres water and bring to the boil. Boil for 1 minute, turn off the heat and cover loosely with a lid. Let the ginger mixture cool to room temperature. It can be used straight away or, for a stronger flavour, leave for 24 hours. Strain the ginger liquid through a fine sieve into a large jug; discard the solids left in the sieve. Add the juice of 1 lemon. Fill glasses with ice cubes and pour over the ginger beer. Top up with soda water, garnish with lime wedges to squeeze over and enjoy! This will keep for 3 days in the fridge.

PORK TERRINE

This rustic terrine is really worth the effort. It's a luxurious addition to any picnic. Serve in thick slices with a tomato or marrow chutney (page 404) or red-onion marmalade (page 404). You can make this 4 days in advance and keep it covered in the fridge, but leave out the egg as it will turn grey at the edges.

SERVES 8

50g smoked bacon lardons

100g chicken livers, roughly chopped

400g lean minced pork

1 duck breast, skinned

50g breadcrumbs

50ml milk

2 shallots, peeled and chopped

1 large garlic clove, peeled and chopped

20g salted butter

1 tablespoon coriander seeds

1 teaspoon black peppercorns

1–2 tablespoons Cognac

2 medium free-range eggs, whisked

30g dried sour cherries, chopped

30g pistachios, chopped

salt

1 packet smoked streaky bacon

4 medium eggs, cooked for 5 minutes and peeled but kept whole (optional)

Preheat the oven to 160°C/gas 3. In a food processor, blend the bacon, livers, pork and duck breast in batches to a coarse texture, then tip into a large bowl. Place the breadcrumbs in a separate bowl, add the milk and allow to soak for 5 minutes. Soften the shallots and garlic in the butter and cool slightly, then add to the food processor with the milk and breadcrumbs. Process to a rough texture, then add to the bowl with the meat, mixing well.

Grind the coriander seeds and peppercorns to a coarse powder using a pestle and mortar. Add to the bowl along with the Cognac, whisked eggs, sour cherries and pistachios and season well with salt. Mix together very thoroughly until combined.

Line a 900g loaf tin with the bacon rashers, reserving 3 slices for the top. Put half the terrine mixture into the tin, pressing it carefully into the corners. If using them, sit the cooked eggs in a line along the centre. Carefully spoon the remaining terrine mixture on top, pressing into the corners again. Arrange the reserved streaky bacon rashers over the top, tucking in the ends. Cover the dish tightly with foil, then put in a roasting tin with sides. Pour boiling water into the tin to come halfway up the sides of the dish. Bake for 2 hours, remove the foil, then bake for a further 15 minutes to brown the top. Cool completely, then wrap in fresh foil and chill overnight. Serve cold or at room temperature.

🍷 *A chilled Beaujolais.*

TIP: *To freeze the terrine, make it as above, cool and then freeze for up to 1 month. Defrost in the fridge before serving.*

REFUELLING SNACKS

These energy-giving bites are ideal on a walking or biking adventure for a mid-afternoon pick-me-up along with thirst-quenchers (page 375). They are just the sort of thing you'll need to get you to the top of that next hill or to settle into a satisfied sugary slumber. These will all keep for 3 days in an airtight container.

FLAPJACKS Makes 16 squares

Preheat the oven to 180°C/gas 4 and grease and line a 23cm square cake tin. Put 180g unsalted butter, 200g soft light brown sugar and 150ml golden syrup in a saucepan and heat, stirring occasionally, until the butter has melted and the sugar has dissolved. Add 400g porridge oats, 125g dried fruits (such as a mixture of dried apricots, dried cherries, sultanas and raisins) and 50g dessicated coconut (or mixed seeds), then mix well. Transfer the oat mixture to the tin and smooth down using the back of a tablespoon. Bake in the oven for 25–30 minutes, until light golden. Cool in the tin, turn out and cut into squares.

TRIPLE-CHOCOLATE TIFFIN Makes 16 squares

Line a 20cm square cake tin with baking parchment. Place a large bowl over a pan of simmering water, and put 100g unsalted butter, 300g milk chocolate and 8 tablespoons golden syrup in it. Stir together with a wooden spoon and, once melted, leave to cool for a few minutes.

Place 100g chopped good-quality dark chocolate (70% cocoa solids), 50g white chocolate chips, 100g raisins and 275g broken Rich Tea biscuits in a large bowl and stir together with the melted chocolate sauce. Pour into the lined tin, pressing into the edges and leave to set in the fridge for a minimum of 2 hours. Remove from the tin and slice into squares.

BANANA BREAD Serves 8–10

Lightly grease a 900g loaf tin and preheat the oven to 180°C/gas 4. In a large mixing bowl, beat together 100g softened, unsalted butter and 175g light brown sugar. Sift 225g self-raising flour and 1 teaspoon baking powder into the bowl and mix together until well combined. Peel and mash 3 large bananas and stir them into the mixture with 1 large egg, and mix well again. Pour the mixture into the tin and sprinkle the top with brown sugar, then bake in the oven for 50 minutes until the cake is well risen. Leave to cool slightly in the tin for 5–10 minutes, then remove from the tin and allow to cool completely on a wire rack. It can be frozen for up to 1 month.

Ging gang goolie goolie goolie goolie watcha,
Ging gang goo, ging gang goo,
Ging gang goolie goolie goolie goolie watcha,
Ging gang goo, ging gang goo.

'Ging Gang Goolie', Robert Baden-Powell

CAMPING

Camping is a celebration of being outdoors – rather like a picnic, but it brings an extra sense of camaraderie and adventure. Sleeping under canvas makes you feel removed from everything, whether you are pitching a tent at the bottom of the garden or in the wilds of the countryside by a wood or in a field. Most of my childhood camping memories take me back to sleepovers in my parents' garden or those of my friends'. Of course, we were never that far from the house, so perhaps not quite as courageous as we thought we were, but there was a certain novelty and excitement about sleeping outside, surrounded by the slightly spooky sounds of nature, sharing midnight feasts in the dark. We would spend the entire day preparing for it, gathering ingredients from the kitchen and foraging outside, setting up our camp. We would roast sticky sweet snacks on the fire, then at night we would talk around a lit torch until way past our normal bedtime – our chatter occasionally interrupted by the sound of the rain gently hitting the canvas or of some nocturnal creature nearby. If the night was particularly warm, we'd start off outside in our sleeping bags until the dew started to fall. Being out in the open air, exposed to the elements, brought a real sense of exhilaration . . . even if we had set up camp just yards from the back door (our parents would leave us the spare key, just in case).

Away from modern comforts and often with no mobile signal, camping can be therapeutic and provide a break from routine. There are no rules. The pace of day-to-day activities is dictated by nature's clock – falling asleep with the rising moon, the air chilled in the blackened night and waking with the morning light. There is something quite charming about a simple, nomadic existence, making a home away from home and tuning in to the rhythms of the earth. Life slows down, and even the smallest chores can turn into adventures: boiling water for tea, toasting bread or baking a banana in the embers of a fire.

Camping means different things to everyone, but it is almost universally accessible and can be enjoyed by all. It's not only affordable, but can be tailored to suit most needs, be it a bells-and-whistles 'glamping' experience, a backpacker-style adventure in the wilderness, a family holiday by the sea or a children's sleepover party in a garden. Whatever form it takes, camping is earthy, soul-enriching and character-building, and there can be few such satisfying moments as having your tent pitched and the smoke rising from your campfire as the golden sun sets on the horizon – even if it's just for a fleeting moment before the rain spoils everything.

DISCOVERING THE GREAT BRITISH COUNTRYSIDE *The enthusiasm for camping and the romanticisation of the countryside in Britain came about in the second half of the nineteenth century. Dramatic urbanisation meant that thousands of people had left rural Britain for work in the city; the countryside thus became a place associated with pleasure, to be explored and enjoyed, rather than providing a livelihood. Masses of city-dwellers would grab their bikes, which were safe, inexpensive and easy to ride, and the first lightweight tents of their kind, and head for the hills. Sleeping under the stars had truly caught on.*

PLANNING AND EQUIPMENT

If you are going on a backpacking adventure, it's particularly important to ensure that you have everything you need and that it's compact and lightweight. If you have your car nearby or are in sight of the house then you don't need to be quite so organised.

THE CAMPSITE

Check that your camping spot is not on restricted land and familiarise yourself with any rules and regulations. If you're planning to walk to your campsite, rucksacks are the most practical way of transporting everything. Always carry bags for rubbish and empties. You should leave the campsite without any traces of your being there.

PACKING

Check your tent before you leave, in case you need to make repairs. Traditional bell tents and teepees can be hired and bought online. Bring the right equipment for the weather conditions (check before you go): sun cream, hat and a towel for swimming, or waterproofs. Pack plenty of layers for when it gets cooler at night: fleeces, blankets, bed socks and beanies (even hot-water bottles). Make a checklist — it's easy to forget essentials, and it's useful to have when you arrive home to make sure nothing is missing. A few fun items that might add to the experience include long forks or skewers for roasting food over the fire, while folding chairs and tables can be useful for mealtimes. Children can perch on logs.

> ### USEFUL EQUIPMENT
>
> - *Tents, groundsheets, sleeping bags and blankets.*
> - *Torches (head torches are best!) and an LED hook light.*
> - *Firelighters and matches.*
> - *All-weather kit.*
> - *Swiss Army knife with tin and bottle opener, rubbish bags.*
> - *First-aid kit.*

FOOD AND DRINK

Plan what utensils you'll need (a ladle for serving stew, tongs for a barbecue or flasks to keep hot drinks warm). Rather than taking whole packets and bottles of food and drink, measure out what you'll need into smaller containers. Enamel, plastic or biodegradable plates, bowls and mugs are most practical. Foil is great for cooking and to keep things warm, and use ziplock bags for marinades and dressings. Bring plenty of water and cool bags. A 'brewing kit' for hot drinks with individually wrapped sachets will help guard against things getting damp. Long-life UHT is more practical than fresh milk.

TIPS: *Wrap cutlery in bandanas which are useful as napkins, neckties, pot-holders, or even eye-masks if you want to sleep past dawn.* • *Pack after-dinner grub in paper bags fastened with clothes pegs to keep insects and hands from creeping in.*

SETTING UP CAMP

It's imperative to pick a camping spot that is flat, well-drained and free from stones or sharp objects – grass is ideal. Test this out by lying on your chosen territory.

PITCHING THE TENT

Your tent needs to be sheltered from the wind, but if the weather is hot, angle it so that the breeze can flow through. If a slope is unavoidable, make sure your feet are facing down the hill to sleep. Hammer pegs in with a wooden mallet, and check that they're secure. It can be fun to have an encampment of several tents with bunting strung between them if you're celebrating a particular occasion; pitch them in a semicircle with a campfire in the middle, downwind. It's worth taking the time to practise putting up new tents beforehand, or to check for damaged or missing parts on old ones.

CAMOUFLAGE DENS *This is a great activity to keep kids busy while you set things up. Divide them into pairs and give them a limited time to create a camouflaged den or teepee using natural materials: pieces of wood, netting, rope, string, leaves and branches (anything they can find). If you like, pick a winning design based on how well camouflaged it is, how comfy inside, how waterproof and so on, but it doesn't have to be competitive.*

INSIDE THE TENT

When I used to camp in our garden, Dad would always use an outdoor extension cable and plug in an angle-poise lamp inside the tent, making our nights on our own a lot less scary – in hindsight, it was cheating a bit! Battery lanterns and torches are portable and authentic, while LED tent lights have useful hooks so you can hang them up. Try laying old rugs or carpet on the floor, or use sleeping mats, airbeds or camp beds. Hot-water bottles are a welcome luxury; plant them inside sleeping bags early in the evening to keep them warm until bedtime. Nothing can replace pillows, but choose special camping versions if you're pushed for space. Folding tables are useful for meals and games, but even an upturned wooden box covered with a cloth will do the job.

TIP: *Cut out shapes of stars and crescent moons to stick to the inside of the tent with double-sided sticky tape; when it gets dark and the tent is illuminated inside, you'll feel closer to the heavens.*

CAMPING CRAFTS

With adult help, these crafts are good for children to enjoy outdoors. They can communicate between tents with tin-can phones, mark the campsite with a home-made flag and make headdresses to form tribes for the team games on pages 396-7.

TIN-CAN PHONES

I : Pierce a hole in the base of two tin cans (best to get an adult to help with this). 2 : Thread the ends of a 3m length of thin rope or string through the holes in the cans. Tie knots at each end on the inside of the cans to secure. 3 : Keep the cord taut to speak and listen.

HOMEMADE FLAGS

I : Cut a rectangle out of calico, canvas or any plain, medium-weight cotton fabric. 2 : Fold one end around a straight branch or bamboo stick and get an adult to hand sew to secure, or stick with PVA glue. 3 : Paint designs on the fabric with waterproof acrylic paint.

HEADDRESSES AND WAR PAINT

1: Measure a strip of brown card to fit around the child's head allowing extra length to staple the ends together. 2: Decorate the card with geometric shapes and feathers using PVA glue or sticky tape. 3: Apply 'war paint' to faces, by making smudges of paint on each cheek, forehead and nose, but use your imagination for a more camouflaged version.

CAMPING FOODS

Camping provides a great excuse to enjoy food away from the constraints of sitting at the table and your typical routine, but it needs to be simple and easy to eat — especially if you are going to be eating at dusk. The main meals I have included are ideal for camping — one-pot dishes that should suit the mood and the occasion at the end of a day's adventure. They can be prepared at home beforehand and warmed up (if only for authenticity's sake). Dish out with a soup ladle into enamel bowls or hollowed-out bread rolls to capture all the juices. Bring a small bottle of Tabasco sauce to add a fiery finish! Thread some rope through a roll of kitchen towel and tie it up near your campfire for cleaning sticky fingers. Wet wipes, tea towels and bandanas are also useful to have to hand.

COOKING ON A FIRE

If you are a serious camper and plan to prepare your food and drink on the fire, build a campfire (assuming you're allowed to build one at your site). Check that the area is free from any dry tinder or overhanging wood. If it's windy, or you are on a beach, dig a pit and surround the fire with stones or bricks to keep it from spreading. (For tips on how to build a basic fire, see page 77.) Keep your campfire a manageable size, making sure water is always nearby just in case. Light the fire early in the evening as it will take time to give off any real heat and, before you go to bed, check that it is completely out. The best time to cook is when the flames are low and the embers are red-hot (high yellow flames are dangerous and will blacken pans). The main disadvantage of cooking on the fire is that it will give out less light; however, you can always stoke up the flames again after you've cooked everything. You will need a grill rack from your oven and two robust logs or stones on either side of the fire to lay it across to make a sturdy cooking platform. You can find or make a tripod that sits above the fire with a hook from which to hang a cooking pan. Alternatively, use a Dutch oven (a heavy cast-iron casserole with three legs), which can stand directly in the embers. For more about cooking over an open fire, see the Barbecue chapter (page 327).

If you'd rather not use an open fire for cooking, a portable stove or disposable barbecue can provide a more consistent heat source and is worth considering. Trangia stoves in particular are really compact and come with a small gas attachment and lightweight pans.

CAMPING SAUSAGES AND BEANS Serves 8

Kids will love this cowboy-style casserole, and for grown-ups you can add spices and chillies to give it extra bite —
alternatively, wrap strips of bacon around the sausages before cutting them up.

Heat 2 tablespoons olive oil in a large pan with a lid, add 1 peeled and roughly chopped onion and 2 peeled and crushed garlic cloves and sauté for 4–5 minutes, until softened. Add 6 sausages cut into chunks and 10 mini chorizo sausages cut in half (or a chorizo ring cut into bite-size pieces) and fry for a further few minutes, stirring from time to time. Stir in 1 teaspoon smoked paprika and 2 tablespoons tomato purée and mix well. Cook for another minute. Add 200g roasted red peppers from a jar, cut into bite-size pieces, 400g tinned chopped tomatoes and 400g tinned, drained haricot beans. Pour in 250ml chicken or vegetable stock, then bring to the boil and reduce the heat to a gentle simmer. Cover with a lid and allow to simmer gently for 25–30 minutes, removing the lid for the last 5–10 minutes to reduce the liquid and thicken the sauce. Stir in 100g baby leaf spinach, season with salt and freshly ground black pepper to taste and serve with jacket potatoes cooked on the embers of the fire, corn on the cob (page 392), or flat breads and pitta which will travel well.

CHILLI CON CARNE Serves 8

This is ideal spicy food for the great outdoors and can be prepared in advance, requiring just last-minute heating.
Serve in tacos with boil-in-the-bag rice or sweetcorn fritters (page 392).

Heat 1 tablespoon olive oil in a large pan and, once hot, brown 800g beef mince for a few minutes, until nicely coloured. Remove from the pan, drain off the excess fat and set aside. Wipe the pan clean and add 2 tablespoons olive oil. Sauté 2 large peeled and finely chopped onions and 4 peeled and crushed garlic cloves for a few minutes until softened. Add 1 red and 2 green deseeded and finely chopped chillies and cook for a further minute. Stir in ½ teaspoon chilli powder, 1 teaspoon each of cayenne pepper and ground cumin and 3 teaspoons paprika and cook for 1–2 minutes, then add the beef mince back to the pan. Stir in 4 tablespoons tomato purée and heat for 1 minute. Add 400ml red wine, bubble over a high heat for 2–3 minutes to burn off the alcohol and then add two 400g tins chopped tomatoes, 200ml beef stock and 2 cinnamon sticks. Bring to the boil, then reduce the heat, cover with a lid and simmer gently for 45 minutes, adding extra stock if necessary to loosen the sauce. Add 600g tinned, drained and rinsed kidney beans and simmer for another 15 minutes without the lid. Season the chilli with a dash of Tabasco sauce (if you like it hot) and season well with salt and pepper. Serve with sour cream and a generous scattering of grated Cheddar cheese.

A red Rioja, Argentinian Malbec or Chilean Cabernet Sauvignon will go well with both these hearty dishes.

TIP : *If you're planning to be away for a few days, freeze your main dishes prior to leaving (for up to 3 months)*
so they stay chilled for as long as possible. They can also act as ice packs to keep other food and drinks cold.

CAMPFIRE CORN

SWEETCORN FRITTERS Makes 12

I had almost forgotten about these until my dad reminded me how much he liked them on camping trips as a boy.

Sift 100g plain flour and 1½ teaspoons baking powder into a large bowl. Season well. Beat 3 medium eggs and add to the bowl, then mix together. Gradually whisk in 100ml milk to make a smooth batter. Stir in 200g tinned sweetcorn, 6 finely chopped spring onions, the zest of 1 lime and a squeeze of lime juice, 1–2 deseeded and finely chopped red chillies (to taste) and a large handful of chopped coriander. Heat 5 tablespoons vegetable oil in a frying pan. Drop generous spoonfuls of the fritter mixture into the pan and cook in batches for 2–3 minutes on each side until golden. Drain on kitchen towel, and eat immediately.

CORN ON THE COB WITH FLAVOURED BUTTER Serves 8

A classic favourite to cook on an open fire, but prepare the butter at home. You can use soaked corn husks instead of the foil to cook them in.

Place 4 peeled and crushed garlic cloves, 1 deseeded and chopped fresh red chilli, 2 teaspoons sweet paprika, a small handful of chopped fresh mixed herbs, such as parsley, chives and basil, and a squeeze of lime juice, into a food processor and season well with salt and pepper. Blend together until everything is finely chopped, then add 200g softened, unsalted butter and blend again until well combined. Spoon the butter mixture into the centre of a large piece of clingfilm. Wrap it tightly into a log shape, twisting the ends to secure. Chill until firm. Bring a large pan of water to the boil and cook 8 sweetcorn cobs for 6–8 minutes until almost tender. Drain and allow to cool. Place them on to individual sheets of foil and divide the flavoured butter on top. Wrap tightly in foil. Place the parcels on the hot coals for 10–15 minutes, turning frequently. Serve in the foil with the melted butter.

CORN CAKE Makes 16 squares

A cross between a sweet and savoury bread, this make-ahead recipe is inspired by one from a great Venezuelan friend.

Allow 2 squares per person. Preheat the oven to 200°C/gas 6. Grease a 20cm x 30cm tin and line with baking parchment. In a food processor, whizz together 4 x 200g tins drained sweetcorn, 250ml milk, 4 medium eggs, 5 tablespoons caster sugar, 1–1½ teaspoons salt and 150g softened, unsalted butter. Once combined, add 200g quick-cook polenta and 2 teaspoons baking powder and blend until the mixture is just combined and holds together. Do not over-process or it may become liquid. Mix in 75g mature grated Cheddar, then pour the mixture into the tin and bake for 30–35 minutes until golden brown. Serve with the chilli or camping beans (page 391).

FIRESIDE GRUB

These energy-packed snacks are ideal for campfires, or try trail mix (a mixture of nuts and fruit), also known as 'gorp' or 'scroggin'. Use the cookie-dough recipe (page 23), omit the fruit, and use plastic insects to make fossil shapes in the biscuits before baking.

HOT CHOCOLATE SPOONS Serves 8

Make these at home and bring them in a plastic container for a warming fireside treat.

Melt 200g good-quality chocolate in a bowl. Scoop 8 teaspoons into the runny chocolate, one at a time, so that it comes two-thirds of the way up the spoon. Arrange the spoons on baking parchment to set. To use them, dip into warm milk or hot chocolate and serve with marshmallows.

BANANA CANOES Allow 1 banana per person

These are cooked in their own skins in the embers of the fire — making them soft, smoky and sweet.

Slit the banana skins lengthways, cutting right through the flesh but without going through the skin on the other side. Fill with pieces of your favourite chocolate and wrap tightly in foil. Cook in the embers of the fire until gooey. Add a dash of rum for grown-ups.

DAMPERS Serves 8

Make the dough at home and take it with you in a zip-lock bag to toast in your campfire.

In a large bowl, rub together with your fingertips 500g self-raising flour, a generous pinch of salt, 15g caster sugar and 15g cold, cubed butter until the mixture resembles breadcrumbs. Make a well in the centre and gradually add 375ml of milk until it comes together, then turn out on to a lightly floured surface and knead until you have a soft dough. When you're ready to eat, break off a piece of dough, roll it into a 10cm sausage and push a long stick into the middle of it. Place the stick into the embers and toast for a few minutes, until golden. Remove the stick and fill the hole with chocolate spread, jam or golden syrup.

S'MORES Serves 8

These American treats are made using Graham crackers, but this recipe is a yummy British version using digestives.

Break up 200g good-quality chocolate into squares and divide between 8 digestive biscuits — about 4 squares per biscuit. Thread 16 marshmallows on to 8 sticks (2 per stick) and toast in the campfire until just softened and turning golden. Slide the toasted marshmallows off the stick and on to the chocolate, and then sandwich another digestive on top.

GAMES AND ACTIVITIES

This is a time to enjoy being away from computers, televisions and phones. Take plenty of torches, playing cards, travel games and books, such as a pocket illustrated wildlife or astronomy guide that can be read inside the tent. A game like pick up sticks is portable and light, or make your own version by using wooden sticks from the wild. A magnifying glass and some binoculars will help identify some of nature's wonders. For late-afternoon antics before the light fails, here are a few games and activities to keep kids busy.

MIDGIE BITES

Give each player a set of small round stickers (each player should have their own colour) – these represent midgie bites. The purpose of the game is to subtly 'bite' other players by planting stickers on their clothes without them noticing. The person who gets rid of all their stickers first, without being bitten themselves, is the winner.

CRAMBO

One player leaves the group and waits out of earshot. Everyone else comes up with a word. When the player comes back, they are given a word that rhymes with the chosen word. So for 'seat', the clue might be 'heat'. The 'guesser' then asks questions without actually saying the word that they suspect to be the answer. The exchange might go something like this: Guesser: Is it a part of the body? Player: No, it is not feet. Guesser: Is it somebody who plays foul in order to win? Player: No, it is not a cheat. Guesser: Is it something you do when you first encounter someone? Player: No, it is not greet. This goes on until the word is eventually guessed correctly. It can be hard for the guesser to frame their indirect questions, but sometimes it's even harder for the other players to work out the word that she or he is getting at. It requires inventiveness and quick thinking from everyone involved.

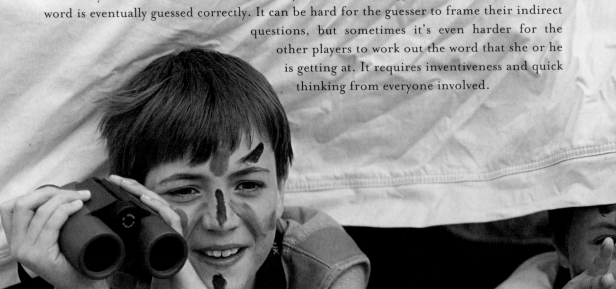

CAPTURE THE FLAG

Divide players into two teams. Lay down some kind of marker for the centre line. Each team takes one half as their territory. At one end of each territory – as far from the centre line as possible – a 'flag' (a scarf or a bandana) is laid down on the ground. The aim is to capture the opposing team's flag. To do this, players must enter the other team's territory, grab the flag and bring it back to their own side. Players defending their flag are allowed to tag members of the opposing team once they have left their own territory. When a player is tagged, they must drop the flag where they are. They are then sent to a designated jail space on the opposition's side, where they remain until one of their team-mates stages a 'jailbreak' (when a player runs and touches their team-mates to save them). Players returning to their own side after a jailbreak are granted 'free walk-backs' and cannot be tagged. The game is won when a player manages to bring the enemy's flag into their team's home territory. To make things harder, let teams hide their flags somewhere out of sight at the start of the game. I've seen players having to climb up trees to capture the enemy's flag. Try playing the game at night and replace the flags with glowsticks or lanterns.

KICK THE CAN

A can is placed on the ground in the middle of the playing area. A seeker is chosen; this person takes the can as their base. They cover their eyes and count to 40 while everyone else runs off to hide. Once the counting is complete, the seeker looks for the other players. If they spot someone hiding, they must run back to the can and – providing they get there first – touch it, while declaring that player 'in the can'. Anyone caught goes to a designated 'jail' area. However, if a player in hiding manages to make it to the can before the seeker does, they can kick it in order to release everyone. The game goes on until the seeker puts all of the other players in jail. At this point, the person who ended up in jail first is declared the seeker and a new game begins.

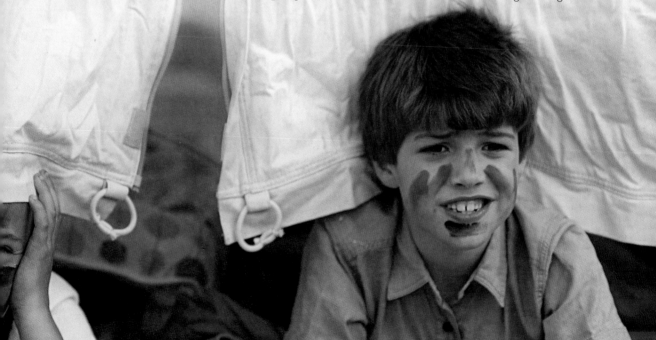

CAMPFIRE SONGS

When night begins to fall and the campers gather around the fire, there's nothing quite like a good old sing-along to bring people together. I have included a few songs that I remember singing as a child around a firebrick barbecue with our next-door neighbour strumming his banjo (a favourite being 'The Quartermaster's Store'). If someone can play an instrument well and lead the sing-along, this can really add to the atmosphere. Look up the lyrics of the songs below before your trip and make up song sheets to hand around.

GING GANG GOOLIE

This song is attributed to Robert Baden-Powell, the founder of the Scouting movement. All kinds of theories have been applied to the origins and meanings of its nonsense language, but perhaps most importantly it means that children of all nationalities can enjoy singing it.

ROW YOUR BOAT

Fun for younger children, this, along with many other songs such as 'London's Burning', 'Drunken Sailor' and 'Ten Green Bottles', can be sung in rounds, adding to the camaraderie.

UNDER THE SPREADING CHESTNUT TREE

This is just a short song: 'Under the spreading chestnut tree, where I held you on my knee / We were happy as can be; under the spreading chestnut tree.' The point is to see how many words in this song you can replace with actions. After you've sung it through a first time as it stands, sing it again and omit 'spreading' and instead spread your hands apart. The second time, omit 'chest' but pat your chest. The third time, also leave out 'nut' and tap the top of your head. Then leave the word 'tree' and instead mime tree branches. Then replace 'knee', by patting your hand to your knee, 'happy' and point to a large grin, and so on. Make it into more of a game if you are a crowd – whoever makes a mistake is out. Start again each time and see if you can get to the end.

THE QUARTERMASTER'S STORE

This song is made up of a verse that keeps changing, followed by a chorus that remains the same (look this up online). You can make up your own lyrics using people's names around the fire, such as 'Jim, nice but dim', or using animals and insects: 'lice, living on the mice'; 'rats, big as alley cats'; 'beans, as big as submarines'; 'snails, crawling on the nails'; 'moths, eating through the cloths'; 'bears, but no one really cares'; 'scouts, eating Brussels sprouts'; 'foxes, stuffed in little boxes' . . .

Many a night I saw the Pleiads,
rising thro' the mellow shade,
Glitter like a swarm of fireflies
tangled in a silver braid.

'Locksley Hall',
Alfred, Lord Tennyson

STAR GAZING

This activity is best in pitch darkness on a very clear night, and can be exciting for even quite young children. Wrap them up warmly and take them out on a late-night walk in the dark with torches. Binoculars are very useful for looking at the craters on the moon and spotting the Milky Way but not for studying individual stars, as they can be difficult to hold steady.

The major patterns in the night sky are easily identifiable when you get to know them. Start with the Milky Way and the Pleiades and then move on to the major constellations and asterisms (often confused with constellations, these are groups of stars that make particular shapes). Learn the names of some of the brighter stars and they will soon become your constant friends.

THE MILKY WAY

Easy to spot, the Milky Way galaxy is a beautiful spiral of stars stretching like a band of hazy light across the night sky. This galaxy contains somewhere between 200 and 400 billion stars and includes the Earth.

THE PLEIADES

The Pleiades is a cluster of hundreds of stars, of which only seven are usually visible to the naked eye. Also known as the Seven Sisters, it is conspicuous in the night sky with a prominent place in ancient mythology. There are wonderful pictures and diagrams of the Milky Way and the Pleiades on the Internet. You'll also find better guidance on how to find them in the night sky than I can manage in this book because it depends on which hemisphere you are in.

THE PLOUGH

An asterism, the Plough (or the Big Dipper) is part of the Great Bear and is always visible in the Northern Hemisphere. The saucepan pattern of its seven brightest stars is easily recognisable and it is very useful for locating Polaris (see below).

THE NORTH STAR (POLARIS)

Although not particularly bright, Polaris is important because it lies more or less along the axis of the Earth's spin. In the Northern Hemisphere it appears to be fixed at due north, with all the other stars rotating around it, so it is a very useful aid to navigation.

ORION

Orion (the Hunter) is only properly visible during the late autumn and winter months in the Northern Hemisphere. The easiest part of the constellation to spot is Orion's belt, a straight row of three stars which line up with other bright stars, such as Sirius, the brightest star in the night sky. Online star maps will show you how to use Orion to find a number of other important stars.

CASSIOPEIA

This is on the opposite side of Polaris from the Plough and has five principal stars in the shape of a 'W'.

Polaris

HOMEMADE PRODUCE

There's something very satisfying about seeing a row of your own homemade jams, chutneys, pickles or liqueurs glowing on the larder shelf. I always look forward to the harvesting times of the year, picking fruits like blackberries and sloes when they're at their best, or at pick-your-own fruit farms, staining my hands in the process. Then returning home to prepare jams and alcohol-based concoctions which takes up the whole weekend and covers the kitchen surfaces in a sticky mess. But that's all part of the process! Once well matured and prettily labelled, your homemade produce will make lovely presents for friends and family, but equally they are something you can enjoy yourself.

PRESERVING TOOLKIT

- **Thermometer**: *a sugar thermometer is the most accurate gauge of the setting point (104°C).*
- **Preserving pan**: *wide and heavy-based, to allow for even, rapid boiling.*
- **Jars and bottles**: *with tight-fitting lids and tops.*
- **Wax discs, elastic bands and labels**: *for sealing and labelling.*
- **Funnel**: *useful for cleanly decanting liquids into bottles.*
- **Muslin**: *for straining liqueurs.*

STERILISING BASICS

This is the most important part of preserving – the containers you use must be completely clean and sterile before you fill them, otherwise the contents will go mouldy. Remember to sterilise the lids and the tools you work with too.

I : Wash your jars, containers and lids in hot, soapy water and rinse well. 2 : Immerse them in boiling water for 10 minutes. 3 : Place the lidless jars upside-down on a baking tray in a preheated oven at 120°C/gas ½ for 10–15 minutes. 4 : Fill the jars while still warm.

PANTRY SUPPLIES

As well as the fruits and vegetables you've gathered, you'll need some basic ingredients.

- **Pectin:** *used to set jam. Some fruits are naturally higher in pectin than others, so will give a firmer set. Lemon juice is also sometimes used to raise the pectin level.*

- **Citric acid:** *used for cordials, this can be bought or ordered from most chemists.*

- **Preserving sugar:** *this sometimes contains added pectin, but granulated sugar also dissolves quickly so is a good substitute. Warm the sugar in the oven before using it.*

- **Vinegar:** *essential for all pickles and chutneys. Keep a variety in stock (red and white wine, malt and cider).*

QUICK STRAWBERRY JAM Makes 8 x 350g jars

This jam is great for using up an abundance of fruit in summer. The recipe is made with strawberries, but use it as a guide and change the fruits as you wish. Once opened it should be kept in the fridge and eaten within two weeks.

• *2.4kg hulled strawberries* • *1.2kg preserving sugar with added pectin.*

Put half the strawberries into a large preserving pan and crush lightly with a potato masher. Add the remainder of the fruit and the sugar, then place over a low heat and stir occasionally until the sugar has dissolved. Turn the heat up to medium and bring to the boil for 5–7 minutes for a loose jam, stirring to prevent catching, adding an extra 2 or 3 minutes if you prefer a firmer set. Remove from the heat, stir well and use a funnel to pour into sterilised jars. Leave to cool a little before covering with sterilised lids. Store in a cool dark place for up to 6 months.

TIP: *You can use any berry or soft fruit for jam, as long as it is not over-ripe; in fact, slightly under-ripe fruit is best. Wash the fruit and cut out any bruises, then peel, de-stone and chop larger fruit where necessary.*

FINDING THE SETTING POINT

There are several ways of checking that the setting point has been reached. The best and easiest is with a sugar thermometer (104°C), accompanied by a saucer test if required. Place a few saucers in the freezer while you make your jam. When the correct temperature has been reached, drop a bit of the mixture on to a cold saucer and let it cool for a moment. If the jam forms a skin and wrinkles when you run your finger through it, it's ready. Take the pan off the heat as soon as you reach the setting point — do not over-boil.

GRANNY'S MARROW CHUTNEY Makes 8 x 350g jars

This is my granny's recipe which has been passed down the family. It's a great way of using up very big marrows, but use large courgettes if you prefer, or experiment with different fruits and vegetables following the same principles.

• 1.8kg marrows, peeled, deseeded and chopped into small chunks • 4 medium onions, peeled and chopped into small chunks • 3 apples, peeled, cored and chopped into small chunks • 225g sultanas or raisins • 225g stoned dates, roughly chopped • 600ml malt vinegar • 900g soft brown sugar • 1 teaspoon salt • 2 tablespoons ground ginger • 2 tablespoons mixed pickling spices, secured in a piece of muslin.

Put the chopped marrow, onions and apples into a large preserving pan, add the rest of the ingredients and the bag of spices and stir together, then place over a medium heat. Bring to a simmer, then reduce the heat and simmer gently for 1½–2 hours or until well blended and thick. Take the pan off the heat, cool and remove the muslin, squeezing the liquid from the bag. Spoon it into sterilised jars with vinegar-proof lids, filling them to within 1cm of the top. Ensure the rims are clean, screw on the sterilised lids and store in a cool place for up to 12 months. Once open, store in the fridge and use within 1 month.

LABELLING & PRESENTATION

Taking care over presentation is all part of the fun. Re-use jars and bottles; just soak off the labels in warm water and sterilise. Kilner jars come in many different sizes; buy clip-top or corked bottles for liqueurs. Cover lids with pretty fabric tied with string and attach paper tag labels (page 266) around bottlenecks with ribbons, add stickers to explain the contents or write with white glass-paint pens straight on to bottles.

RED-ONION MARMALADE Makes 2 x 350g jars

This tangy relish is quick and easy to make and goes very well with cold meats and leftovers (pages 154–5), baked Camembert (page 332) and cheese- or haggis-based canapés (page 187). This is best made as you need it, but will keep for a couple of weeks in a jar in the fridge.

• 4 tablespoons olive oil • 4 red onions, peeled and finely sliced • a pinch of salt • 4 teaspoons soft brown sugar • 2 star anise • 2 cinnamon sticks • 4 tablespoons redcurrant jelly • 200ml red wine • 100ml red wine vinegar.

Heat the oil in a pan, add the onion and salt, cover with a disc of baking parchment and sauté over a low heat for 30 minutes, to soften. Remove the parchment, stir in the remaining ingredients, turn up the heat and simmer, uncovered, for another 30 minutes, stirring occasionally, until thick and syrupy. Cool slightly before storing in sterilised jars with vinegar-proof lids.

ELDERFLOWER CORDIAL Makes 1.5 litres

This delicate summer cordial is wonderfully refreshing in drinks and is delicious on vanilla ice cream, as well as in jellies and fools. It's a British classic, served as a soft drink with sparkling water, or as an alcoholic one with sparkling wine, or vodka, mint and soda.

• *20–25 elderflower heads* • *1.5 litres boiling water* • *1kg white granulated sugar* • *55g citric acid* • *4 lemons, sliced, plus their zest.*

Gently pick over the elderflowers to remove any dirt and briefly stand them, flower-side down, in cold water to remove any little creatures. Pour the boiling water over the sugar in a very large mixing bowl. Stir well and leave to cool slightly, stirring occasionally if necessary to dissolve the sugar. Add the citric acid, the lemon slices and zest, then the flower heads. Cover and leave them to steep in a cool place for 24–48 hours, stirring occasionally. Strain twice through some muslin into a jug and pour through a funnel into sterilised bottles. Label and store the bottles in a cool, dark place, where they will keep for several weeks. Once opened, keep in the fridge in a stoppered bottle for up to one month. You can also freeze the cordial.

TIPS : *The elderflower season is short, from late May until mid-June. Choose a warm sunny morning to get the most flavoursome flowers; pick heads away from roadsides and above waist height.* • *Make the cordial straight away so the flowers don't spoil.*

RASPBERRY VODKA Makes 1 litre

All sorts of fruits and foods can be used to flavour spirits — have a look at the recipes on page 95 for sloe gin and whisky, and for a toffee or chocolate-flavoured vodka. This version is perfect to use in cocktails or even drizzled over white chocolate ice cream. Blackberries or other fruits are easily substituted, or use another clear spirit. Adjust the sugar content depending on the sweetness of the fruit and your own personal taste.

• *400g raspberries* • *400g white caster sugar* • *1 litre vodka.*

Fill a 1-litre sterilised kilner jar with the raspberries and pour in the sugar, then top with the vodka. Seal tightly and give it a good shake. Leave overnight, then shake again. Repeat every day until the sugar is completely dissolved. Using muslin and a funnel, strain into sterilised bottles then store in a cool, dark place for at least 3 months.

TIP : *If you don't have any muslin for straining through, an old, clean pair of tights will do the trick.*

TOP 3 LIQUEURS TO MAKE AT HOME

1: *Raspberry or blackberry vodka*

2: *Sloe gin or whisky (page 95)*

3: *Toffee or After Eight vodka (page 95)*

INDEX

ACKNOWLEDGEMENTS

Writing this book has been an enlightening and thoroughly enjoyable experience but I wouldn't be where I am now without the help and support of many lovely people.

First and foremost I'd like to thank my family for being so understanding and for being the inspiration behind so many of the chapters in this book. In particular, I wish to thank my mother, who has read and reviewed (more than once) every word I have written and who has cheerfully allowed our family home to be taken over for meetings, reviews and photo shoots on more occasions than I can remember.

Thanks to my agent, David Godwin, who got the ball rolling and whose cheeriness and optimism have never wavered.

Special thanks to Sarah Reynolds, my sounding board and friend. Sarah has been an ear to my ideas, an eye to my words, a cook and sharer of recipes, but most importantly a stalwart travelling companion on this literary journey who has stood by me through the highs and lows and never flagged in her dedication.

A huge thank you too to all the Penguins (from Penguin Books), led by Louise Moore, Katy Follain, John Hamilton, Lindsey Evans and Debbie Hatfield in the UK, and Clare Ferraro and Caitlin O'Shaughnessy in the US. I'm not sure they knew what exactly was in store when we started this book but thank you for all your hard work, patience and genuine belief in me and my vision. I also have to mention Sarah Fraser, who tirelessly art-worked all the pages with care. We got there in the end!

David Loftus has been an inspiration with his beautiful photography, in the pursuit of which he went well beyond the call of duty. Amanda Brown organised the photo shoots with meticulous precision and skill and I'm incredibly grateful to all the stylists who spent long hours and days sourcing the right props, along with Katie Cecil, who brought her invaluable stylish flair. Thank you also to the home economists Lisa Harrison, Abi Fawcett and Anna Burges-Lumsden who, with their devoted support team, guided, advised and developed many of the recipes. And not forgetting Sam Duffy for helping me with handicrafts and making all manner of things.

Other special friends have helped me along the way: Rose French, chief recipe tester; Thierry Kelaart, my craft and creative companion; Thomas William Foulser, cocktail confidant of Barts, London; and Ed Pilkington from wine merchants Corney & Barrow. Florist Hannah Bignell, from Ruby & Grace, was generous and inspirational on all things floral, and brothers Simon and Hugo Godwin provided enthusiastic research on historical traditions and games. There are also a number of friends and families who 'celebrated' the chapters with me and brought this book to life.

And finally, thank you to my mentors for their invaluable guidance and support for which I am hugely grateful.